The Lectionary
2024

First published in Great Britain in 2023

Society for Promoting Christian Knowledge
36 Causton Street
London SW1P 4ST
www.spck.org.uk

British Library Cataloguing-in-Publication Data
A catalogue record for this book is available from the British Library

ISBN 978-0-281-08798-3
ISBN 978-0-281-08799-0 (spiral-bound)

1 3 5 7 9 10 8 6 4 2

Designed by Colin Hall, Refined Practice
Typeset by Fakenham Prepress Solutions, Fakenham, Norfolk NR21 8NL
Printed in Great Britain by Ashford Colour Press

Produced on paper from sustainable sources

CONTENTS

UNDERSTANDING THE LECTIONARY

Common Worship on left-hand page

		Sunday Principal Service Weekday Eucharist	Third Service Morning Prayer	Second Service Evening Prayer
June 2024				
1 Saturday	Justin, Martyr at Rome, *c.* 165			
Gr	Com. Martyr *or* *esp.* John 15. 18–21 *also* 1 Macc. 2. 15–22 1 Cor. 1. 18–25	Jude 17, 20–end Ps. 63. 1–6 Mark 11. 27–end	Ps. 20; 21; **23** Josh. 10. 1–15 Luke 11. 37–end	Ps. **24**; 25 Job ch. 12 Rom. 6. 15–end **ct**
2 Sunday	**THE FIRST SUNDAY AFTER TRINITY (Proper 4)**			
G	*Track 1* 1 Sam. 3. 1–10 [11–20] Ps. 139. 1–5, 12–18 2 Cor. 4. 5–12 Mark 2.23 – 3.6	*Track 2* Deut. 5. 12–15 Ps. 81. 1–10 2 Cor. 4. 5–12 Mark 2.23 – 3.6	Ps. 28; 32 Deut. 5. 1–21 Acts 21. 17–39a	Ps. 35 (*or* 35. 1–10) Jer. 5. 1–19 Rom. 7. 7–end *Gospel:* Luke 7. 1–10
3 Monday	*The Martyrs of Uganda, 1885–87 and 1977*			
G **DEL 9**		2 Pet. 1. 2–7 Ps. 91. 1–2, 14–end Mark 12. 1–12	Ps. 27; **30** Josh. ch. 14 Luke 12. 1–12	Ps. 26; **28**; 29 Job ch. 13 Rom. 7. 1–6

Column 1	Column 2	Column 3	Column 4	Column 5
• Date • **Colour:** An upper-case letter indicates the liturgical colour of the day. A lower-case second colour indicates the colour for a Lesser Festival while the upper-case letter indicates the continuing seasonal colour. • **DEL:** Week number of Daily Eucharistic Lectionary.	• Name of the Principal Holy Day, Sunday, Festival or Lesser Festival; • a note of other Commemorations for mention in prayers; • any general note that applies to the whole *Common Worship* provision for the day; • one of the options where there are two options for readings at the Eucharist or Principal Service. **Readings:** Readings occur in this column only in two circumstances. 1. **On Sundays after Trinity** where there are two 'tracks' for the Principal Service readings (where there is a choice of first reading and psalm, but the second reading and Gospel are the same in both tracks), Track I appears in this column. 2. **On Lesser Festivals throughout the year** where there are readings for that festival that are alternative to the semi-continuous Daily Eucharistic Lectionary, these also appear in this column.	On Principal Feasts, Principal Holy Days, Sundays and Festivals this gives the Principal Service Lectionary, intended for use at the main service of the day (in most churches the mid-morning service), whether or not it is a Eucharist. **On other weekdays this gives the Daily Eucharistic Lectionary** for those wanting a semi-continuous pattern of readings and a psalm for Holy Communion. It is most useful in a church where there is a daily celebration and a core community that worships together day by day, though its use is not restricted to that. **On Sundays after Trinity** where there are two 'tracks' for the Principal Service readings (where there is a choice of first reading and psalm, but the second reading and Gospel are the same in both tracks), Track 2 appears in this column.	On Principal Feasts, Principal Holy Days, Sundays and Festivals this gives the Third Service Lectionary. Many churches will have no need of it, for it comes into use only if the Principal and Second Service Lectionaries have been used. Its most likely use is at Morning Prayer (when this is not the Principal Service). Where psalms are recommended for use in the morning, these also appear in this column. **On other weekdays this provides the psalmody and readings for Morning Prayer.** Where two or more psalms are appointed, the psalm in bold italic may be used as the only psalm. Psalms printed in round brackets ( ) may be omitted if they are used as an opening canticle at Morning Prayer. Where † is printed after the psalm number, the psalm may be shortened if desired. For those wishing to follow the Ordinary Time psalm cycle throughout the year (except for the period between 19 December and the Epiphany and from the Monday of Holy Week to the Saturday of Easter Week), this is printed as an alternative to the seasonal provision.	On Principal Feasts, Principal Holy Days, Sundays and Festivals this gives the Second Service Lectionary, intended for use when a second set of readings is required. Its most likely use is in the evening, when the Principal Service Lectionary has been used in the morning. Sometimes it might be used at an evening Eucharist. Where the second reading is not a Gospel reading, an alternative to meet this need is provided. Where psalms are recommended for use in the evening, these also appear in this column. **On other weekdays this provides the psalmody and readings for Evening Prayer.** Where two or more psalms are provided, the psalm in bold italic may be used as the only psalm. Psalms printed in round brackets ( ) may be omitted if they are used as an opening canticle at Evening Prayer. Where † is printed after the psalm number, the psalm may be shortened if desired. For those wishing to follow the Ordinary Time psalm cycle throughout the year (except for the period between 19 December and the Epiphany and from the Monday of Holy Week to the Saturday of Easter Week), this is printed as an alternative to the seasonal provision.

Calendar and Holy Communion	Morning Prayer	Evening Prayer	NOTES

Nicomede, Priest and Martyr at Rome (date unknown)

Gr	Com. Martyr	Josh. 10. 1–15 Luke 11. 37–end	Job ch. 12 Rom. 6. 15–end	
			ct	

THE FIRST SUNDAY AFTER TRINITY

G	2 Sam. 9. 6–end Ps. 41. 1–4 1 John 4. 7–end Luke 16. 19–31	Ps. 28; 32 Deut. 5. 1–21 Acts 21. 17–39a	Ps. 35 (or 35. 1–10) Jer. 5. 1–19 Rom. 7. 7–end	

G		Josh. ch. 14 Luke 12. 1–12	Job ch. 13 Rom. 7. 1–6	

Column 6
- Liturgical colour (see column 1).

Column 7
- The name of the Principal Holy Day, Sunday, Festival or Lesser Festival;
- any general note that applies to the whole Prayer Book provision for the day and an indication of points at which users may wish to draw on Common Worship material on the opposite page where the BCP has no provision;
- the Lectionary for the Eucharist on any day for which provision is made.

Column 8
This provides the readings for Morning Prayer, together with psalm provision where it varies from the BCP monthly cycle.

Column 9
This provides the readings for Evening Prayer, together with psalm provision where it varies from the BCP monthly cycle.

A letter to indicate liturgical colour in this column indicates a change of colour for Evening Prayer. The symbol in bold lower case, **ct**, indicates that the Collect at Evening Prayer should be that of the following day. This also applies to column 5.

Column 10
Space for notes.

ABBREVIATIONS OF BOOKS OF THE BIBLE

Old Testament

Gen. (Genesis)	Kings	Song of Sol. (Song of Solomon)	Obad. (Obadiah)
Exod. (Exodus)	Chron. (Chronicles)	Isa. (Isaiah)	Jonah
Lev. (Leviticus)	Ezra	Jer. (Jeremiah)	Mic. (Micah)
Num. (Numbers)	Neh. (Nehemiah)	Lam. (Lamentations)	Nahum
Deut. (Deuteronomy)	Esth. (Esther)	Ezek. (Ezekiel)	Hab. (Habakkuk)
Josh. (Joshua)	Job	Dan. (Daniel)	Zeph. (Zephaniah)
Judg. (Judges)	Ps. (Psalms)	Hos. (Hosea)	Hag. (Haggai)
Ruth	Prov. (Proverbs)	Joel	Zech. (Zechariah)
Sam. (Samuel)	Eccles. (Ecclesiastes)	Amos	Mal. (Malachi)

Apocrypha

Esdras	Wisd. (Wisdom of Solomon)	Song of the Three (Song of the Three Children)	Prayer of Manasseh
Tobit	Ecclus. (Ecclesiasticus)		Macc. (Maccabees)
Judith	Baruch	Susanna (The History of Susanna)	

New Testament

Matt. (Matthew)	Cor. (Corinthians)	Tim. (Timothy)	John (letters of John)
Mark	Gal. (Galatians)	Titus	Jude
Luke	Eph. (Ephesians)	Philem. (Philemon)	Rev. (Revelation)
John	Phil. (Philippians)	Heb. (Hebrews)	
Acts (Acts of the Apostles)	Col. (Colossians)	Jas. (James)	
Rom. (Romans)	Thess. (Thessalonians)	Pet. (Peter)	

MAKING CHOICES IN *COMMON WORSHIP*

Common Worship makes provision for a variety of pastoral and liturgical circumstances. It needs to, for it has to serve some church communities where Morning Prayer, Holy Communion and Evening Prayer are all celebrated every day, and yet be useful also in a church with only one service a week, and that service varying in form and time from week to week.

At the beginning of the year, some decisions in principle need to be taken.

In relation to the Calendar, whether to keep The Epiphany on Saturday 6 January or on Sunday 7 January, whether to keep The Presentation of Christ (Candlemas) on Friday 2 February or on Sunday 28 January, and whether to keep the Feast of All Saints on Friday 1 November or on Sunday 3 November.

In relation to the Lectionary, the initial choices every year to decide in relation to Sundays are:

- which of the services on a Principal Feast, Principal Holy Day, Sunday or Festival constitutes the 'Principal Service'; then use the Principal Service Lectionary (column 3) consistently for that service through the year;

- during the Sundays after Trinity, whether to use Track 1 of the Principal Service Lectionary (column 2), where the first reading stays over several weeks with one Old Testament book read semi-continuously, or Track 2 (column 3), where the first reading is chosen for its relationship to the Gospel reading of the day;

- which, if any, service on a Principal Feast, Principal Holy Day, Sunday or Festival constitutes the 'Second Service'; then use the Second Service Lectionary (column 5) consistently for that service through the year;

- which, if any, service on a Principal Feast, Principal Holy Day, Sunday or Festival constitutes the 'Third Service'; then use the Third Service Lectionary (column 4) consistently for that service through the year.

And in relation to weekdays:

- whether to use the Daily Eucharistic Lectionary (column 3) consistently for weekday celebrations of Holy Communion (with the exception of Principal Feasts, Principal Holy Days and Festivals) or to make some use of the Lesser Festival provision;

- whether to follow the first psalm provision in column 4 (morning) and column 5 (evening), where psalms during the seasons have a seasonal flavour but in ordinary time follow a sequential pattern; or to follow the alternative provision in the same columns, where psalms follow the sequential pattern throughout the year, except for the period between 19 December and The Epiphany and from the Monday of Holy Week to the Saturday of Easter Week; or to follow the psalm cycle in the Book of Common Prayer, where they are nearly always used 'in course';

- whether to use the Additional Weekday Lectionary (which begins on page 116) for weekday services (other than Holy Communion). It provides a one-year cycle of two readings for each day (except for Sundays, Principal Feasts, Principal Holy Days, Festivals and during Holy Week). Since each of the readings is designed to 'stand alone' (that is, it is complete in itself and will make sense to the worshipper who has not attended on the previous day and who will not be present on the next day), it is intended particularly for use in those churches and cathedrals that attract occasional rather than regular congregations.

The flexibility of *Common Worship* is intended to enable the church and the minister to find the most helpful provision for them. But once a decision is made, it is advisable to stay with that decision through the year or at the very least through a complete season.

Square brackets indicate optional additional verses or psalms. A choice between alternative readings is denoted by an italicized *or*, positioned between references.

All Bible references (except to the psalms) are to the New Revised Standard Version, Anglicized edition (1995). Those who use other Bible translations should check the verse numbers against the NRSV. References to the psalms are to the *Common Worship* Psalter.

BOOK OF COMMON PRAYER

A separate Lectionary for the Book of Common Prayer is no longer issued. Provision is made on the right-hand pages of this Lectionary for BCP worship on all Sundays in the year, for the major festivals and for Morning and Evening Prayer. The Epistles and Gospels for Holy Communion are those of 1662, with the additions and variations of 1928, now authorized under the *Common Worship* overall provision. The Old Testament readings and psalms for these services, formerly appended to the Series One Holy Communion service, may be used but are not mandatory with the 1662 order.

Readings for Morning and Evening Prayer, which are the same as those for *Common Worship*, are set out in the BCP section for Sundays and weekdays. The special psalm provision of the BCP is given; however, where the *Common Worship* psalm provision is used, verse numbering may occasionally differ slightly from that in the BCP Psalter, and appropriate adjustment will have to be made (a table of variations in verse numbering can be found at www.churchofengland.org/prayer-and-worship/worship-texts-and-resources/common-worship/daily-prayer/psalter/psalter-verse). Otherwise the Psalter is read in course daily through each month.

The Calendar observes BCP dates when these differ from those of *Common Worship*; for example, St

Thomas on 21 December. Additional commemorations in the *Common Worship* Calendar are not included, but those who wish to observe them may use the *Collects and Post Communions in Traditional Language: Lesser Festivals, Common of the Saints, Special Occasions* (Church House Publishing).

The Lectionaries of 1871 and 1922, to be found in many copies of the BCP, are still authorized and may be used, but – with the exception of the psalms and readings for Holy Communion mentioned above – the Additional Alternative Lectionary (1961) is no longer authorized for public worship.

Although those who use the BCP, for private or public worship or both, are free to follow any of the authorized lectionaries, there is much to be said for common usage across the Church of England, so that the same passages are being read by all. It is of course appropriate that BCP readings should be taken from the Authorized or King James Version for harmony of style, with the daily recitation of the BCP Psalter.

The integrity of the BCP as the traditional source of worship in the Church of England is not in any way affected by the use of a common lectionary for the daily offices.

CERTAIN DAYS AND OCCASIONS COMMONLY OBSERVED

Plough Sunday may be observed on 7 January 2024.

The Week of Prayer for Christian Unity may be observed from 18 to 25 January 2024.

Education Sunday may be observed on 8 September 2024.

Rogation Sunday may be observed on 5 May 2024.

The Feast of Dedication is observed on the anniversary of the dedication or consecration of a church, or, when the actual date is unknown, on 6 October 2024. In *Common Worship*, 27 October 2024 is an alternative date.

Ember Days. *Common Worship* encourages the bishop to set the Ember Days in each diocese in the week before the ordinations, whereas in BCP the dates are fixed.

Days of Discipline and Self-Denial in *Common Worship* are the weekdays of Lent and all Fridays in the year, except all Principal Feasts and festivals outside Lent and Fridays between Easter Day and Pentecost. The eves of Principal Feasts are also appropriately kept as days of discipline and self-denial in preparation for the feast.

Days of Fasting and Abstinence according to the BCP are the forty days of Lent, the Ember Days at the four seasons, the three Rogation Days, and all Fridays in the year except Christmas Day. The BCP also orders the observance of the Evens or Vigils before The Nativity of our Lord, The Purification of the Blessed Virgin Mary, The Annunciation of the Blessed Virgin Mary, Easter Day, Ascension Day, Pentecost, and before the following saints' days: Matthias, John the Baptist, Peter, James, Bartholomew, Matthew, Simon and Jude, Andrew, Thomas, and All Saints. (If any of these days falls on Monday, the Vigil is to be kept on the previous Saturday.)

KEY TO LITURGICAL COLOURS

Common Worship suggests appropriate liturgical colours. They are not mandatory, and traditional or local use may be followed.

For a detailed discussion of when colours may be used, see Common Worship: Services and Prayers for the Church of England (Church House Publishing), New Handbook of Pastoral Liturgy (SPCK) or A Companion to Common Worship: Volume I (SPCK).

When a lower-case letter accompanies an upper-case letter, the lower-case letter indicates the liturgical colour appropriate to the Lesser Festival of that day, while the upper-case letter indicates the continuing seasonal colour.

W White
𝖜 Gold or white
R Red
P Purple (may vary from 'Roman purple' to violet, with blue as an alternative; a Lent array of sackcloth may be used in Lent, and rose pink on The Third Sunday of Advent and Fourth Sunday of Lent)
G Green

PRINCIPAL FEASTS, HOLY DAYS AND FESTIVALS

Principal Feasts and other Principal Holy Days (Ash Wednesday, Maundy Thursday, Good Friday) are printed in **LARGE BOLD CAPITALS** in the Lectionary.

There are no longer proper readings relating to the Holy Spirit on the six days after Pentecost. Instead they have been located on the nine days before Pentecost.

When Patronal and Dedication Festivals are kept as Principal Feasts, they may be transferred to the nearest Sunday, unless that day is already either a Principal Feast or The First Sunday of Advent, The Baptism of Christ, The First Sunday of Lent or Palm Sunday.

Festivals are printed in the Lectionary in **SMALL BOLD CAPITALS.**

For each day there is a full liturgical provision for the Holy Communion and for Morning and Evening Prayer. Most holy days that are in the category 'Festival' are provided with an optional First Evening Prayer. Its use is entirely at the discretion of the minister. Where it is used, the liturgical colour for the next day should be used at that First Evening Prayer, and this has been indicated in the provision on the following pages.

LESSER FESTIVALS AND COMMEMORATIONS

Lesser Festivals (printed in **medium-bold roman** typeface) are observed at the level appropriate to a particular church. The readings and psalms for The Common of the Saints are listed on page 10. In addition, there are special readings appropriate to the Festival listed in the first column. The daily psalms and readings at Morning and Evening Prayer are not usually superseded by those for Lesser Festivals, but the readings and psalms for Holy Communion may on occasion be used at Morning or Evening Prayer.

Commemorations are printed in the Lectionary in italic typeface. They do not have collect, psalm or readings, but may be observed by mention in prayers of intercession and thanksgiving. For local reasons,

or where there is an established tradition in the wider Church, they may be kept as Lesser Festivals using the appropriate material from The Common of the Saints. Equally, it may be desirable to observe some Lesser Festivals as Commemorations.

If a Lesser Festival or a Commemoration falls on a Principal Feast, Principal Holy Day, Sunday or Festival, it is not normally observed that year, although it may be celebrated, where there is sufficient reason, on the nearest available day. Lesser Festivals and Commemorations which, for this reason, would not be celebrated in 2023–24 are listed on pages 9–10, so that, if desired, they may be mentioned in prayers of intercession and thanksgiving.

LESSER FESTIVALS AND COMMEMORATIONS NOT OBSERVED IN 2023-24

The Lesser Festivals and Commemorations (shown in italics) listed below fall on a Sunday or during Holy Week or Easter Week this year, and are thus not observed in this Lectionary.

COMMON WORSHIP

2023

December

3 *Francis Xavier, Missionary, Apostle of the Indies, 1552*

17 *Eglantine Jebb, Social Reformer, Founder of 'Save the Children', 1928*

31 *John Wyclif, Reformer, 1384*

2024

January

21 Agnes, Child Martyr at Rome, 304

28 Thomas Aquinas, Priest, Philosopher, Teacher, 1274

February

4 *Gilbert of Sempringham, Founder of the Gilbertine Order, 1189*

14 Cyril and Methodius, Missionaries to the Slavs, 869 and 885

Valentine, Martyr at Rome, c. 269

March

17 Patrick, Bishop, Missionary, Patron of Ireland, c. 460

24 *Walter Hilton of Thurgarton, Augustinian Canon, Mystic, 1396*

Paul Couturier, Priest, Ecumenist, 1953

Oscar Romero, Archbishop of San Salvador, Martyr, 1980

26 *Harriet Monsell, Founder of the Community of St John the Baptist, Clewer, 1883*

31 *John Donne, Priest, Poet, 1631*

April

1 *Frederick Denison Maurice, Priest, Teacher, 1872*

21 Anselm, Abbot of Le Bec, Archbishop of Canterbury, Teacher, 1109

28 *Peter Chanel, Missionary in the South Pacific, Martyr, 1841*

May

12 *Gregory Dix, Priest, Monk, Scholar, 1952*

19 Dunstan, Archbishop of Canterbury, Restorer of Monastic Life, 988

26 Augustine, first Archbishop of Canterbury, 605

John Calvin, Reformer, 1564

Philip Neri, Founder of the Oratorians, Spiritual Guide, 1595

June

9 Columba, Abbot of Iona, Missionary, 597

Ephrem of Syria, Deacon, Hymn Writer, Teacher, 373

16 Richard, Bishop of Chichester, 1253

Joseph Butler, Bishop of Durham, Philosopher, 1752

23 Etheldreda, Abbess of Ely, c. 678

July

14 John Keble, Priest, Tractarian, Poet, 1866

August

4 *Jean-Baptiste Vianney, Curé d'Ars, Spiritual Guide, 1859*

11 Clare of Assisi, Founder of the Minoresses (Poor Clares), 1253

September

1 *Giles of Provence, Hermit, c. 710*

8 The Birth of the Blessed Virgin Mary

15 Cyprian, Bishop of Carthage, Martyr, 258

October

6 William Tyndale, Translator of the Scriptures, Reformation Martyr, 1536

13 Edward the Confessor, King of England, 1066

November

3 Richard Hooker, Priest, Anglican Apologist, Teacher, 1600

Martin of Porres, Friar, 1639

10 Leo the Great, Bishop of Rome, Teacher, 461

17 Hugh, Bishop of Lincoln, 1200

December

1 *Charles de Foucauld, Hermit in the Sahara, 1916*

8 The Conception of the Blessed Virgin Mary

29 Thomas Becket, Archbishop of Canterbury, Martyr, 1170

2024

January
21 Agnes, Child Martyr at Rome, 304

February
14 Valentine, Martyr at Rome, c. 269

April
3 Richard, Bishop of Chichester, 1253
4 Ambrose, Bishop of Milan, 397

May
19 Dunstan, Archbishop of Canterbury, Restorer of Monastic Life, 988
26 Augustine, first Archbishop of Canterbury, 605

September
1 Giles of Provence, Hermit, c. 710
8 The Nativity of the Blessed Virgin Mary

October
6 Faith of Aquitaine, Martyr, c. 304
13 Edward the Confessor, King of England, 1066, translated 1163

November
17 Hugh, Bishop of Lincoln, 1200

December
29 Thomas Becket, Archbishop of Canterbury, Martyr, 1170

THE COMMON OF THE SAINTS

The Blessed Virgin Mary
Genesis 3. 8–15, 20; Isaiah 7. 10–14; Micah 5. 1–4
Psalms 45. 10–17; 113; 131
Acts 1. 12–14; Romans 8. 18–30; Galatians 4. 4–7
Luke 1. 26–38; I. 39–47; John 19. 25–27

Martyrs
2 Chronicles 24. 17–21; Isaiah 43. 1–7;
    Jeremiah 11. 18–20; Wisdom 4. 10–15
Psalms 3; 11; 31. 1–5; 44. 18–24; 126
Romans 8. 35–end; 2 Corinthians 4. 7–15;
    2 Timothy 2. 3–7 [8–13]; Hebrews 11. 32–end;
    1 Peter 4. 12–end; Revelation 12. 10–12a
Matthew 10. 16–22; 10. 28–39; 16. 24–26;
    John 12. 24–26; 15. 18–21

Teachers of the Faith and Spiritual Writers
I Kings 3. [6–10] 11–14; Proverbs 4. 1–9;
    Wisdom 7. 7–10, 15–16; Ecclesiasticus 39. 1–10
Psalms 19. 7–10; 34. 11–17; 37. 31–35; 119. 89–96;
    119. 97–104
I Corinthians 1. 18–25; 2. 1–10; 2. 9–end;
    Ephesians 3. 8–12; 2 Timothy 4. 1–8; Titus 2. 1–8
Matthew 5. 13–19; 13. 52–end; 23. 8–12; Mark 4. 1–9;
    John 16. 12–15

Bishops and Other Pastors
I Samuel 16. I, 6–13; Isaiah 6. 1–8; Jeremiah 1. 4–10;
    Ezekiel 3. 16–21; Malachi 2. 5–7
Psalms 1; 15; 16. 5–end; 96; 110
Acts 20. 28–35; I Corinthians 4. 1–5;
    2 Corinthians 4. 1–10 (or 1–2, 5–7);
    5. 14–20; 1 Peter 5. 1–4

Matthew 11. 25–end; 24. 42–46; John 10. 11–16;
    15. 9–17; 21. 15–17

Members of Religious Communities
I Kings 19. 9–18; Proverbs 10. 27–end;
    Song of Solomon 8. 6–7; Isaiah 61.10 – 62.5;
    Hosea 2. 14–15, 19–20
Psalms 34. 1–8; 112. 1–9; 119. 57–64; 123; 131
Acts 4. 32–35; 2 Corinthians 10.17 – 11.2;
    Philippians 3. 7–14; 1 John 2. 15–17;
    Revelation 19. 1, 5–9
Matthew 11. 25–end; 19. 3–12; 19. 23–end;
    Luke 9. 57–end; 12. 32–37

Missionaries
Isaiah 52. 7–10; 61. 1–3a; Ezekiel 34. 11–16; Jonah 3. 1–5
Psalms 67; 87; 97; 100; 117
Acts 2. 14, 22–36; 13. 46–49; 16. 6–10; 26. 19–23;
    Romans 15. 17–21; 2 Corinthians 5.11 – 6.2
Matthew 9. 35–end; 28. 16–end; Mark 16. 15–20;
    Luke 5. 1–11; 10. 1–9

Any Saint
Genesis 12. 1–4; Proverbs 8. 1–11; Micah 6. 6–8;
    Ecclesiasticus 2. 7–13 [14–end]
Psalms 32; 33. 1–5; 119. 1–8; 139. 1–4 [5–12]; 145. 8–14
Ephesians 3. 14–19; 6. 11–18; Hebrews 13. 7–8, 15–16;
    James 2. 14–17; 1 John 4. 7–16; Revelation 21. [1–4]
    5–7
Matthew 19. 16–21; 25. 1–13; 25. 14–30; John 15. 1–8;
    17. 20–end

SPECIAL OCCASIONS

The Guidance of the Holy Spirit
Proverbs 24. 3–7; Isaiah 30. 15–21; Wisdom 9. 13–17
Psalms 25. 1–9; 104. 26–33; 143. 8–10
Acts 15. 23–29; Romans 8. 22–27;
   1 Corinthians 12. 4–13
Luke 14. 27–33; John 14. 23–26; 16. 13–15

The Commemoration of the Faithful Departed
Lamentations 3. 17–26, 31–33 or Wisdom 3. 1–9
Psalm 23 or 27. 1–6, 16–end
Romans 5. 5–11 or I Peter 1. 3–9
John 5. 19–25 or 6. 37–40

Rogation Days
Deuteronomy 8. 1–10; 1 Kings 8. 35–40; Job 28. 1–11
Psalms 104. 21–30; 107. 1–9; 121
Philippians 4. 4–7; 2 Thessalonians 3. 6–13;
   1 John 5. 12–15
Matthew 6. 1–15; Mark 11. 22–24; Luke 11. 5–13

Harvest Thanksgiving

Year A
Deuteronomy 8. 7–18 or 28. 1–14
Psalm 65
2 Corinthians 9. 6–end
Luke 12. 16–30 or 17. 11–19

Year B
Joel 2. 21–27
Psalm 126
1 Timothy 2. 1–7 or 6. 6–10
Matthew 6. 25–33

Year C
Deuteronomy 26. 1–11
Psalm 100
Philippians 4. 4–9 or Revelation 14. 14–18
John 6. 25–35

Mission and Evangelism
Isaiah 49. 1–6; 52. 7–10; Micah 4. 1–5
Psalms 2; 46; 67
Acts 17. 12–end; 2 Corinthians 5.14 – 6.2;
   Ephesians 2. 13–end
Matthew 5. 13–16; 28. 16–end; John 17. 20–end

The Unity of the Church
Jeremiah 33. 6–9a; Ezekiel 36. 23–28;
   Zephaniah 3. 16–end
Psalms 100; 122; 133
Ephesians 4. 1–6; Colossians 3. 9–17;
   1 John 4. 9–15
Matthew 18. 19–22; John 11. 45–52; 17. 11b–23

The Peace of the World
Isaiah 9. 1–6; 57. 15–19; Micah 4. 1–5
Psalms 40. 14–17; 72. 1–7; 85. 8–13
Philippians 4. 6–9; 1 Timothy 2. 1–6;
   James 3. 13–18
Matthew 5. 43–end; John 14. 23–29; 15. 9–17

Social Justice and Responsibility
Isaiah 32. 15–end; Amos 5. 21–24; 8. 4–7;
   Acts 5. 1–11
Psalms 31. 21–24; 85. 1–7; 146. 5–10
Colossians 3. 12–15; James 2. 1–4
Matthew 5. 1–12; 25. 31–end;
   Luke 16. 19–end

Ministry (including Ember Days)
Numbers 11. 16–17, 24–29; 27. 15–end;
   1 Samuel 16. 1–13a; Isaiah 6. 1–8; 61. 1–3;
   Jeremiah 1. 4–10
Psalms 40. 8–13; 84. 8–12; 89. 19–25;
   101. 1–5, 7; 122
Acts 20. 28–35; 1 Corinthians 3. 3–11;
   Ephesians 4. 4–16; Philippians 3. 7–14
Luke 4. 16–21; 12. 35–43; 22. 24–27;
   John 4. 31–38; 15. 5–17

In Time of Trouble
Genesis 9. 8–17; Job 1. 13–end; Isaiah 38. 6–11
Psalms 86. 1–7; 107. 4–15; 142. 1–7
Romans 3. 21–26; 8. 18–25;
   2 Corinthians 8. 1–5, 9
Mark 4. 35–end; Luke 12. 1–7; John 16. 31–end

For the Sovereign
Joshua 1. 1–9; Proverbs 8. 1–16
Psalms 20; 101; 121
Romans 13. 1–10; Revelation 21.22 – 22.4
Matthew 22. 16–22; Luke 22. 24–30

		Sunday Principal Service / Weekday Eucharist	Third Service / Morning Prayer	Second Service / Evening Prayer

3 Sunday — THE FIRST SUNDAY OF ADVENT
Common Worship Year B begins

P		Isa. 64. 1–9 Ps. 80. 1–8, 18–20 (*or* 80. 1–8) 1 Cor. 1. 3–9 Mark 13. 24–end	Ps. 44 Isa. 2. 1–5 Luke 12. 35–48	Ps. 25 (*or* 25. 1–9) Isa. 1. 1–20 Matt. 21. 1–13

4 Monday — *John of Damascus, Monk, Teacher, c. 749; Nicholas Ferrar, Deacon, Founder of the Little Gidding Community, 1637*
Daily Eucharistic Lectionary Year 2 begins

P		Isa. 2. 1–5 Ps. 122 Matt. 8. 5–11	Ps. *50*; 54 *alt.* Ps. *1*; 2; 3 Isa. 25. 1–9 Matt. 12. 1–21	Ps. 70; *71* *alt.* Ps. *4*; 7 Isa. 42. 18–end Rev. ch. 19

5 Tuesday

P		Isa. 11. 1–10 Ps. 72. 1–4, 18–19 Luke 10. 21–24	Ps. *80*; 82 *alt.* Ps. *5*; 6; (8) Isa. 26. 1–13 Matt. 12. 22–37	Ps. *74*; 75 *alt.* Ps. *9*; 10† Isa. 43. 1–13 Rev. ch. 20

6 Wednesday — Nicholas, Bishop of Myra, c. 326

Pw	Com. Bishop *also* Isa. 61. 1–3 1 Tim. 6. 6–11 Mark 10. 13–16	*or* Isa. 25. 6–10a Ps. 23 Matt. 15. 29–37	Ps. 5; *7* *alt.* Ps. 119. 1–32 Isa. 28. 1–13 Matt. 12. 38–end	Ps. 76; *77* *alt.* Ps. *11*; 12; 13 Isa. 43. 14–end Rev. 21. 1–8

7 Thursday — Ambrose, Bishop of Milan, Teacher, 397

Pw	Com. Teacher *also* Isa. 41. 9b–13 Luke 22. 24–30	*or* Isa. 26. 1–6 Ps. 118. 18–27a Matt. 7. 21, 24–27	Ps. *42*; 43 *alt.* Ps. 14; *15*; 16 Isa. 28. 14–end Matt. 13. 1–23	Ps. *40*; 46 *alt.* Ps. 18† Isa. 44. 1–8 Rev. 21. 9–21

8 Friday — The Conception of the Blessed Virgin Mary

Pw	Com. BVM	*or* Isa. 29. 17–end Ps. 27. 1–4, 16–17 Matt. 9. 27–31	Ps. *25*; 26 *alt.* Ps. 17; *19* Isa. 29. 1–14 Matt. 13. 24–43	Ps. 16; *17* *alt.* Ps. 22 Isa. 44. 9–23 Rev. 21.22 – 22.5

9 Saturday

P		Isa. 30. 19–21, 23–26 Ps. 146. 4–9 Matt. 9.35 – 10.1, 6–8	Ps. *9*; 10 *alt.* Ps. 20; 21; *23* Isa. 29. 15–end Matt. 13. 44–end	Ps. *27*; 28 *alt.* Ps. *24*; 25 Isa. 44.24 – 45.13 Rev. 22. 6–end **ct**

10 Sunday — THE SECOND SUNDAY OF ADVENT

P		Isa. 40. 1–11 Ps. 85. 1–2, 8–end (*or* 85. 8–end) 2 Pet. 3. 8–15a Mark 1. 1–8	Ps. 80 Baruch 5. 1–9 *or* Zeph. 3. 14–end Luke 1. 5–20	Ps. 40 (*or* 40. 12–end) 1 Kings 22. 1–28 Rom. 15. 4–13 *Gospel*: Matt. 11. 2–11

11 Monday

P		Isa. ch. 35 Ps. 85. 7–end Luke 5. 17–26	Ps. 44 *alt.* Ps. 27; *30* Isa. 30. 1–18 Matt. 14. 1–12	Ps. *144*; 146 *alt.* Ps. 26; *28*; 29 Isa. 45. 14–end 1 Thess. ch. 1

	Calendar and Holy Communion	Morning Prayer	Evening Prayer	NOTES
	THE FIRST SUNDAY IN ADVENT Advent 1 Collect until Christmas Eve			
P	Mic. 4. 1–4, 6–7 Ps. 25. 1–9 Rom. 13. 8–14 Matt. 21. 1–13	Ps. 44 Isa. 2. 1–5 Luke 12. 35–48	Ps. 9 Isa. 1. 1–20 Mark 13. 24–end	
P		Isa. 25. 1–9 Matt. 12. 1–21	Isa. 42. 18–end Rev. ch. 19	
P		Isa. 26. 1–13 Matt. 12. 22–37	Isa. 43. 1–13 Rev. ch. 20	
	Nicholas, Bishop of Myra, c. 326			
Pw	Com. Bishop	Isa. 28. 1–13 Matt. 12. 38–end	Isa. 43. 14–end Rev. 21. 1–8	
P		Isa. 28. 14–end Matt. 13. 1–23	Isa. 44. 1–8 Rev. 21. 9–21	
	The Conception of the Blessed Virgin Mary			
Pw		Isa. 29. 1–14 Matt. 13. 24–43	Isa. 44. 9–23 Rev. 21.22 – 22.5	
P		Isa. 29. 15–end Matt. 13. 44–end	Isa. 44.24 – 45.13 Rev. 22. 6–end	
			ct	
	THE SECOND SUNDAY IN ADVENT			
P	2 Kings 22. 8–10; 23. 1–3 Ps. 50. 1–6 Rom. 15. 4–13 Luke 21. 25–33	Ps. 80 Baruch 5. 1–9 or Zeph. 3. 14–end Luke 1. 5–20	Ps. 40 (or 40. 12–end) 1 Kings 22. 1–28 2 Pet. 3. 8–15a	
P		Isa. 30. 1–18 Matt. 14. 1–12	Isa. 45. 14–end 1 Thess. ch. 1	

		Sunday Principal Service Weekday Eucharist	Third Service Morning Prayer	Second Service Evening Prayer
12 Tuesday				
P		Isa. 40. 1–11 Ps. 96. 1, 10–end Matt. 18. 12–14	Ps. *56*; 57 *alt.* Ps. 32; *36* Isa. 30. 19–end Matt. 14. 13–end	Ps. *11*; 12; 13 *alt.* Ps. 33 Isa. ch. 46 1 Thess. 2. 1–12
13 Wednesday	**Lucy, Martyr at Syracuse, 304** Ember Day* *Samuel Johnson, Moralist, 1784*			
Pr	Com. Martyr *or* *also* Wisd. 3. 1–7 2 Cor. 4. 6–15	Isa. 40. 25–end Ps. 103. 8–13 Matt. 11. 28–end	Ps. *62*; 63 *alt.* Ps. 34 Isa. ch. 31 Matt. 15. 1–20	Ps. *10*; 14 *alt.* Ps. 119. 33–56 Isa. ch. 47 1 Thess. 2. 13–end
14 Thursday	**John of the Cross, Poet, Teacher, 1591**			
Pw	Com. Teacher *or* *esp.* 1 Cor. 2. 1–10 *also* John 14. 18–23	Isa. 41. 13–20 Ps. 145. 1, 8–13 Matt. 11. 11–15	Ps. 53; *54*; 60 *alt.* Ps. 37† Isa. ch. 32 Matt. 15. 21–28	Ps. 73 *alt.* Ps. 39; *40* Isa. 48. 1–11 1 Thess. ch. 3
15 Friday	Ember Day*			
P		Isa. 48. 17–19 Ps. 1 Matt. 11. 16–19	Ps. 85; *86* *alt.* Ps. 31 Isa. 33. 1–22 Matt. 15. 29–end	Ps. 82; *90* *alt.* Ps. 35 Isa. 48. 12–end 1 Thess. 4. 1–12
16 Saturday	Ember Day*			
P		Ecclus. 48. 1–4, 9–11 *or* 2 Kings 2. 9–12 Ps. 80. 1–4, 18–19 Matt. 17. 10–13	Ps. 145 *alt.* Ps. 41; *42*; 43 Isa. ch. 35 Matt. 16. 1–12	Ps. 93; *94* *alt.* Ps. 45; *46* Isa. 49. 1–13 1 Thess. 4. 13–end **ct**
17 Sunday	**THE THIRD SUNDAY OF ADVENT** O Sapientia**			
P		Isa. 61. 1–4, 8–end Ps. 126 *or Canticle:* Magnificat 1 Thess. 5. 16–24 John 1. 6–8, 19–28	Ps. 50. 1–6; 62 Isa. ch. 12 Luke 1. 57–66	Ps. 68. 1–19 (*or* 68. 1–8) Mal. 3. 1–4; ch. 4 Phil. 4. 4–7 *Gospel:* Matt. 14. 1–12
18 Monday				
P		Jer. 23. 5–8 Ps. 72. 1–2, 12–13, 18–end Matt. 1. 18–24	Ps. 40 *alt.* Ps. 44 Isa. 38. 1–8, 21–22 Matt. 16. 13–end	Ps. 25; *26* *alt.* Ps. *47*; 49 Isa. 49. 14–25 1 Thess. 5. 1–11
19 Tuesday				
P		Judg. 13. 2–7, 24–end Ps. 71. 3–8 Luke 1. 5–25	Ps. 144; *146* Isa. 38. 9–20 Matt. 17. 1–13	Ps. 10; *57* Isa. ch. 50 1 Thess. 5. 12–end

*For Ember Day provision, see p. 11.
**Evening Prayer readings from the Additional Weekday Lectionary (see p. 119) may be used from 17 to 23 December.

	Calendar and Holy Communion	Morning Prayer	Evening Prayer	NOTES
P		Isa. 30. 19–end Matt. 14. 13–end	Isa. ch. 46 1 Thess. 2. 1–12	
	Lucy, Martyr at Syracuse, 304 Ember Day			
Pr	Com. Virgin Martyr *or* Ember CEG	Isa. ch. 31 Matt. 15. 1–20	Isa. ch. 47 1 Thess. 2. 13–end	
P		Isa. ch. 32 Matt. 15. 21–28	Isa. 48. 1–11 1 Thess. ch. 3	
	Ember Day			
P	Ember CEG	Isa. 33. 1–22 Matt. 15. 29–end	Isa. 48. 12–end 1 Thess. 4. 1–12	
	O Sapientia Ember Day			
P	Ember CEG	Isa. ch. 35 Matt. 16. 1–12	Isa. 49. 1–13 1 Thess. 4. 13–end	
			ct	
	THE THIRD SUNDAY IN ADVENT			
P	Isa. ch. 35 Ps. 80. 1–7 1 Cor. 4. 1–5 Matt. 11. 2–10	Ps. 62 Isa. ch. 12 Luke 1. 57–66	Ps. 68. 1–19 (*or* 68. 1–8) Mal. 3. 1–4; ch. 4 Matt. 14. 1–12	
P		Isa. 38. 1–8, 21–22 Matt. 16. 13–end	Isa. 49. 14–25 1 Thess. 5. 1–11	
P		Isa. 38. 9–20 Matt. 17. 1–13	Isa. ch. 50 1 Thess. 5. 12–end	

		Sunday Principal Service Weekday Eucharist	Third Service Morning Prayer	Second Service Evening Prayer
20 Wednesday				
P		Isa. 7. 10–14 Ps. 24. 1–6 Luke 1. 26–38	Ps. *46*; 95 Isa. ch. 39 Matt. 17. 14–21	Ps. *4*; 9 Isa. 51. 1–8 2 Thess. ch. 1
21 Thursday*				
P		Zeph. 3. 14–18 Ps. 33. 1–4, 11–12, 20–end Luke 1. 39–45	Ps. *121*; 122; 123 Zeph. 1.1 - 2.3 Matt. 17. 22–end	Ps. 80; *84* Isa. 51. 9–16 2 Thess. ch. 2
22 Friday				
P		1 Sam. 1. 24–end Ps. 113 Luke 1. 46–56	Ps. *124*; 125; 126; 127 Zeph. 3. 1–13 Matt. 18. 1–20	Ps. 24; *48* Isa. 51. 17–end 2 Thess. ch. 3
23 Saturday				
P		Mal. 3. 1–4; 4. 5–end Ps. 25. 3–9 Luke 1. 57–66	Ps. 128; 129; *130*; 131 Zeph. 3. 14–end Matt. 18. 21–end	Ps. 89. 1–37 Isa. 52. 1–12 Jude **ct**
24 Sunday	**THE FOURTH SUNDAY OF ADVENT** **CHRISTMAS EVE**			
P		2 Sam. 7. 1–11, 16 *Canticle*: Magnificat or Ps. 89. 1–4, 19–26 (or 1–8) Rom. 16. 25–end Luke 1. 26–38	Ps. 144 Isa. 7. 10–16 Rom. 1. 1–7	*Evening Prayer* Ps. 85 Zech. ch. 2 Rev. 1. 1–8
25 Monday	**CHRISTMAS DAY**			
w	*Any of the following sets of readings may be used on the evening of Christmas Eve and on Christmas Day. Set III should be used at some service during the celebration.*	I Isa. 9. 2–7 Ps. 96 Titus 2. 11–14 Luke 2. 1–14 [15–20] II Isa. 62. 6–end Ps. 97 Titus 3. 4–7 Luke 2. [1–7] 8–20 III Isa. 52. 7–10 Ps. 98 Heb. 1. 1–4 [5–12] John 1. 1–14	*MP*: Ps. *110*; 117 Isa. 62. 1–5 Matt. 1. 18–end	*EP*: Ps. 8 Isa. 65. 17–25 Phil. 2. 5–11 or Luke 2. 1–20 *if it has not been used at the principal service of the day*

*Thomas the Apostle may be celebrated on 21 December instead of 3 July.

	Calendar and Holy Communion	Morning Prayer	Evening Prayer	NOTES
P		Isa. ch. 39 Matt. 17. 14–21	Isa. 51. 1–8 2 Thess. ch. 1 *or First EP of Thomas the Apostle* (Ps. 27) Isa. ch. 35 Heb. 10.35 – 11.1 **R ct**	
	THOMAS THE APOSTLE			
R	Job 42. 1–6 Ps. 139. 1–11 Eph. 2. 19–end John 20. 24–end	(Ps. 92; 146) 2 Sam. 15. 17–21 *or* Ecclus. ch. 2 John 11. 1–16	(Ps. 139) Hab. 2. 1–4 1 Pet. 1. 3–12	
P		Zeph. 3. 1–13 Matt. 18. 1–20	Isa. 51. 17–end 2 Thess. ch. 3	
P		Zeph. 3. 14–end Matt. 18. 21–end	Isa. 52. 1–12 Jude **ct**	
	THE FOURTH SUNDAY IN ADVENT **CHRISTMAS EVE**			
P	Collect (1) Advent 4 (2) Advent 1 Isa. 40. 1–9 Ps. 145. 17–end Phil. 4. 4–7 John 1. 19–28	Ps. 144 Isa. 7. 10–16 Rom. 1. 1–7	Ps. 85 Zech. ch. 2 Rev. 1. 1–8	
	CHRISTMAS DAY			
w	Isa. 9. 2–7 Ps. 98 Heb. 1. 1–12 John 1. 1–14	Ps. 110; 117 Isa. 62. 1–5 Matt. 1. 18–end	Ps. 8 Isa. 65. 17–25 Phil. 2. 5–11 *or* Luke 2. 1–20	

		Sunday Principal Service Weekday Eucharist	Third Service Morning Prayer	Second Service Evening Prayer
26 Tuesday	**STEPHEN, DEACON, FIRST MARTYR**			
R	*The reading from Acts must be used as either the first or second reading at the Eucharist.*	2 Chron. 24. 20–22 or Acts 7. 51–end Ps. 119. 161–168 Acts 7. 51–end or Gal. 2. 16b–20 Matt. 10. 17–22	MP: Ps. *13*; 31. 1–8; 150 Jer. 26. 12–15 Acts ch. 6	EP: Ps. 57; *86* Gen. 4. 1–10 Matt. 23. 34–end
27 Wednesday	**JOHN, APOSTLE AND EVANGELIST**			
W		Exod. 33. 7–11a Ps. 117 1 John ch. 1 John 21. 19b–end	MP: Ps. *21*; 147. 13–end Exod. 33. 12–end 1 John 2. 1–11	EP: Ps. 97 Isa. 6. 1–8 1 John 5. 1–12
28 Thursday	**THE HOLY INNOCENTS**			
R		Jer. 31. 15–17 Ps. 124 1 Cor. 1. 26–29 Matt. 2. 13–18	MP: Ps. *36*; 146 Baruch 4. 21–27 or Gen. 37. 13–20 Matt. 18. 1–10	EP: Ps. 123; *128* Isa. 49. 14–25 Mark 10. 13–16
29 Friday	**Thomas Becket, Archbishop of Canterbury, Martyr, 1170**			
Wr	Com. Martyr or *esp.* Matt. 10. 28–33 *also* Ecclus. 51. 1–8	1 John 2. 3–11 Ps. 96. 1–4 Luke 2. 22–35	Ps. *19*; 20 Jonah ch. 1 Col. 1. 1–14	Ps. 131; *132* Isa. 57. 15–end John 1. 1–18
30 Saturday				
W		1 John 2. 12–17 Ps. 96. 7–10 Luke 2. 36–40	Ps. 111; 112; *113* Jonah ch. 2 Col. 1. 15–23	Ps. *65*; 84 Isa. 59. 1–15a John 1. 19–28 **ct**
31 Sunday	**THE FIRST SUNDAY OF CHRISTMAS**			
W		Isa. 61.10 – 62.3 Ps. 148 (or 148. 7–end) Gal. 4. 4–7 Luke 2. 15–21	Ps. 105. 1–11 Isa. 63. 7–9 Eph. 3. 5–12	Ps. 132 Isa. ch. 35 Col. 1. 9–20 *or* Luke 2. 41–end *or First EP of The Naming of Jesus* Ps. 148 Jer. 23. 1–6 Col. 2. 8–15

January 2024

1 Monday	**THE NAMING AND CIRCUMCISION OF JESUS**			
W		Num. 6. 22–end Ps. 8 Gal. 4. 4–7 Luke 2. 15–21	MP: Ps. *103*; 150 Gen. 17. 1–13 Rom. 2. 17–end	EP: Ps. 115 Deut. 30. [1–10] 11–end Acts 3. 1–16

	Calendar and Holy Communion	Morning Prayer	Evening Prayer	NOTES
	STEPHEN, DEACON, FIRST MARTYR			
R	Collect (1) Stephen (2) Christmas 2 Chron. 24. 20–22 Ps. 119. 161–168 Acts 7. 55–end Matt. 23. 34–end	(Ps. 13; 31. 1–8; 150) Jer. 26. 12–15 Acts ch. 6	(Ps. 57; 86) Gen. 4. 1–10 Matt. 10. 17–22	
	JOHN, APOSTLE AND EVANGELIST			
W	Collect (1) John (2) Christmas Exod. 33. 18–end Ps. 92. 11–end 1 John ch. 1 John 21. 19b–end	(Ps. 21; 147. 13–end) Exod. 33. 7–11a 1 John 2. 1–11	(Ps. 97) Isa. 6. 1–8 1 John 5. 1–12	
	THE HOLY INNOCENTS			
R	Collect (1) Innocents (2) Christmas Jer. 31. 10–17 Ps. 123 Rev. 14. 1–5 Matt. 2. 13–18	(Ps. 36; 146) Baruch 4. 21–27 or Gen. 37. 13–20 Matt. 18. 1–10	(Ps. 124; 128) Isa. 49. 14–25 Mark 10. 13–16	
W	CEG of Christmas	Jonah ch. 1 Col. 1. 1–14	Isa. 57. 15–end John 1. 1–18	
W	CEG of Christmas	Jonah ch. 2 Col. 1. 15–23	Isa. 59. 1–15a John 1. 19–28 **ct**	
	THE SUNDAY AFTER CHRISTMAS DAY			
W	Isa. 62. 10–12 Ps. 45. 1–7 Gal. 4. 1–7 Matt. 1. 18–end	Ps. 105. 1–11 Isa. 63. 7–9 Eph. 3. 5–12	Ps. 132 Isa. ch. 35 1 John 1. 1–7 or First EP of the Circumcision of Christ Ps. 148 Jer. 23. 1–6 Col. 2. 8–15	
	THE CIRCUMCISION OF CHRIST			
W	Additional collect Gen. 17. 3b–10 Ps. 98 Rom. 4. 8–13 or Eph. 2. 11–18 Luke 2. 15–21	(Ps. 103; 150) Gen. 17. 1–13 Rom. 2. 17–end	(Ps. 115) Deut. 30. [1–10] 11–end Acts 3. 1–16	

	Sunday Principal Service Weekday Eucharist	Third Service Morning Prayer	Second Service Evening Prayer
2 Tuesday **Basil the Great and Gregory of Nazianzus, Bishops, Teachers, 379 and 389** *Seraphim, Monk of Sarov, Spiritual Guide, 1833; Vedanayagam Samuel Azariah, Bishop in South India, Evangelist, 1945*			
W	Com. Teacher *or* *esp.* 2 Tim. 4. 1–8 Matt. 5. 13–19	1 John 2. 22–28 Ps. 98. 1–4 John 1. 19–28	Ps. 18. 1–30 Ruth ch. 1 Col. 2. 8–end	Ps. 45; *46* Isa. 60. 1–12 John 1. 35–42
3 Wednesday			
W		1 John 2.29 – 3.6 Ps. 98. 2–7 John 1. 29–34	Ps. *127*; 128; 131 Ruth ch. 2 Col. 3. 1–11	Ps. *2*; 110 Isa. 60. 13–end John 1. 43–end
4 Thursday			
W		1 John 3. 7–10 Ps. 98. 1, 8–end John 1. 35–42	Ps. 89. 1–37 Ruth ch. 3 Col. 3.12 – 4.1	Ps. 85; *87* Isa. ch. 61 John 2. 1–12
5 Friday			
W		1 John 3. 11–21 Ps. 100 John 1. 43–end	Ps. 8; *48* Ruth 4. 1–7 Col. 4. 2–end	*First EP of The Epiphany* Ps. 96; *97* Isa. 49. 1–13 John 4. 7–26 𝖂 ct *or, if The Epiphany is celebrated on 7 January:* Ps. 96; *97* Isa. ch. 62 John 2. 13–end
6 Saturday **THE EPIPHANY**			
𝖂	Isa. 60. 1–6 Ps. 72. [1–9] 10–15 Eph. 3. 1–12 Matt. 2. 1–12	*MP*: Ps. *132*; 113 Jer. 31. 7–14 John 1. 29–34	*EP*: Ps. *98*; 100 Baruch 4.36 – 5.end *or* Isa. 60. 1–9 John 2. 1–11
W	*or, if The Epiphany is celebrated on 7 January:* 1 John 5. 5–13 Ps. 147. 13–end Mark 1. 7–11	Ps. *99*; 147. 1–12 Baruch 1.15 – 2.10 *or* Jer. 23. 1–8 Matt. 20. 1–16	*First EP of The Epiphany* Ps. 96; 97 Isa. 49. 1–13 John 4. 7–26 𝖂 ct
7 Sunday **THE BAPTISM OF CHRIST (THE FIRST SUNDAY OF EPIPHANY)** *or transferred to 8 January if The Epiphany is celebrated today. (For The Epiphany, see provision on 6 January.)*			
𝖂	Gen. 1. 1–5 Ps. 29 Acts 19. 1–7 Mark 1. 4–11	Ps. 89. 19–29 1 Sam. 16. 1–3, 13 John 1. 29–34	Ps. 46; [47] Isa. 42. 1–9 Eph. 2. 1–10 *Gospel*: Matt. 3. 13–end
8 Monday For The Baptism, see provision on 7 January.			
W **DEL 1**	1 Sam. 1. 1–8 Ps. 116. 10–15 Mark 1. 14–20	Ps. *2*; 110 *alt.* Ps. 71 Gen. 1. 1–19 Matt. 21. 1–17	Ps. *34*; 36 *alt.* Ps. *72*; 75 Amos ch. 1 1 Cor. 1. 1–17

	Calendar and Holy Communion	Morning Prayer	Evening Prayer	NOTES
W		Ruth ch. 1 Col. 2. 8–end	Isa. 60. 1–12 John 1. 35–42	
W		Ruth ch. 2 Col. 3. 1–11	Isa. 60. 13–end John 1. 43–end	
W		Ruth ch. 3 Col. 3.12 – 4.1	Isa. ch. 61 John 2. 1–12	
W		Ruth 4. 1–7 Col. 4. 2–end	*First EP of The Epiphany* Ps. 96; 97 Isa. 49. 1–13 John 4. 7–26 𝔚 ct	

THE EPIPHANY

𝔚	Isa. 60. 1–9 Ps. 100 Eph. 3. 1–12 Matt. 2. 1–12	Ps. 132; 113 Jer. 31. 7–14 John 1. 29–34	Ps. 72; 98 Baruch 4.36 - 5.end *or* Isa. 60. 1–9 John 2. 1–11	

THE FIRST SUNDAY AFTER THE EPIPHANY
To celebrate The Baptism of Christ, see *Common Worship* provision.

W *or* G	Zech. 8. 1–8 Ps. 72. 1–8 Rom. 12. 1–5 Luke 2. 41–end	Ps. 89. 19–29 1 Sam. 16. 1–3, 13 John 1. 29–34	Ps. 46; [47] Isa. 42. 1–9 Eph. 2. 1–10	

Lucian, Priest and Martyr, 290

Wr *or* Gr	Com. Martyr	Gen. 1. 1–19 Matt. 21. 1–17	Amos ch. 1 1 Cor. 1. 1–17	

		Sunday Principal Service Weekday Eucharist	Third Service Morning Prayer	Second Service Evening Prayer
9 Tuesday				
W		1 Sam. 1. 9–20 *Canticle*: 1 Sam. 2. 1, 4–8 *or* Magnificat Mark 1. 21–28	Ps. 8; *9* *alt.* Ps. 73 Gen. 1.20 – 2.3 Matt. 21. 18–32	Ps. *45*; 46 *alt.* Ps. 74 Amos ch. 2 1 Cor. 1. 18–end
10 Wednesday	*William Laud, Archbishop of Canterbury, 1645*			
W		1 Sam. 3. 1–10, 19–20 Ps. 40. 1–4, 7–10 Mark 1. 29–39	Ps. 19; *20* *alt.* Ps. 77 Gen. 2. 4–end Matt. 21. 33–end	Ps. *47*; 48 *alt.* Ps. 119. 81–104 Amos ch. 3 1 Cor. ch. 2
11 Thursday	*Mary Slessor, Missionary in West Africa, 1915*			
W		1 Sam. 4. 1–11 Ps. 44. 10–15, 24–25 Mark 1. 40–end	Ps. *21*; 24 *alt.* Ps. 78. 1–39† Gen. ch. 3 Matt. 22. 1–14	Ps. *61*; 65 *alt.* Ps. 78. 40–end† Amos ch. 4 1 Cor. ch. 3
12 Friday	*Aelred of Hexham, Abbot of Rievaulx, 1167* *Benedict Biscop, Abbot of Wearmouth, Scholar, 689*			
W	Com. Religious *or* *also* Ecclus. 15. 1–6	1 Sam. 8. 4–7, 10–end Ps. 89. 15–18 Mark 2. 1–12	Ps. *67*; 72 *alt.* Ps. 55 Gen. 4. 1–16, 25–26 Matt. 22. 15–33	Ps. 68 *alt.* Ps. 69 Amos 5. 1–17 1 Cor. ch. 4
13 Saturday	*Hilary, Bishop of Poitiers, Teacher, 367* *Kentigern (Mungo), Missionary Bishop in Strathclyde and Cumbria, 603; George Fox, Founder of the Society of Friends (the Quakers), 1691*			
W	Com. Teacher *or* *also* 1 John 2. 18–25 John 8. 25–32	1 Sam. 9. 1–4, 17–19; 10. 1a Ps. 21. 1–6 Mark 2. 13–17	Ps. 29; *33* *alt.* Ps. *76*; 79 Gen. 6. 1–10 Matt. 22. 34–end	Ps. 84; *85* *alt.* Ps. 81; *84* Amos 5. 18–end 1 Cor. ch. 5 **ct**
14 Sunday	**THE SECOND SUNDAY OF EPIPHANY**			
W		1 Sam. 3. 1–10 [11–20] Ps. 139. 1–5, 12–18 (*or* 1–9) Rev. 5. 1–10 John 1. 43–end	Ps. 145. 1–12 Isa. 62. 1–5 1 Cor. 6. 11–end	Ps. 96 Isa. 60. 9–end Heb. 6.17 – 7.10 *Gospel:* Matt. 8. 5–13
15 Monday				
W **DEL 2**		1 Sam. 15. 16–23 Ps. 50. 8–10, 16–17, 24 Mark 2. 18–22	Ps. 145; *146* *alt.* Ps. *80*; 82 Gen. 6.11 – 7.10 Matt. 24. 1–14	Ps. 71 *alt.* Ps. *85*; 86 Amos ch. 6 1 Cor. 6. 1–11
16 Tuesday				
W		1 Sam. 16. 1–13 Ps. 89. 19–27 Mark 2. 23–end	Ps. *132*; 147. 1–12 *alt.* Ps. 87; *89. 1–18* Gen. 7. 11–end Matt. 24. 15–28	Ps. 89. 1–37 *alt.* Ps. 89. 19–end Amos ch. 7 1 Cor. 6. 12–end
17 Wednesday	*Antony of Egypt, Hermit, Abbot, 356* *Charles Gore, Bishop, Founder of the Community of the Resurrection, 1932*			
W	Com. Religious *or* *esp.* Phil. 3. 7–14 *also* Matt. 19. 16–26	1 Sam. 17. 32–33, 37, 40–51 Ps. 144. 1–2, 9–10 Mark 3. 1–6	Ps. *81*; 147. 13–end *alt.* Ps. 119. 105–128 Gen. 8. 1–14 Matt. 24. 29–end	Ps. *97*; 98 *alt.* Ps. *91*; 93 Amos ch. 8 1 Cor. 7. 1–24

	Calendar and Holy Communion	Morning Prayer	Evening Prayer	NOTES
W or G		Gen. 1.20 – 2.3 Matt. 21. 18–32	Amos ch. 2 1 Cor. 1. 18–end	
W or G		Gen. 2. 4–end Matt. 21. 33–end	Amos ch. 3 1 Cor. ch. 2	
W or G		Gen. ch. 3 Matt. 22. 1–14	Amos ch. 4 1 Cor. ch. 3	
W or G		Gen. 4. 1–16, 25–26 Matt. 22. 15–33	Amos 5. 1–17 1 Cor. ch. 4	
	Hilary, Bishop of Poitiers, Teacher, 367			
W or Gw	Com. Doctor	Gen. 6. 1–10 Matt. 22. 34–end	Amos 5. 18–end 1 Cor. ch. 5	
			ct	
THE SECOND SUNDAY AFTER THE EPIPHANY				
W or G	2 Kings 4. 1–17 Ps. 107. 13–22 Rom. 12. 6–16a John 2. 1–11	Ps. 145. 1–12 Isa. 62. 1–5 1 Cor. 6. 11–end	Ps. 96 Isa. 60. 9–end Heb. 6.17 – 7.10	
W or G		Gen. 6.11 – 7.10 Matt. 24. 1–14	Amos ch. 6 1 Cor. 6. 1–11	
W or G		Gen. 7. 11–end Matt. 24. 15–28	Amos ch. 7 1 Cor. 6. 12–end	
W or G		Gen. 8. 1–14 Matt. 24. 29–end	Amos ch. 8 1 Cor. 7. 1–24	

		Sunday Principal Service Weekday Eucharist	Third Service Morning Prayer	Second Service Evening Prayer
18 Thursday	*Amy Carmichael, Founder of the Dohnavur Fellowship, Spiritual Writer, 1951* The Week of Prayer for Christian Unity until 25 January			
W		1 Sam. 18. 6–9; 19. 1–7 Ps. 56. 1–2, 8–end Mark 3. 7–12	Ps. *76*; 148 *alt.* Ps. 90; *92* Gen. 8.15 – 9.7 Matt. 25. 1–13	Ps. 99; 100; *111* *alt.* Ps. 94 Amos ch. 9 1 Cor. 7. 25–end
19 Friday	**Wulfstan, Bishop of Worcester, 1095**			
W	Com. Bishop *or* *esp.* Matt. 24. 42–46	1 Sam. 24. 3–22a Ps. 57. 1–2, 8–end Mark 3. 13–19	Ps. *27*; 149 *alt.* Ps. *88*; (95) Gen. 9. 8–19 Matt. 25. 14–30	Ps. 73 *alt.* Ps. 102 Hos. 1.1 – 2.1 1 Cor. ch. 8
20 Saturday	*Richard Rolle of Hampole, Spiritual Writer, 1349*			
W		2 Sam. 1. 1–4, 11–12, 17–19, 23–end Ps. 80. 1–6 Mark 3. 20–21	Ps. *122*; 128; 150 *alt.* Ps. 96; *97*; 100 Gen. 11. 1–9 Matt. 25. 31–end	Ps. *61*; 66 *alt.* Ps. 104 Hos. 2. 2–17 1 Cor. 9. 1–14 ct
21 Sunday	**THE THIRD SUNDAY OF EPIPHANY**			
W		Gen. 14. 17–20 Ps. 128 Rev. 19. 6–10 John 2. 1–11	Ps. 113 Jonah 3. 1–5, 10 John 3. 16–21	Ps. 33 (*or* 33. 1–12) Jer. 3.21 – 4.2 Titus 2. 1–8, 11–14 *Gospel:* Matt. 4. 12–23
22 Monday	*Vincent of Saragossa, Deacon, first Martyr of Spain, 304*			
W DEL 3		2 Sam. 5. 1–7, 10 Ps. 89. 19–27 Mark 3. 22–30	Ps. 40; *108* *alt.* Ps. *98*; 99; 101 Gen. 11.27 – 12.9 Matt. 26. 1–16	Ps. *138*; 144 *alt.* Ps. 105† (*or* Ps. 103) Hos. 2.18 – 3.end 1 Cor. 9. 15–end
23 Tuesday				
W		2 Sam. 6. 12–15, 17–19 Ps. 24. 7–end Mark 3. 31–end	Ps. 34; *36* *alt.* Ps. 106† (*or* Ps. 103) Gen. 13. 2–end Matt. 26. 17–35	Ps. 145 *alt.* Ps. 107† Hos. 4. 1–16 1 Cor. 10. 1–13
24 Wednesday	**Francis de Sales, Bishop of Geneva, Teacher, 1622**			
W	Com. Teacher *or* *also* Prov. 3. 13–18 John 3. 17–21	2 Sam. 7. 4–17 Ps. 89. 19–27 Mark 4. 1–20	Ps. 45; *46* *alt.* Ps. 110; *111*; 112 Gen. ch. 14 Matt. 26. 36–46	Ps. 21; *29* *alt.* Ps. 119. 129–152 Hos. 5. 1–7 1 Cor. 10.14 – 11.1 *or First EP of The* *Conversion of Paul* Ps. 149 Isa. 49. 1–13 Acts 22. 3–16 ct
25 Thursday	**THE CONVERSION OF PAUL**			
W		Jer. 1. 4–10 *or* Acts 9. 1–22 Ps. 67 Acts 9. 1–22 *or* Gal. 1. 11–16a Matt. 19. 27–end	*MP:* Ps. 66; 147. 13–end Ezek. 3. 22–end Phil. 3. 1–14	*EP:* Ps. 119. 41–56 Ecclus. 39. 1–10 *or* Isa. 56. 1–8 Col. 1.24 – 2.7

	Calendar and Holy Communion	Morning Prayer	Evening Prayer	NOTES
	Prisca, Martyr at Rome, *c.* **265** For the Week of Prayer for Christian Unity, see *Common Worship* provision.			
Wr or **Gr**	Com. Virgin Martyr	Gen. 8.15 – 9.7 Matt. 25. 1–13	Amos ch. 9 1 Cor. 7. 25–end	
W or **G**		Gen. 9. 8–19 Matt. 25. 14–30	Hos. 1.1 – 2.1 1 Cor. ch. 8	
	Fabian, Bishop of Rome, Martyr, 250			
Wr or **Gr**	Com. Martyr	Gen. 11. 1–9 Matt. 25. 31–end	Hos. 2. 2–17 1 Cor. 9. 1–14	
			ct	
	THE THIRD SUNDAY AFTER THE EPIPHANY			
W or **G**	2 Kings 6. 14b–23 Ps. 102. 15–22 Rom. 12. 16b–end Matt. 8. 1–13	Ps. 113 Jonah 3. 1–5, 10 John 3. 16–21	Ps. 33 (or 33. 1–12) Jer. 3.21 – 4.2 Titus 2. 1–8, 11–14	
	Vincent of Saragossa, Deacon, first Martyr of Spain, 304			
Wr or **Gr**	Com. Martyr	Gen. 11.27 – 12.9 Matt. 26. 1–16	Hos. 2.18 – 3.end 1 Cor. 9. 15–end	
W or **G**		Gen. 13. 2–end Matt. 26. 17–35	Hos. 4. 1–16 1 Cor. 10. 1–13	
W or **G**		Gen. ch. 14 Matt. 26. 36–46	Hos. 5. 1–7 1 Cor. 10.14 – 11.1 or First EP of The Conversion of Paul (Ps. 149) Isa. 49. 1–13 Acts 22. 3–16	
			W ct	
	THE CONVERSION OF PAUL			
W	Josh. 5. 13–end Ps. 67 Acts 9. 1–22 Matt. 19. 27–end	(Ps. 66; 147. 13–end) Ezek. 3. 22–end Phil. 3. 1–14	(Ps. 119. 41–56) Ecclus. 39. 1–10 or Isa. 56. 1–8 Col. 1.24 – 2.7	

		Sunday Principal Service Weekday Eucharist	Third Service Morning Prayer	Second Service Evening Prayer
26 Friday	**Timothy and Titus, Companions of Paul**			
W	Isa. 61. 1–3a *or* Ps. 100 2 Tim. 2. 1–8 *or* Titus 1. 1–5 Luke 10. 1–9	2 Sam. 11. 1–10, 13–17 Ps. 51. 1–6, 9 Mark 4. 26–34	Ps. 61; **65** *alt.* Ps. 139 Gen. ch. 16 Matt. 26. 57–end	Ps. **67**; 77 *alt.* Ps. **130**; 131; 137 Hos. 6.7 – 7.2 1 Cor. 11. 17–end
27 Saturday				
W		2 Sam. 12. 1–7, 10–17 Ps. 51. 11–16 Mark 4. 35–end	Ps. 68 *alt.* Ps. 120; **121**; 122 Gen. 17. 1–22 Matt. 27. 1–10	Ps. **72**; 76 *alt.* Ps. 118 Hos. ch. 8 1 Cor. 12. 1–11 **ct**
28 Sunday	**THE FOURTH SUNDAY OF EPIPHANY** *or The Presentation of Christ in the Temple (Candlemas)**			
W		Deut. 18. 15–20 Ps. 111 Rev. 12. 1–5a Mark 1. 21–28	Ps. 71. 1–6, 15–17 Jer. 1. 4–10 Mark 1. 40–end	Ps. 34 (or 34. 1–10) 1 Sam. 3. 1–20 1 Cor. 14. 12–20 *Gospel:* Matt. 13. 10–17
29 Monday				
W [G]** DEL 4		2 Sam. 15. 13–14, 30; 16. 5–13 Ps. 3 Mark 5. 1–20	***Ps. **57**; 96 *alt.* Ps. 123; 124; 125; **126** Gen. 18. 1–15 Matt. 27. 11–26	***Ps. 2; **20** *alt.* Ps. **127**; 128; 129 Hos. ch. 9 1 Cor. 12. 12–end
30 Tuesday	**Charles, King and Martyr, 1649**			
Wr [Gr]	Com. Martyr *or* *also* Ecclus. 2. 12–17 1 Tim. 6. 12–16	2 Sam. 18.9–10, 14, 24–25, 30 – 19.3 Ps. 86. 1–6 Mark. 5. 21–end	***Ps. **93**; 97 *alt.* Ps. **132**; 133 Gen. 18. 16–end Matt. 27. 27–44	***Ps. **19**; 21 *alt.* Ps. (134); **135** Hos. ch. 10 1 Cor. ch. 13
31 Wednesday	*John Bosco, Priest, Founder of the Salesian Teaching Order, 1888*			
W [G]		2 Sam. 24. 2, 9–17 Ps. 32. 1–8 Mark 6. 1–6a	***Ps. **95**; 98 *alt.* Ps. 119. 153–end Gen. 19. 1–3, 12–29 Matt. 27. 45–56	***Ps. **81**; 111 *alt.* Ps. 136 Hos. 11. 1–11 1 Cor. 14. 1–19

February 2024

1 Thursday	*Brigid, Abbess of Kildare, c. 525*			
W [G]		1 Kings 2. 1–4, 10–12 *Canticle:* 1 Chron. 29. 10–12 *or* Ps. 145. 1–5 Mark 6. 7–13	***Ps. 99; **110** *alt.* Ps. **143**; 146 Gen. 21. 1–21 Matt. 27. 57–end	*First EP of The Presentation* Ps. 118 1 Sam. 1. 19b–end Heb. 4. 11–end **𝖂 ct** *or, if The Presentation was kept on 28 January:* Ps. **138**; 140; 141 Hos. 11.12 – 12.end 1 Cor. 14. 20–end

*See provision for First EP on 1 February and throughout the day for The Presentation on 2 February.
**Ordinary Time begins today if The Presentation was observed on 28 January.
***If The Presentation was observed on 28 January, the alternative psalms are used.

	Calendar and Holy Communion	Morning Prayer	Evening Prayer	NOTES
W *or* **G**		Gen. ch. 16 Matt. 26. 57–end	Hos. 6.7 – 7.2 1 Cor. 11. 17–end	
W *or* **G**		Gen. 17. 1–22 Matt. 27. 1–10	Hos. ch. 8 1 Cor. 12. 1–11 **ct**	
SEPTUAGESIMA				
W *or* **G**	Gen. 1. 1–5 Ps. 9. 10–20 1 Cor. 9. 24–end Matt. 20. 1–16	Ps. 71. 1–6, 15–17 Jer. 1. 4–10 Mark 1. 40–end	Ps. 34 (*or* 34. 1–10) 1 Sam. 3. 1–20 1 Cor. 14. 12–20	
W *or* **G**		Gen. 18. 1–15 Matt. 27. 11–26	Hos. ch. 9 1 Cor. 12. 12–end	
Charles, King and Martyr, 1649				
Wr *or* **Gr**	Com. Martyr	Gen. 18. 16–end Matt. 27. 27–44	Hos. ch. 10 1 Cor. ch. 13	
W *or* **G**		Gen. 19. 1–3, 12–29 Matt. 27. 45–56	Hos. 11. 1–11 1 Cor. 14. 1–19	
W *or* **G**		Gen. 21. 1–21 Matt. 27. 57–end	*First EP of The Presentation* Ps. 118 1 Sam. 1. 19b–end Heb. 4. 11–end 𝔚 **ct**	

		Sunday Principal Service Weekday Eucharist	Third Service Morning Prayer	Second Service Evening Prayer
2 Friday	**THE PRESENTATION OF CHRIST IN THE TEMPLE (CANDLEMAS)**			
𝔚		Mal. 3. 1–5 Ps. 24. [1–6] 7–end Heb. 2. 14–end Luke 2. 22–40	*MP*: Ps. ***48***; 146 Exod. 13. 1–16 Rom. 12. 1–5	*EP*: Ps. 122; ***132*** Hag. 2. 1–9 John 2. 18–22
	or, if The Presentation is observed on 28 January:			
G		Ecclus. 47. 2–11 Ps. 18. 31–36, 50–end Mark 6. 14–29	Ps. 142; ***144*** Gen. 22. 1–19 Matt. 28. 1–15	Ps. 145 Hos. 13. 1–14 1 Cor. 16. 1–9
3 Saturday	**Anskar, Archbishop of Hamburg, Missionary in Denmark and Sweden, 865** *Ordinary Time starts today (or on 29 January if The Presentation is observed on 28 January)*			
Gw	Com. Missionary *or* *esp.* Isa. 52. 7–10 *also* Rom. 10. 11–15	1 Kings 3. 4–13 Ps. 119. 9–16 Mark 6. 30–34	Ps. 147 Gen. ch. 23 Matt. 28. 16–end	Ps. ***148***; 149; 150 Hos. ch. 14 1 Cor. 16. 10–end **ct**
4 Sunday	**THE SECOND SUNDAY BEFORE LENT**			
G		Prov. 8. 1, 22–31 Ps. 104. 26–end Col. 1. 15–20 John 1. 1–14	Ps. 29; 67 Deut. 8. 1–10 Matt. 6. 25–end	Ps. 65 Gen. 2. 4b–end Luke 8. 22–35
5 Monday				
G **DEL 5**		1 Kings 8. 1–7, 9–13 Ps. 132. 1–9 Mark 6. 53–end	Ps. ***1***; 2; 3 Gen. 29.31 – 30.24 2 Tim. 4. 1–8	Ps. ***4***; 7 Eccles. 7. 1–14 John 19. 1–16
6 Tuesday	*The Martyrs of Japan, 1597*			
G		1 Kings 8. 22–23, 27–30 Ps. 84. 1–10 Mark 7. 1–13	Ps. ***5***; 6; (8) Gen. 31. 1–24 2 Tim. 4. 9–end	Ps. ***9***; 10† Eccles. 7. 15–end John 19. 17–30
7 Wednesday				
G		1 Kings 10. 1–10 Ps. 37. 3–6, 30–32 Mark 7. 14–23	Ps. 119. 1–32 Gen. 31.25 – 32.2 Titus ch. 1	Ps. ***11***; 12; 13 Eccles. ch. 8 John 19. 31–end
8 Thursday				
G		1 Kings 11. 4–13 Ps. 106. 3, 35–41 Mark 7. 24–30	Ps. 14; ***15***; 16 Gen. 32. 3–30 Titus ch. 2	Ps. 18† Eccles. ch. 9 John 20. 1–10
9 Friday				
G		1 Kings 11. 29–32; 12. 19 Ps. 81. 8–14 Mark 7. 31–end	Ps. 17; ***19*** Gen. 33. 1–17 Titus ch. 3	Ps. 22 Eccles. 11. 1–8 John 20. 11–18
10 Saturday	*Scholastica, sister of Benedict, Abbess of Plombariola*, c. *543*			
G		1 Kings 12.26–32; 13. 33–end Ps. 106. 6–7, 20–23 Mark 8. 1–10	Ps. 20; 21; ***23*** Gen. ch. 35 Philem.	Ps. ***24***; 25 Eccles. 11.9 – 12.end John 20. 19–end **ct**

	Calendar and Holy Communion	Morning Prayer	Evening Prayer	NOTES
	THE PRESENTATION OF CHRIST IN THE TEMPLE			
W	Mal. 3. 1–5 Ps. 48. 1–7 Gal. 4. 1–7 Luke 2. 22–40	Ps. 48; 146 Exod. 13. 1–16 Rom. 12. 1–5	Ps. 122; 132 Hag. 2. 1–9 John 2. 18–22	
	Blasius, Bishop of Sebastopol, Martyr, c. 316			
Gr	Com. Martyr	Gen. ch. 23 Matt. 28. 16–end	Hos. ch. 14 1 Cor. 16. 10–end	
			ct	
	SEXAGESIMA			
G	Gen. 3. 9–19 Ps. 83. 1–2, 13–end 2 Cor. 11. 19–31 Luke 8. 4–15	Ps. 29; 67 Deut. 8. 1–10 Matt. 6. 25–end	Ps. 65 Gen. 2. 4b–end Luke 8. 22–35	
	Agatha, Martyr in Sicily, 251			
Gr	Com. Virgin Martyr	Gen. 29.31 – 30.24 2 Tim. 4. 1–8	Eccles. 7. 1–14 John 19. 1–16	
G		Gen. 31. 1–24 2 Tim. 4. 9–end	Eccles. 7. 15–end John 19. 17–30	
G		Gen. 31.25 – 32.2 Titus ch. 1	Eccles. ch. 8 John 19. 31–end	
G		Gen. 32. 3–30 Titus ch. 2	Eccles. ch. 9 John 20. 1–10	
G		Gen. 33. 1–17 Titus ch. 3	Eccles. 11. 1–8 John 20. 11–18	
G		Gen. ch. 35 Philem.	Eccles. 11.9 – 12.end John 20. 19–end	
			ct	

	Sunday Principal Service Weekday Eucharist	Third Service Morning Prayer	Second Service Evening Prayer
11 Sunday THE SUNDAY NEXT BEFORE LENT			
G	2 Kings 2. 1–12 Ps. 50. 1–6 2 Cor. 4. 3–6 Mark 9. 2–9	Ps. 27; 150 Exod. 24. 12–end 2 Cor. 3. 12–end	Ps. 2; [99] 1 Kings 19. 1–16 2 Pet. 1. 16–end *Gospel:* Mark 9. [2–8] 9–13
12 Monday			
G **DEL 6**	Jas. 1. 1–11 Ps. 119. 65–72 Mark 8. 11–13	Ps. 27; *30* Gen. 37. 1–11 Gal. ch. 1	Ps. 26; *28*; 29 Jer. ch. 1 John 3. 1–21
13 Tuesday			
G	Jas. 1. 12–18 Ps. 94. 12–18 Mark 8. 14–21	Ps. 32; *36* Gen. 37. 12–end Gal. 2. 1–10	Ps. 33 Jer. 2. 1–13 John 3. 22–end
14 Wednesday ASH WEDNESDAY			
P	Joel 2. 1–2, 12–17 *or* Isa. 58. 1–12 Ps. 51. 1–18 2 Cor. 5.20b – 6.10 Matt. 6. 1–6, 16–21 *or* John 8. 1–11	*MP*: Ps. 38 Dan. 9. 3–6, 17–19 1 Tim. 6. 6–19	*EP*: Ps. *51* or Ps. 102 (*or* 102. 1–18) Isa. 1. 10–18 Luke 15. 11–end
15 Thursday *Sigfrid, Bishop, Apostle of Sweden, 1045; Thomas Bray, Priest, Founder of the SPCK and the SPG, 1730*			
P	Deut. 30. 15–end Ps. 1 Luke 9. 22–25	Ps. 77 *alt.* Ps. 37† Gen. ch. 39 Gal. 2. 11–end	Ps. 74 *alt.* Ps. 39; *40* Jer. 2. 14–32 John 4. 1–26
16 Friday			
P	Isa. 58. 1–9a Ps. 51. 1–5, 17–18 Matt. 9. 14–15	Ps. *3*; 7 *alt.* Ps. 31 Gen. ch. 40 Gal. 3. 1–14	Ps. 31 *alt.* Ps. 35 Jer. 3. 6–22 John 4. 27–42
17 Saturday Janani Luwum, Archbishop of Uganda, Martyr, 1977			
Pr	Com. Martyr *or* Isa. 58. 9b–end *also* Ecclus. 4. 20–28 Ps. 86. 1–7 John 12. 24–32 Luke 5. 27–32	Ps. 71 *alt.* Ps. 41; *42*; 43 Gen. 41. 1–24 Gal. 3. 15–22	Ps. 73 *alt.* Ps. 45; *46* Jer. 4. 1–18 John 4. 43–end **ct**
18 Sunday THE FIRST SUNDAY OF LENT			
P	Gen. 9. 8–17 Ps. 25. 1–9 1 Pet. 3. 18–end Mark 1. 9–15	Ps. 77 Exod. 34. 1–10 Rom. 10. 8b–13	Ps. 119. 17–32 Gen. 2. 15–17; 3. 1–7 Rom. 5. 12–19 *or* Luke 13. 31–end

	Calendar and Holy Communion	Morning Prayer	Evening Prayer
	QUINQUAGESIMA		
G	Gen. 9. 8–17 Ps. 77. 11–end 1 Cor. ch. 13 Luke 18. 31–43	Ps. 27; 150 Exod. 24. 12–end 2 Cor. 3. 12–end	Ps. 2; [99] 1 Kings 19. 1–16 2 Pet. 1. 16–end
G		Gen. 37. 1–11 Gal. ch. 1	Jer. ch. 1 John 3. 1–21
G		Gen. 37. 12–end Gal. 2. 1–10	Jer. 2. 1–13 John 3. 22–end
	ASH WEDNESDAY		
P	Ash Wednesday Collect until 30 March Commination Joel 2. 12–17 Ps. 57 Jas. 4. 1–10 Matt. 6. 16–21	Ps. 38 Dan. 9. 3–6, 17–19 1 Tim. 6. 6–19	Ps. 51 *or* Ps. 102 (*or* 102. 1–18) Isa. 1. 10–18 Luke 15. 11–end
P	Exod. 24. 12–end Matt. 8. 5–13	Gen. ch. 39 Gal. 2. 11–end	Jer. 2. 14–32 John 4. 1–26
P	1 Kings 19. 3b–8 Matt. 5.43 – 6.6	Gen. ch. 40 Gal. 3. 1–14	Jer. 3. 6–22 John 4. 27–42
P	Isa. 38. 1–6a Mark 6. 45–end	Gen. 41. 1–24 Gal. 3. 15–22	Jer. 4. 1–18 John 4. 43–end
			ct
	THE FIRST SUNDAY IN LENT		
P	Collect (1) Lent 1 (2) Ash Wednesday Ember until 24 February Gen. 3. 1–6 Ps. 91. 1–12 2 Cor. 6. 1–10 Matt. 4. 1–11	Ps. 77 Exod. 34. 1–10 Rom. 10. 8b–13	Ps. 119. 17–32 Gen. 2. 15–17; 3. 1–7 Rom. 5. 12–19 *or* Luke 13. 31–end

NOTES

		Sunday Principal Service Weekday Eucharist	Third Service Morning Prayer	Second Service Evening Prayer
19 Monday				
P		Lev. 19. 1–2, 11–18 Ps. 19. 7–end Matt. 25. 31–end	Ps. 10; *11* *alt.* Ps. 44 Gen. 41. 25–45 Gal. 3.23 – 4.7	Ps. 12; *13*; 14 *alt.* Ps. *47*; 49 Jer. 4. 19–end John 5. 1–18
20 Tuesday				
P		Isa. 55. 10–11 Ps. 34. 4–6, 21–22 Matt. 6. 7–15	Ps. 44 *alt.* Ps. *48*; 52 Gen. 41.46 – 42.5 Gal. 4. 8–20	Ps. 46; *49* *alt.* Ps. 50 Jer. 5. 1–19 John 5. 19–29
21 Wednesday Ember Day*				
P		Jonah ch. 3 Ps. 51. 1–5, 17–18 Luke 11. 29–32	Ps. *6*; 17 *alt.* Ps. 119. 57–80 Gen. 42. 6–17 Gal. 4.21 – 5.1	Ps. 9; *28* *alt.* Ps. *59*; 60 (67) Jer. 5. 20–end John 5. 30–end
22 Thursday				
P		Esth. 14. 1–5, 12–14 *or* Isa. 55. 6–9 Ps. 138 Matt. 7. 7–12	Ps. *42*; 43 *alt.* Ps. 56; *57*; (63†) Gen. 42. 18–28 Gal. 5. 2–15	Ps. 137; 138; *142* *alt.* Ps. 61; *62*; 64 Jer. 6. 9–21 John 6. 1–15
23 Friday **Polycarp, Bishop of Smyrna, Martyr, *c.* 155** Ember Day*				
Pr	Com. Martyr *also* Rev. 2. 8–11	*or* Ezek. 18. 21–28 Ps. 130 Matt. 5. 20–26	Ps. 22 *alt.* Ps. *51*; 54 Gen. 42. 29–end Gal. 5. 16–end	Ps. 54; *55* *alt.* Ps. 38 Jer. 6. 22–end John 6. 16–27
24 Saturday** Ember Day*				
P		Deut. 26. 16–end Ps. 119. 1–8 Matt. 5. 43–end	Ps. 59; *63* *alt.* Ps. 68 Gen. 43. 1–15 Gal. ch. 6	Ps. *4*; 16 *alt.* Ps. 65; *66* Jer. 7. 1–20 John 6. 27–40 **ct**
25 Sunday **THE SECOND SUNDAY OF LENT**				
P		Gen. 17. 1–7, 15–16 Ps. 22. 23–end Rom. 4. 13–end Mark 8. 31–end	Ps. 105. 1–6, 37–end Isa. 51. 1–11 Gal. 3. 1–9, 23–end	Ps. 135 (*or* 135. 1–14) Gen. 12. 1–9 Heb. 11. 1–3, 8–16 *Gospel:* John 8. 51–end
26 Monday				
P		Dan. 9. 4–10 Ps. 79. 8–9, 12, 14 Luke 6. 36–38	Ps. 26; *32* *alt.* Ps. 71 Gen. 43. 16–end Heb. ch. 1	Ps. 70; *74* *alt.* Ps. *72*; 75 Jer. 7. 21–end John 6. 41–51

*For Ember Day provision, see p. 11.
**Matthias may be celebrated on 24 February instead of 14 May.

	Calendar and Holy Communion	Morning Prayer	Evening Prayer	NOTES
P	Ezek. 34. 11–16a Matt. 25. 31–end	Gen. 41. 25–45 Gal. 3.23 – 4.7	Jer. 4. 19–end John 5. 1–18	
P	Isa. 55. 6–11 Matt. 21. 10–16	Gen. 41.46 – 42.5 Gal. 4. 8–20	Jer. 5. 1–19 John 5. 19–29	
	Ember Day			
P	Ember CEG *or* Isa. 58. 1–9a Matt. 12. 38–end	Gen. 42. 6–17 Gal. 4.21 – 5.1	Jer. 5. 20–end John 5. 30–end	
P	Isa. 58. 9b–end John 8. 31–45	Gen. 42. 18–28 Gal. 5. 2–15	Jer. 6. 9–21 John 6. 1–15	
	Ember Day			
P	Ember CEG *or* Ezek. 18. 20–25 John 5. 2–15	Gen. 42. 29–end Gal. 5. 16–end	Jer. 6. 22–end John 6. 16–27 *or First EP of Matthias* (Ps. 147) Isa. 22. 15–22 Phil. 3.13b – 4.1 **R ct**	
	MATTHIAS THE APOSTLE Ember Day			
R	1 Sam. 2. 27–35 Ps. 16. 1–7 Acts 1. 15–end Matt. 1. 25–end	(Ps. 15) Jonah 1. 1–9 Acts 2. 37–end	(Ps. 80) 1 Sam. 16. 1–13a Matt. 7. 15–27	
	THE SECOND SUNDAY IN LENT			
P	Jer. 17. 5–10 Ps. 25. 13–end 1 Thess. 4. 1–8 Matt. 15. 21–28	Ps. 105. 1–6, 37–end Isa. 51. 1–11 Gal. 3. 1–9, 23–end	Ps. 135 (*or* 135. 1–14) Gen. 12. 1–9 Heb. 11. 1–3, 8–16	
P	Heb. 2. 1–10 John 8. 21–30	Gen. 43. 16–end Heb. ch. 1	Jer. 7. 21–end John 6. 41–51	

	Sunday Principal Service Weekday Eucharist	Third Service Morning Prayer	Second Service Evening Prayer

27 Tuesday   George Herbert, Priest, Poet, 1633

Pw	Com. Pastor *or* Isa. 1. 10, 16–20	Ps. 50	Ps. *52*; 53; 54
	esp. Mal. 2. 5–7 Ps. 50. 8, 16–end	*alt.* Ps. 73	*alt.* Ps. 74
	Matt. 11. 25–30 Matt. 23. 1–12	Gen. 44. 1–17	Jer. 8. 1–15
	also Rev. 19. 5–9	Heb. 2. 1–9	John 6. 52–59

28 Wednesday

P	Jer. 18. 18–20	Ps. 35	Ps. *3*; 51
	Ps. 31. 4–5, 14–18	*alt.* Ps. 77	*alt.* Ps. 119. 81–104
	Matt. 20. 17–28	Gen. 44. 18–end	Jer. 8.18 – 9.11
		Heb. 2. 10–end	John 6. 60–end

29 Thursday

P	Jer. 17. 5–10	Ps. 34	Ps. 71
	Ps. 1	*alt.* Ps. 78. 1–39†	*alt.* Ps. 78. 40–end†
	Luke 16. 19–end	Gen. 45. 1–15	Jer. 9. 12–24
		Heb. 3. 1–6	John 7. 1–13

March 2024

1 Friday   David, Bishop of Menevia, Patron of Wales, c. 601

Pw	Com. Bishop *or* Gen. 37. 3–4, 12–13,	Ps. 40; *41*	Ps. *6*; 38
	also 2 Sam. 23. 1–4 17–28	*alt.* Ps. 55	*alt.* Ps. 69
	Ps. 89. 19–22, 24 Ps. 105. 16–22	Gen. 45. 16–end	Jer. 10. 1–16
	Matt. 21. 33–43, 45–46	Heb. 3. 7–end	John 7. 14–24

2 Saturday   Chad, Bishop of Lichfield, Missionary, 672*

Pw	Com. Missionary *or* Mic. 7. 14–15, 18–20	Ps. 3; *25*	Ps. *23*; 27
	also 1 Tim. 6. 11b–16 Ps. 103. 1–4, 9–12	*alt.* Ps. *76*; 79	*alt.* Ps. 81; *84*
	Luke 15. 1–3, 11–end	Gen. 46. 1–7, 28–end	Jer. 10. 17–24
		Heb. 4. 1–13	John 7. 25–36
			ct

3 Sunday   THE THIRD SUNDAY OF LENT

P	Exod. 20. 1–17	Ps. 18. 1–25	Ps. 11; 12
	Ps. 19 (*or* 19. 7–end)	Jer. ch. 38	Exod. 5.1 – 6.1
	1 Cor. 1. 18–25	Phil. 1. 1–26	Phil. 3. 4b–14
	John 2. 13–22		*or* Matt. 10. 16–22

4 Monday**

P	2 Kings 5. 1–15	Ps. *5*; 7	Ps. 11; *17*
	Ps. 42. 1–2; 43. 1–4	*alt.* Ps. *80*; 82	*alt.* Ps. *85*; 86
	Luke 4. 24–30	Gen. 47. 1–27	Jer. 11. 1–17
		Heb. 4.14 – 5.10	John 7. 37–52

5 Tuesday

P	Song of the Three 2,	Ps. 6; *9*	Ps. 61; 62; *64*
	11–20	*alt.* Ps. 87; *89. 1–18*	*alt.* Ps. 89. 19–end
	or Dan. 2. 20–23	Gen. 47.28 – 48.end	Jer. 11.18 – 12.6
	Ps. 25. 3–10	Heb. 5.11 – 6.12	John 7.53 – 8.11
	Matt. 18. 21–end		

*Chad may be celebrated with Cedd on 26 October instead of 2 March.
**The following readings may replace those provided for Holy Communion on any day during the Third Week of Lent: Exod. 17. 1–7; Ps. 95. 1–2, 6–end; John 4. 5–42.

	Calendar and Holy Communion	Morning Prayer	Evening Prayer	NOTES
P	Heb. 2. 11–end Matt. 23. 1–12	Gen. 44. 1–17 Heb. 2. 1–9	Jer. 8. 1–15 John 6. 52–59	
P	Heb. 3. 1–6 Matt. 20. 17–28	Gen. 44. 18–end Heb. 2. 10–end	Jer. 8.18 – 9.11 John 6. 60–end	
P	Heb. 3. 7–end John 5. 30–end	Gen. 45. 1–15 Heb. 3. 1–6	Jer. 9. 12–24 John 7. 1–13	

David, Bishop of Menevia, Patron of Wales, c. 601

Pw	Com. Bishop or Heb. ch. 4 Matt. 21. 33–end	Gen. 45. 16–end Heb. 3. 7–end	Jer. 10. 1–16 John 7. 14–24	

Chad, Bishop of Lichfield, Missionary, 672

Pw	Com. Bishop or Heb. ch. 5 Luke 15. 11–end	Gen. 46. 1–7, 28–end Heb. 4. 1–13	Jer. 10. 17–24 John 7. 25–36	

ct

THE THIRD SUNDAY IN LENT

P	Num. 22. 21–31 Ps. 9. 13–end Eph. 5. 1–14 Luke 11. 14–28	Ps. 18. 1–25 Jer. ch. 38 Phil. 1. 1–26	Ps. 11; 12 Exod. 5.1 – 6.1 Phil. 3. 4b–14 or Matt. 10. 16–22	
P	Heb. 6. 1–10 Luke 4. 23–30	Gen. 47. 1–27 Heb. 4.14 – 5.10	Jer. 11. 1–17 John 7. 37–52	
P	Heb. 6. 11–end Matt. 18. 15–22	Gen. 47.28 – 48.end Heb. 5.11 – 6.12	Jer. 11.18 – 12.6 John 7.53 – 8.11	

		Sunday Principal Service Weekday Eucharist	Third Service Morning Prayer	Second Service Evening Prayer
6	Wednesday			
	P	Deut. 4. 1, 5–9 Ps. 147. 13–end Matt. 5. 17–19	Ps. 38 *alt.* Ps. 119. 105–128 Gen. 49. 1–32 Heb. 6. 13–end	Ps. 36; *39* *alt.* Ps. *91*; 93 Jer. 13. 1–11 John 8. 12–30
7	Thursday	**Perpetua, Felicity and their Companions, Martyrs at Carthage, 203**		
	Pr	Com. Martyr *or* Jer. 7. 23–28 *esp.* Rev. 12. 10–12a Ps. 95. 1–2, 6–end *also* Wisd. 3. 1–7 Luke 11. 14–23	Ps. *56*; 57 *alt.* Ps. 90; *92* Gen. 49.33 – 50.end Heb. 7. 1–10	Ps. *59*; 60 *alt.* Ps. 94 Jer. ch. 14 John 8. 31–47
8	Friday	**Edward King, Bishop of Lincoln, 1910** *Felix, Bishop, Apostle to the East Angles, 647; Geoffrey Studdert Kennedy, Priest, Poet, 1929*		
	Pw	Com. Bishop *or* Hos. ch. 14 *also* Heb. 13. 1–8 Ps. 81. 6–10, 13, 16 Mark 12. 28–34	Ps. 22 *alt.* Ps. *88*; (95) Exod. 1. 1–14 Heb. 7. 11–end	Ps. 69 *alt.* Ps. 102 Jer. 15. 10–end John 8. 48–end
9	Saturday			
	P	Hos. 5.15 – 6.6 Ps. 51. 1–2, 17–end Luke 18. 9–14	Ps. 31 *alt.* Ps. 96; *97*; 100 Exod. 1.22 – 2.10 Heb. ch. 8	Ps. *116*; 130 *alt.* Ps. 104 Jer. 16.10 – 17.4 John 9. 1–17 ct
10	Sunday	**THE FOURTH SUNDAY OF LENT** (Mothering Sunday)		
	P	Num. 21. 4–9 Ps. 107. 1–3, 17–22 (*or* 107. 1–9) Eph. 2. 1–10 John 3. 14–21	Ps. 27 1 Sam. 16. 1–13 John 9. 1–25	Ps. 13; 14 Exod. 6. 2–13 Rom. 5. 1–11 *Gospel:* John 12. 1–8 If the Principal Service readings for The Fourth Sunday of Lent are displaced by Mothering Sunday provisions, they may be used at the Second Service.
		or, for Mothering Sunday Exod. 2. 1–10 *or* 1 Sam. 1. 20–end Ps. 34. 11–20 *or* Ps. 127. 1–4 2 Cor. 1. 3–7 *or* Col. 3. 12–17 Luke 2. 33–35 *or* John 19. 25b–27			
11	Monday*			
	P	Isa. 65. 17–21 Ps. 30. 1–5, 8, 11–end John 4. 43–end	Ps. 70; *77* *alt.* Ps. *98*; 99; 101 Exod. 2. 11–22 Heb. 9. 1–14	Ps. *25*; 28 *alt.* Ps. *105*† (or 103) Jer. 17. 5–18 John 9. 18–end

*The following readings may replace those provided for Holy Communion on any day during the Fourth Week of Lent: Mic. 7. 7–9; Ps. 27. 1, 9–10, 16–17; John ch. 9.

	Calendar and Holy Communion	Morning Prayer	Evening Prayer	NOTES
P	Heb. 7. 1–10 Matt. 15. 1–20	Gen. 49. 1–32 Heb. 6. 13–end	Jer. 13. 1–11 John 8. 12–30	

Perpetua, Martyr at Carthage, 203

Pr	Com. Martyr *or* Heb. 7. 11–25 John 6. 26–35	Gen. 49.33 – 50.end Heb. 7. 1–10	Jer. ch. 14 John 8. 31–47	
P	Heb. 7. 26–end John 4. 5–26	Exod. 1. 1–14 Heb. 7. 11–end	Jer. 15. 10–end John 8. 48–end	
P	Heb. 8. 1–6 John 8. 1–11	Exod. 1.22 – 2.10 Heb. ch. 8	Jer. 16.10 – 17.4 John 9. 1–17	

ct

THE FOURTH SUNDAY IN LENT
To celebrate Mothering Sunday, see *Common Worship* provision.

P	Exod. 16. 2–7a Ps. 122 Gal. 4. 21–end *or* Heb. 12. 22–24 John 6. 1–14	Ps. 27 1 Sam. 16. 1–13 John 9. 1–25	Ps. 13; 14 Exod. 6. 2–13 Rom. 5. 1–11	
P	Heb. 11. 1–6 John 2. 13–end	Exod. 2. 11–22 Heb. 9. 1–14	Jer. 17. 5–18 John 9. 18–end	

	Sunday Principal Service Weekday Eucharist	Third Service Morning Prayer	Second Service Evening Prayer
12 Tuesday			
P	Ezek. 47. 1–9, 12 Ps. 46. 1–8 John 5. 1–3, 5–16	Ps. 54; *79* *alt.* Ps. *106*† (*or* 103) Exod. 2.23 – 3.20 Heb. 9. 15–end	Ps. *80*; 82 *alt.* Ps. 107† Jer. 18. 1–12 John 10. 1–10
13 Wednesday			
P	Isa. 49. 8–15 Ps. 145. 8–18 John 5. 17–30	Ps. *63*; 90 *alt.* Ps. 110; *111*; 112 Exod. 4. 1–23 Heb. 10. 1–18	Ps. 52; *91* *alt.* Ps. 119. 129–152 Jer. 18. 13–end John 10. 11–21
14 Thursday			
P	Exod. 32. 7–14 Ps. 106. 19–23 John 5. 31–end	Ps. 53; *86* *alt.* Ps. 113; *115* Exod. 4.27 – 6.1 Heb. 10. 19–25	Ps. 94 *alt.* Ps. 114; *116*; 117 Jer. 19. 1–13 John 10. 22–end
15 Friday			
P	Wisd. 2. 1, 12–22 *or* Jer. 26. 8–11 Ps. 34. 15–end John 7. 1–2, 10, 25–30	Ps. 102 *alt.* Ps. 139 Exod. 6. 2–13 Heb. 10. 26–end	Ps. 13; *16* *alt.* Ps. *130*; 131; 137 Jer. 19.14 – 20.6 John 11. 1–16
16 Saturday			
P	Jer. 11. 18–20 Ps. 7. 1–2, 8–10 John 7. 40–52	Ps. 32 *alt.* Ps. 120; *121*; 122 Exod. 7. 8–end Heb. 11. 1–16	Ps. *140*; 141; 142 *alt.* Ps. 118 Jer. 20. 7–end John 11. 17–27 **ct**
17 Sunday **THE FIFTH SUNDAY OF LENT (Passiontide begins)**			
P	Jer. 31. 31–34 Ps. 51. 1–13 *or* Ps. 119. 9–16 Heb. 5. 5–10 John 12. 20–33	Ps. 107. 1–22 Exod. 24. 3–8 Heb. 12. 18–end	Ps. 34 (*or* 34. 1–10) Exod. 7. 8–24 Rom. 5. 12–end *Gospel:* Luke 22. 1–13
18 Monday* *Cyril, Bishop of Jerusalem, Teacher, 386*			
P	Susanna 1–9, 15–17, 19–30, 33–62 (*or* 41b–62) *or* Josh. 2. 1–14 Ps. 23 John 8. 1–11	Ps. *73*; 121 *alt.* Ps. 123; 124; 125; *126* Exod. 8. 1–19 Heb. 11. 17–31	Ps. *26*; 27 *alt.* Ps. *127*; 128; 129 Jer. 21. 1–10 John 11. 28–44 *or First EP of Joseph* Ps. 132 Hos. 11. 1–9 Luke 2. 41–end **W ct**
19 Tuesday **JOSEPH OF NAZARETH**			
W	2 Sam. 7. 4–16 Ps. 89. 26–36 Rom. 4. 13–18 Matt. 1. 18–end	*MP:* Ps. 25; 147. 1–12 Isa. 11. 1–10 Matt. 13. 54–end	*EP:* Ps. 1; 112 Gen. 50. 22–end Matt. 2. 13–end

*The following readings may replace those provided for Holy Communion on any day, except St Joseph's Day, during the Fifth Week of Lent: 2 Kings 4. 18–21, 32–37; Ps. 17. 1–8, 16; John 11. 1–45.

	Calendar and Holy Communion	Morning Prayer	Evening Prayer	NOTES
	Gregory the Great, Bishop of Rome, 604			
Pw	Com. Doctor *or* Heb. 11. 13–16a John 7. 14–24	Exod. 2.23 – 3.20 Heb. 9. 15–end	Jer. 18. 1–12 John 10. 1–10	
P	Heb. 12. 1–11 John 9. 1–17	Exod. 4. 1–23 Heb. 10. 1–18	Jer. 18. 13–end John 10. 11–21	
P	Heb. 12. 12–17 John 5. 17–27	Exod. 4.27 – 6.1 Heb. 10. 19–25	Jer. 19. 1–13 John 10. 22–end	
P	Heb. 12. 22–end John 11. 33–46	Exod. 6. 2–13 Heb. 10. 26–end	Jer. 19.14 – 20.6 John 11. 1–16	
P	Heb. 13. 17–21 John 8. 12–20	Exod. 7. 8–end Heb. 11. 1–16	Jer. 20. 7–end John 11. 17–27	
			ct	
	THE FIFTH SUNDAY IN LENT			
P	Exod. 24. 4–8 Ps. 143 Heb. 9. 11–15 John 8. 46–end	Ps. 107. 1–22 Jer. 31. 31–34 Heb. 5. 5–10	Ps. 34 (*or* 34. 1–10) Exod. 7. 8–24 Rom. 5. 12–end	
	Edward, King of the W. Saxons, 978			
Pr	Com. Martyr *or* Col. 1. 13–23a John 7. 1–13	Exod. 8. 1–19 Heb. 11. 17–31	Jer. 21. 1–10 John 11. 28–44	
	To celebrate Joseph, see *Common Worship* provision.			
P	Col. 2. 8–12 John 7. 32–39	Exod. 8. 20–end Heb. 11.32 – 12.2	Jer. 22. 1–5, 13–19 John 11. 45–end	

		Sunday Principal Service Weekday Eucharist	Third Service Morning Prayer	Second Service Evening Prayer

20 Wednesday   **Cuthbert, Bishop of Lindisfarne, Missionary, 687***

Pw	Com. Missionary *or* *esp.* Ezek. 34. 11–16 *also* Matt. 18. 12–14	Dan. 3. 14–20, 24–25, 28 *Canticle:* Bless the Lord John 8. 31–42	Ps. **55**; 124 *alt.* Ps. 119. 153–end Exod. 9. 1–12 Heb. 12. 3–13	Ps. 56; **62** *alt.* Ps. 136 Jer. 22.20 – 23.8 John 12. 1–11

21 Thursday   **Thomas Cranmer, Archbishop of Canterbury, Reformation Martyr, 1556**

Pr	Com. Martyr *or*	Gen. 17. 3–9 Ps. 105. 4–9 John 8. 51–end	Ps. **40**; 125 *alt.* Ps. **143**; 146 Exod. 9. 13–end Heb. 12. 14–end	Ps. 42; **43** *alt.* Ps. **138**; 140; 141 Jer. 23. 9–32 John 12. 12–19

22 Friday

P		Jer. 20. 10–13 Ps. 18. 1–6 John 10. 31–end	Ps. **22**; 126 *alt.* Ps. 142; **144** Exod. ch. 10 Heb. 13. 1–16	Ps. 31 *alt.* Ps. 145 Jer. ch. 24 John 12. 20–36a

23 Saturday

P		Ezek. 37. 21–end *Canticle:* Jer. 31. 10–13 *or* Ps. 121 John 11. 45–end	Ps. **23**; 127 *alt.* Ps. 147 Exod. ch. 11 Heb. 13. 17–end	Ps. 128; 129; **130** *alt.* Ps. **148**; 149; 150 Jer. 25. 1–14 John 12. 36b–end **ct**

24 **Sunday**   **PALM SUNDAY**

R	*Liturgy of the Palms* Mark 11. 1–11 *or* John 12. 12–16 Ps. 118. 1–2, 19–end (*or* 118. 19–end)	*Liturgy of the Passion* Isa. 50. 4–9a Ps. 31. 9–16 (*or* 31. 9–18) Phil. 2. 5–11 Mark 14.1 – 15.end *or* Mark 15. 1–39 [40–end]	Ps. 61; 62 Zech. 9. 9–12 1 Cor. 2. 1–12	Ps. 69. 1–20 Isa. 5. 1–7 Mark 12. 1–12

25 Monday   **MONDAY OF HOLY WEEK**
(The Annunciation transferred to 8 April)

R		Isa. 42. 1–9 Ps. 36. 5–11 Heb. 9. 11–15 John 12. 1–11	*MP*: Ps. 41 Lam. 1. 1–12a Luke 22. 1–23	*EP*: Ps. 25 Lam. 2. 8–19 Col. 1. 18–23

26 Tuesday   **TUESDAY OF HOLY WEEK**

R		Isa. 49. 1–7 Ps. 71. 1–14 (*or* 71. 1–8) 1 Cor. 1. 18–31 John 12. 20–36	*MP*: Ps. 27 Lam. 3. 1–18 Luke 22. [24–38] 39–53	*EP*: Ps. 55. 13–24 Lam. 3. 40–51 Gal. 6. 11–end

27 Wednesday   **WEDNESDAY OF HOLY WEEK**

R		Isa. 50. 4–9a Ps. 70 Heb. 12. 1–3 John 13. 21–32	*MP*: Ps. 102 (*or* 102. 1–18) Wisd. 1.16 – 2.1, 12–22 *or* Jer. 11. 18–20 Luke 22. 54–end	*EP*: Ps. 88 Isa. 63. 1–9 Rev. 14.18 – 15.4

*Cuthbert may be celebrated on 4 September instead of 20 March.

	Calendar and Holy Communion	Morning Prayer	Evening Prayer	NOTES
P	Col. 2. 13–19 John 7. 40–end	Exod. 9. 1–12 Heb. 12. 3–13	Jer. 22.20 – 23.8 John 12. 1–11	
	Benedict, Abbot of Monte Cassino, c. 550			
Pw	Com. Abbot or Col. 3. 8–11 John 10. 22–38	Exod. 9. 13–end Heb. 12. 14–end	Jer. 23. 9–32 John 12. 12–19	
P	Col. 3. 12–17 John 11. 47–54	Exod. ch. 10 Heb. 13. 1–16	Jer. ch. 24 John 12. 20–36a	
P	Col. 4. 2–6 John 6. 53–end	Exod. ch. 11 Heb. 13. 17–end	Jer. 25. 1–14 John 12. 36b–end	
			ct	
	THE SUNDAY NEXT BEFORE EASTER (PALM SUNDAY)			
R	Zech. 9. 9–12 Ps. 73. 22–end Phil. 2. 5–11 Passion acc. to Matthew Matt. 27. 1–54 or Matt. 26.1 – 27.61 or Matt. 21. 1–13	Ps. 61; 62 Isa. 42. 1–9 1 Cor. 2. 1–12	Ps. 69. 1–20 Isa. 5. 1–7 Mark 12. 1–12	
	MONDAY IN HOLY WEEK (The Annunciation transferred to 8 April)			
R	Isa. 63. 1–19 Ps. 55. 1–8 Gal. 6. 1–11 Mark ch. 14	Ps. 41 Lam. 1. 1–12a John 12. 1–11	Ps. 25 Lam. 2. 8–19 Col. 1. 18–23	
	TUESDAY IN HOLY WEEK			
R	Isa. 50. 5–11 Ps. 13 Rom. 5. 6–19 Mark 15. 1–39	Ps. 27 Lam. 3. 1–18 John 12. 20–36	Ps. 55. 13–24 Lam. 3. 40–51 Gal. 6. 11–end	
	WEDNESDAY IN HOLY WEEK			
R	Isa. 49. 1–9a Ps. 54 Heb. 9. 16–end Luke ch. 22	Ps. 102 (or 102. 1–18) Wisd. 1.16 – 2.1, 12–22 or Jer. 11. 18–20 John 13. 21–32	Ps. 88 Isa. 63. 1–9 Rev. 14.18 – 15.4	

	Sunday Principal Service Weekday Eucharist	Third Service Morning Prayer	Second Service Evening Prayer
28 Thursday	**MAUNDY THURSDAY**		
W(HC)R	Exod. 12. 1–4 [5–10], 11–14 Ps. 116. 1, 10–end (or 116. 9–end) 1 Cor. 11. 23–26 John 13. 1–17, 31b–35	*MP*: Ps. 42; 43 Lev. 16. 2–24 Luke 23. 1–25	*EP*: Ps. 39 Exod. ch. 11 Eph. 2. 11–18
29 Friday	**GOOD FRIDAY**		
R	Isa. 52.13 – 53.end Ps. 22 (or 22. 1–11 or 22. 1–21) Heb. 10. 16–25 or Heb. 4. 14–16; 5. 7–9 John 18.1 – 19.end	*MP*: Ps. 69 Gen. 22. 1–18 *A part of John 18 – 19 if not read at the Principal Service* or Heb. 10. 1–10	*EP*: Ps. 130; 143 Lam. 5. 15–end *A part of John 18 – 19 if not read at the Principal Service, especially* John 19. 38–end or Col. 1. 18–23
30 Saturday	**EASTER EVE**		
	These readings are for use at services other than the Easter Vigil Job 14. 1–14 or Lam. 3. 1–9, 19–24 Ps. 31. 1–4, 15–16 (or 31. 1–5) 1 Pet. 4. 1–8 Matt. 27. 57–end or John 19. 38–end	Ps. 142 Hos. 6. 1–6 John 2. 18–22	Ps. 116 Job 19. 21–27 1 John 5. 5–12
31 Sunday	**EASTER DAY**		
𝔴	*The following readings and psalms (or canticles) are provided for use at the Easter Vigil. A minimum of three Old Testament readings should be chosen. The reading from Exodus ch. 14 should always be used.* Gen. 1.1 – 2.4a & Ps. 136. 1–9, 23–end Gen. 7. 1–5, 11–18; 8. 6–18; 9. 8–13 & Ps. 46 Gen. 22. 1–18 & Ps. 16 Exod. 14. 10–end; 15. 20–21 & *Canticle*: Exod. 15. 1b–13, 17–18 Isa. 55. 1–11 & *Canticle*: Isa. 12. 2–end Baruch 3.9–15, 32 – 4.4 & Ps. 19 or Prov. 8. 1–8, 19–21; 9. 4b–6 & Ps. 19 Ezek. 36. 24–28 & Ps. 42; 43 Ezek. 37. 1–14 & Ps. 143 Zeph. 3. 14–end & Ps. 98 Rom. 6. 3–11 & Ps. 114 Mark 16. 1–8		
𝔴	*Easter Day Services The reading from Acts must be used as either the first or second reading at the Principal Service.* Acts 10. 34–43 or Isa. 25. 6–9 Ps. 118. 1–2, 14–24 (or 118. 14–24) 1 Cor. 15. 1–11 or Acts 10. 34–43 John 20. 1–18 or Mark 16. 1–8	*MP*: Ps. 114; 117 Gen. 1. 1–5, 26–end 2 Cor. 5.14 – 6.2	*EP*: Ps. 105 or Ps. 66. 1–11 Ezek. 37. 1–14 Luke 24. 13–35

April 2024

	Sunday Principal Service Weekday Eucharist	Third Service Morning Prayer	Second Service Evening Prayer
1 Monday	**MONDAY OF EASTER WEEK**		
W	Acts 2. 14, 22–32 Ps. 16. 1–2, 6–end Matt. 28. 8–15	Ps. *111*; 117; 146 Exod. 12. 1–14 1 Cor. 15. 1–11	Ps. 135 Song of Sol. 1.9 – 2.7 Mark 16. 1–8

	Calendar and Holy Communion	Morning Prayer	Evening Prayer	NOTES

MAUNDY THURSDAY

W **(HC)** **R**	Exod. 12. 1–11 Ps. 43 1 Cor. 11. 17–end Luke 23. 1–49	Ps. 42; 43 Lev. 16. 2–24 John 13. 1–17, 31b–35	Ps. 39 Exod. ch. 11 Eph. 2. 11–18

GOOD FRIDAY

R	Alt. Collect Passion acc. to John Alt. Gospel, if Passion is read Num. 21. 4–9 Ps. 140. 1–9 Heb. 10. 1–25 John 19. 1–37 *or* John 19. 38–end	Ps. 69 Gen. 22. 1–18 John ch. 18	Ps. 130; 143 Lam. 5. 15–end John 19. 38–end

EASTER EVE

	Job 14. 1–14 1 Pet. 3. 17–22 Matt. 27. 57–end	Ps. 142 Hos. 6. 1–6 John 2. 18–22	Ps. 116 Job 19. 21–27 1 John 5. 5–12

EASTER DAY

𝔴	Exod. 12. 21–28 Ps. 111 Col. 3. 1–7 John 20. 1–10	Ps. 114; 117 Gen. 1. 1–5, 26–end 2 Cor. 5.14 – 6.2	Ps. 105 *or* Ps. 66. 1–11 Isa. 25. 6–9 Luke 24. 13–35

MONDAY IN EASTER WEEK

W	Hos. 6. 1–6 Easter Anthems Acts 10. 34–43 Luke 24. 13–35	Exod. 12. 1–14 1 Cor. 15. 1–11	Song of Sol. 1.9 – 2.7 Mark 16. 1–8

		Sunday Principal Service / Weekday Eucharist	Third Service / Morning Prayer	Second Service / Evening Prayer
2 Tuesday	**TUESDAY OF EASTER WEEK**			
W		Acts 2. 36–41 / Ps. 33. 4–5, 18–end / John 20. 11–18	Ps. *112*; 147. 1–12 / Exod. 12. 14–36 / 1 Cor. 15. 12–19	Ps. 136 / Song of Sol. 2. 8–end / Luke 24. 1–12
3 Wednesday	**WEDNESDAY OF EASTER WEEK**			
W		Acts 3. 1–10 / Ps. 105. 1–9 / Luke 24. 13–35	Ps. *113*; 147. 13–end / Exod. 12. 37–end / 1 Cor. 15. 20–28	Ps. 105 / Song of Sol. ch. 3 / Matt. 28. 16–end
4 Thursday	**THURSDAY OF EASTER WEEK**			
W		Acts 3. 11–end / Ps. 8 / Luke 24. 35–48	Ps. *114*; 148 / Exod. 13. 1–16 / 1 Cor. 15. 29–34	Ps. 106 / Song of Sol. 5.2 – 6.3 / Luke 7. 11–17
5 Friday	**FRIDAY OF EASTER WEEK**			
W		Acts 4. 1–12 / Ps. 118. 1–4, 22–26 / John 21. 1–14	Ps. *115*; 149 / Exod. 13.17 – 14.14 / 1 Cor. 15. 35–50	Ps. 107 / Song of Sol. 7.10 – 8.4 / Luke 8. 41–end
6 Saturday	**SATURDAY OF EASTER WEEK**			
W		Acts 4. 13–21 / Ps. 118. 1–4, 14–21 / Mark 16. 9–15	Ps. *116*; 150 / Exod. 14. 15–end / 1 Cor. 15. 51–end	Ps. 145 / Song of Sol. 8. 5–7 / John 11. 17–44 / ct
7 **Sunday**	**THE SECOND SUNDAY OF EASTER**			
W		*The reading from Acts must be used as either the first or second reading at the Principal Service.* Acts 4. 32–35 [or Exod. 14. 10–end; 15. 20–21] / Ps. 133 / 1 John 1.1 – 2.2 / John 20. 19–end	Ps. 22. 20–end / Isa. 53. 6–12 / Rom. 4. 13–25	*First EP of The Annunciation* Ps. 85 / Wisd. 9. 1–12 / *or* Gen. 3. 8–15 / Gal. 4. 1–5 / 𝖂 ct
8 Monday	**THE ANNUNCIATION OF OUR LORD TO THE BLESSED VIRGIN MARY** (transferred from 25 March)			
𝖜		Isa. 7. 10–14 / Ps. 40. 5–11 / Heb. 10. 4–10 / Luke 1. 26–38	*MP*: Ps. 111; 113 / 1 Sam. 2. 1–10 / Rom. 5. 12–end	*EP*: Ps. 131; 146 / Isa. 52. 1–12 / Heb. 2. 5–end
9 Tuesday	*Dietrich Bonhoeffer, Lutheran Pastor, Martyr, 1945*			
W		Acts 4. 32–end / Ps. 93 / John 3. 7–15	Ps. *8*; 20; 21 / *alt.* Ps. *5*; 6; (8) / Exod. 15.22 – 16.10 / Col. 1. 15–end	Ps. 104 / *alt.* Ps. 9; *10*† / Deut. 1. 19–40 / John 20. 11–18
10 Wednesday	**William Law, Priest, Spiritual Writer, 1761** / *William of Ockham, Friar, Philosopher, Teacher, 1347*			
W		Com. Teacher *or* / *esp.* 1 Cor. 2. 9–end / *also* Matt. 17. 1–9	Acts 5. 17–26 / Ps. 34. 1–8 / John 3. 16–21	Ps. 16; *30* / *alt.* Ps. 119. 1–32 / Exod. 16. 11–end / Col. 2. 1–15	Ps. 33 / *alt.* Ps. *11*; 12; 13 / Deut. 3. 18–end / John 20. 19–end

	Calendar and Holy Communion	Morning Prayer	Evening Prayer	NOTES
	TUESDAY IN EASTER WEEK			
W	1 Kings 17. 17–end Ps. 16. 9–end Acts 13. 26–41 Luke 24. 36b–48	Exod. 12. 14–36 1 Cor. 15. 12–19	Song of Sol. 2. 8–end Luke 24. 1–12	
W	Isa. 42. 10–16 Ps. 111 Acts 3. 12–18 John 20. 11–18	Exod. 12. 37–end 1 Cor. 15. 20–28	Song of Sol. ch. 3 Matt. 28. 16–end	
W	Isa. 43. 16–21 Ps. 113 Acts 8. 26–end John 21. 1–14	Exod. 13. 1–16 1 Cor. 15. 29–34	Song of Sol. 5.2 – 6.3 Luke 7. 11–17	
W	Ezek. 37. 1–14 Ps. 116. 1–9 1 Pet. 3. 18–end Matt. 28. 16–end	Exod. 13.17 – 14.14 1 Cor. 15. 35–50	Song of Sol. 7.10 – 8.4 Luke 8. 41–end	
W	Zech. 8. 1–8 Ps. 118. 14–21 1 Pet. 2. 1–10 John 20. 24–end	Exod. 14. 15–end 1 Cor. 15. 51–end	Song of Sol. 8. 5–7 John 11. 17–44 **ct**	
	THE FIRST SUNDAY AFTER EASTER			
W	Ezek. 37. 1–10 Ps. 81. 1–4 1 John 5. 4–12 John 20. 19–23	Ps. 22. 20–end Isa. 53. 6–12 Rom. 4. 13–25	*First EP of The* *Annunciation* Ps. 85 Wisd. 9. 1–12 *or* Gen. 3. 8–15 Gal. 4. 1–5 𝖂 ct	
	THE ANNUNCIATION OF THE BLESSED VIRGIN MARY (transferred from 25 March)			
𝖂	Isa. 7. 10–14 [15] Ps. 113 Rom. 5. 12–19 Luke 1. 26–38	Ps. 111 1 Sam. 2. 1–10 Heb. 10. 4–10	Ps. 131; 146 Isa. 52. 1–12 Heb. 2. 5–end	
W		Exod. 15.22 – 16.10 Col. 1. 15–end	Deut. 1. 19–40 John 20. 11–18	
W		Exod. 16. 11–end Col. 2. 1–15	Deut. 3. 18–end John 20. 19–end	

		Sunday Principal Service / Weekday Eucharist	Third Service / Morning Prayer	Second Service / Evening Prayer

11 Thursday   *George Augustus Selwyn, first Bishop of New Zealand, 1878*

W		Acts 5. 27–33 Ps. *34*. 1, 15–end John 3. 31–end	Ps. *28*; 29 *alt.* Ps. 14; *15*; 16 Exod. ch. 17 Col. 2.16 – 3.11	Ps. 34 *alt.* Ps. 18† Deut. 4. 1–14 John 21. 1–14

12 Friday

W		Acts 5. 34–42 Ps. 27. 1–5, 16–17 John 6. 1–15	Ps. 57; *61* *alt.* Ps. 17; *19* Exod. 18. 1–12 Col. 3.12 – 4.1	Ps. 118 *alt.* Ps. 22 Deut. 4. 15–31 John 21. 15–19

13 Saturday

W		Acts 6. 1–7 Ps. 33. 1–5, 18–19 John 6. 16–21	Ps. 63; *84* *alt.* Ps. 20; 21; *23* Exod. 18. 13–end Col. 4. 2–end	Ps. 66 *alt.* Ps. *24*; 25 Deut. 4. 32–40 John 21. 20–end **ct**

14 Sunday   **THE THIRD SUNDAY OF EASTER**

W	*The reading from Acts must be used as either the first or second reading at the Principal Service.*	Acts 3. 12–19 [or Zeph. 3. 14–end] Ps. 4 1 John 3. 1–7 Luke 24. 36b–48	Ps. 77. 11–20 Isa. 63. 7–15 1 Cor. 10. 1–13	Ps. 142 Deut. 7. 7–13 Rev. 2. 1–11 *Gospel:* Luke 16. 19–end

15 Monday

W		Acts 6. 8–15 Ps. 119. 17–24 John 6. 22–29	Ps. *96*; 97 *alt.* Ps. 27; *30* Exod. ch. 19 Luke 1. 1–25	Ps. *61*; 65 *alt.* Ps. 26; *28*; 29 Deut. 5. 1–22 Eph. 1. 1–14

16 Tuesday   *Isabella Gilmore, Deaconess, 1923*

W		Acts 7.51 – 8.1a Ps. 31. 1–5, 16 John 6. 30–35	Ps. *98*; 99; 100 *alt.* Ps. 32; *36* Exod. 20. 1–21 Luke 1. 26–38	Ps. 71 *alt.* Ps. 33 Deut. 5. 22–end Eph. 1. 15–end

17 Wednesday

W		Acts 8. 1b–8 Ps. 66. 1–6 John 6. 35–40	Ps. 105 *alt.* Ps. 34 Exod. ch. 24 Luke 1. 39–56	Ps. 67; *72* *alt.* Ps. 119. 33–56 Deut. ch. 6 Eph. 2. 1–10

18 Thursday

W		Acts 8. 26–end Ps. 66. 7–8, 14–end John 6. 44–51	Ps. 136 *alt.* Ps. 37† Exod. 25. 1–22 Luke 1. 57–end	Ps. 73 *alt.* Ps. 39; *40* Deut. 7. 1–11 Eph. 2. 11–end

19 Friday   **Alphege, Archbishop of Canterbury, Martyr, 1012**

Wr	Com. Martyr *also* Heb. 5. 1–4 *or*	Acts 9. 1–20 Ps. 117 John 6. 52–59	Ps. 107 *alt.* Ps. 31 Exod. 28. 1–4a, 29–38 Luke 2. 1–20	Ps. 77 *alt.* Ps. 35 Deut. 7. 12–end Eph. 3. 1–13

	Calendar and Holy Communion	Morning Prayer	Evening Prayer	NOTES
W		Exod. ch. 17 Col. 2.16 – 3.11	Deut. 4. 1–14 John 21. 1–14	
W		Exod. 18. 1–12 Col. 3.12 – 4.1	Deut. 4. 15–31 John 21. 15–19	
W		Exod. 18. 13–end Col. 4. 2–end	Deut. 4. 32–40 John 21. 20–end	
			ct	

THE SECOND SUNDAY AFTER EASTER

	Calendar and Holy Communion	Morning Prayer	Evening Prayer	NOTES
W	Ezek. 34. 11–16a Ps. 23 1 Pet. 2. 19–end John 10. 11–16	Ps. 77. 11–20 Isa. 63. 7–15 1 Cor. 10. 1–13	Ps. 142 Deut. 7. 7–13 Rev. 2. 1–11	
W		Exod. ch. 19 Luke 1. 1–25	Deut. 5. 1–22 Eph. 1. 1–14	
W		Exod. 20. 1–21 Luke 1. 26–38	Deut. 5. 22–end Eph. 1. 15–end	
W		Exod. ch. 24 Luke 1. 39–56	Deut. ch. 6 Eph. 2. 1–10	
W		Exod. 25. 1–22 Luke 1. 57–end	Deut. 7. 1–11 Eph. 2. 11–end	

Alphege, Archbishop of Canterbury, Martyr, 1012

	Calendar and Holy Communion	Morning Prayer	Evening Prayer	NOTES
Wr	Com. Martyr	Exod. 28. 1–4a, 29–38 Luke 2. 1–20	Deut. 7. 12–end Eph. 3. 1–13	

		Sunday Principal Service Weekday Eucharist	Third Service Morning Prayer	Second Service Evening Prayer

20 Saturday

W		Acts 9. 31–42 Ps. 116. 10–15 John 6. 60–69	Ps. 108; *110*; 111 *alt.* Ps. 41; *42*; 43 Exod. 29. 1–9 Luke 2. 21–40	Ps. 23; *27* *alt.* Ps. 45; *46* Deut. ch. 8 Eph. 3. 14–end **ct**

21 Sunday THE FOURTH SUNDAY OF EASTER

W	*The reading from Acts must be used as either the first or second reading at the Principal Service.*	Acts 4. 5–12 [Gen. 7. 1–5, 11–18; 8. 6–18; 9. 8–13] Ps. 23 1 John 3. 16–end John 10. 11–18	Ps. 119. 89–96 Neh. 7.73b – 8.12 Luke 24. 25–32	Ps. 81. 8–16 Exod. 16. 4–15 Rev. 2. 12–17 *Gospel:* John 6. 30–40

22 Monday

W		Acts 11. 1–18 Ps. 42. 1–2; 43. 1–4 John 10. 1–10 (*or* 11–18)	Ps. 103 *alt.* Ps. 44 Exod. 32. 1–14 Luke 2. 41–end	Ps. 112; 113; *114* *alt.* Ps. *47*; 49 Deut. 9. 1–21 Eph. 4. 1–16 *or First EP of George* Ps. 111; 116 Jer. 15. 15–end Heb. 11.32 – 12.2 **R ct**

23 Tuesday GEORGE, MARTYR, PATRON OF ENGLAND, *c.* 304

R		1 Macc. 2. 59–64 *or* Rev. 12. 7–12 Ps. 126 2 Tim. 2. 3–13 John 15. 18–21	*MP:* Ps. 5; 146 Josh. 1. 1–9 Eph. 6. 10–20	*EP:* Ps. 3; 11 Isa. 43. 1–7 John 15. 1–8

24 Wednesday *Mellitus, Bishop of London, first Bishop at St Paul's, 624; The Seven Martyrs of the Melanesian Brotherhood, Solomon Islands, 2003*

W		Acts 12.24 – 13.5 Ps. 67 John 12. 44–end	Ps. 135 *alt.* Ps. 119. 57–80 Exod. ch. 33 Luke 3. 15–22	Ps. *47*; 48 *alt.* Ps. *59*; 60 (67) Deut. 10. 12–end Eph. 5. 1–14 *or First EP of Mark* Ps. 19 Isa. 52. 7–10 Mark 1. 1–15 **R ct**

25 Thursday MARK THE EVANGELIST

R		Prov. 15. 28–end *or* Acts 15. 35–end Ps. 119. 9–16 Eph. 4. 7–16 Mark 13. 5–13	*MP:* Ps. 37. 23–end; 148 Isa. 62. 6–10 *or* Ecclus. 51. 13–end Acts 12.25 – 13.13	*EP:* Ps. 45 Ezek. 1. 4–14 2 Tim. 4. 1–11

26 Friday

W		Acts 13. 26–33 Ps. 2 John 14. 1–6	Ps. 33 *alt.* Ps. *51*; 54 Exod. 35.20 – 36.7 Luke 4. 14–30	Ps. *36*; 40 *alt.* Ps. 38 Deut. 12. 1–14 Eph. 6. 1–9

	Calendar and Holy Communion	Morning Prayer	Evening Prayer	NOTES
W		Exod. 29. 1–9 Luke 2. 21–40	Deut. ch. 8 Eph. 3. 14–end	
			ct	

THE THIRD SUNDAY AFTER EASTER

	Calendar and Holy Communion	Morning Prayer	Evening Prayer	NOTES
W	Gen. 45. 3–10 Ps. 57 1 Pet. 2. 11–17 John 16. 16–22	Ps. 119. 89–96 Neh. 7.73b – 8.12 Luke 24. 25–32	Ps. 81. 8–16 Exod. 16. 4–15 Rev. 2. 12–17	
W		Exod. 32. 1–14 Luke 2. 41–end	Deut. 9. 1–21 Eph. 4. 1–16	

George, Martyr, Patron of England, c. 304
To celebrate George, see *Common Worship* provision.

	Calendar and Holy Communion	Morning Prayer	Evening Prayer	NOTES
Wr	Com. Martyr	Exod. 32. 15–34 Luke 3. 1–14	Deut. 9.23 – 10.5 Eph. 4. 17–end	
W		Exod. ch. 33 Luke 3. 15–22	Deut. 10. 12–end Eph. 5. 1–14 *or First EP of Mark* (Ps. 19) Isa. 52. 7–10 Mark 1. 1–15	
			R ct	

MARK THE EVANGELIST

	Calendar and Holy Communion	Morning Prayer	Evening Prayer	NOTES
R	Prov. 15. 28–end Ps. 119. 9–16 Eph. 4. 7–16 John 15. 1–11	(Ps. 37. 23–end; 148) Isa. 62. 6–10 *or* Ecclus. 51. 13–end Acts 12.25 – 13.13	(Ps. 45) Ezek. 1. 4–14 2 Tim. 4. 1–11	
W		Exod. 35.20 – 36.7 Luke 4. 14–30	Deut. 12. 1–14 Eph. 6. 1–9	

		Sunday Principal Service Weekday Eucharist	Third Service Morning Prayer	Second Service Evening Prayer
27 Saturday	*Christina Rossetti, Poet, 1894*			
W		Acts 13. 44–end Ps. 98. 1–5 John 14. 7–14	Ps. 34 *alt.* Ps. 68 Exod. 40. 17–end Luke 4. 31–37	Ps. *84*; 86 *alt.* Ps. 65; **66** Deut. 15. 1–18 Eph. 6. 10–end **ct**
28 Sunday	**THE FIFTH SUNDAY OF EASTER**			
W	*The reading from Acts must be used as either the first or second reading at the Principal Service.*	Acts 8. 26–end [Baruch 3.9–15, 32 – 4.4 *or* Gen. 22. 1–18] Ps. 22. 25–end 1 John 4. 7–end John 15. 1–8	Ps. 44. 16–end 2 Macc. 7. 7–14 *or* Dan. 3. 16–28 Heb. 11.32 – 12.2	Ps. 96 Isa. 60. 1–14 Rev. 3. 1–13 *Gospel:* Mark 16. 9–16
29 Monday	**Catherine of Siena, Teacher, 1380**			
W	Com. Teacher *or* *also* Prov. 8. 1, 6–11 John 17. 12–end	Acts 14. 5–18 Ps. 118. 1–3, 14–15 John 14. 21–26	Ps. 145 *alt.* Ps. 71 Num. 9. 15–end; 10. 33–end Luke 4. 38–end	Ps. 105 *alt.* Ps. **72**; 75 Deut. 16. 1–20 1 Pet. 1. 1–12
30 Tuesday	*Pandita Mary Ramabai, Translator of the Scriptures, 1922*			
W		Acts 14. 19–end Ps. 145. 10–end John 14. 27–end	Ps. *19*; 147. 1–12 *alt.* Ps. 73 Num. 11. 1–33 Luke 5. 1–11	Ps. 96; **97** *alt.* Ps. 74 Deut. 17. 8–end 1 Pet. 1. 13–end *or First EP of Philip and James* Ps. 25 Isa. 40. 27–end John 12. 20–26 **R ct**

May 2024

		Sunday Principal Service Weekday Eucharist	Third Service Morning Prayer	Second Service Evening Prayer
1 Wednesday	**PHILIP AND JAMES, APOSTLES**			
R		Isa. 30. 15–21 Ps. 119. 1–8 Eph. 1. 3–10 John 14. 1–14	*MP*: Ps. 139; 146 Prov. 4. 10–18 Jas. 1. 1–12	*EP*: Ps. 149 Job 23. 1–12 John 1. 43–end
2 Thursday	**Athanasius, Bishop of Alexandria, Teacher, 373**			
W	Com. Teacher *or* *also* Ecclus. 4. 20–28 Matt. 10. 24–27	Acts 15. 7–21 Ps. 96. 1–3, 7–10 John 15. 9–11	Ps. *57*; 148 *alt.* Ps. 78. 1–39† Num. 13. 1–3, 17–end Luke 5. 27–end	Ps. 104 *alt.* Ps. 78. 40–end† Deut. ch. 19 1 Pet. 2. 11–end
3 Friday				
W		Acts 15. 22–31 Ps. 57. 8–end John 15. 12–17	Ps. *138*; 149 *alt.* Ps. 55 Num. 14. 1–25 Luke 6. 1–11	Ps. 66 *alt.* Ps. 69 Deut. 21.22 – 22.8 1 Pet. 3. 1–12

	Calendar and Holy Communion	Morning Prayer	Evening Prayer	NOTES
W		Exod. 40. 17–end Luke 4. 31–37	Deut. 15. 1–18 Eph. 6. 10–end	
			ct	

THE FOURTH SUNDAY AFTER EASTER

	Calendar and Holy Communion	Morning Prayer	Evening Prayer	NOTES
W	Job 19. 21–27a Ps. 66. 14–end Jas. 1. 17–21 John 16. 5–15	Ps. 44. 16–end 2 Macc. 7. 7–14 or Dan. 3. 16–28 Heb. 11.32 – 12.2	Ps. 96 Isa. 60. 1–14 Rev. 3. 1–13	
W		Num. 9. 15–end; 10. 33–end Luke 4. 38–end	Deut. 16. 1–20 1 Pet. 1. 1–12	
W		Num. 11. 1–33 Luke 5. 1–11	Deut. 17. 8–end 1 Pet. 1. 13–end or First EP of Philip and James (Ps. 119. 1–8) Isa. 40. 27–end John 12. 20–26	
			R ct	

PHILIP AND JAMES, APOSTLES

	Calendar and Holy Communion	Morning Prayer	Evening Prayer	NOTES
R	Prov. 4. 10–18 Ps. 25. 1–9 Jas. 1. [1] 2–12 John 14. 1–14	(Ps. 139; 146) Isa. 30. 1–5 John 12. 20–26	(Ps. 149) Job 23. 1–12 John 1. 43–end	
W		Num. 13. 1–3, 17–end Luke 5. 27–end	Deut. ch. 19 1 Pet. 2. 11–end	

The Invention of the Cross

	Calendar and Holy Communion	Morning Prayer	Evening Prayer	NOTES
Wr		Num. 14. 1–25 Luke 6. 1–11	Deut. 21.22 – 22.8 1 Pet. 3. 1–12	

		Sunday Principal Service Weekday Eucharist	Third Service Morning Prayer	Second Service Evening Prayer
4 Saturday	**English Saints and Martyrs of the Reformation Era**			
W	Isa. 43. 1–7 *or* *or* Ecclus. 2. 10–17 Ps. 87 2 Cor. 4. 5–12 John 12. 20–26	Acts 16. 1–10 Ps. 100 John 15. 18–21	Ps. *146*; 150 *alt.* Ps. *76*; 79 Num. 14. 26–end Luke 6. 12–26	Ps. 118 *alt.* Ps. 81; *84* Deut. 24. 5–end 1 Pet. 3. 13–end **ct**
5 Sunday	**THE SIXTH SUNDAY OF EASTER**			
W	*The reading from* *Acts must be used* *as either the first or* *second reading at the* *Principal Service.*	Acts 10. 44–end [Isa. 55. 1–11] Ps. 98 1 John 5. 1–6 John 15. 9–17	Ps. 104. 26–32 Ezek. 47. 1–12 John 21. 1–19	Ps. 45 Song of Sol. 4.16 – 5.2; 8. 6–7 Rev. 3. 14–end *Gospel:* Luke 22. 24–30
6 Monday	Rogation Day*			
W		Acts 16. 11–15 Ps. 149. 1–5 John 15.26 – 16.4	Ps. *65*; 67 *alt.* Ps. *80*; 82 Num. 16. 1–35 Luke 6. 27–38	Ps. *121*; 122; 123 *alt.* Ps. *85*; 86 Deut. ch. 26 1 Pet. 4. 1–11
7 Tuesday	Rogation Day*			
W		Acts 16. 22–34 Ps. 138 John 16. 5–11	Ps. 124; 125; *126*; 127 *alt.* Ps. 87; *89. 1–18* Num. 16. 36–end Luke 6. 39–end	Ps. *128*; 129; 130; 131 *alt.* Ps. 89. 19–end Deut. 28. 1–14 1 Pet. 4. 12–end
8 Wednesday	**Julian of Norwich, Spiritual Writer,** *c.* **1417** Rogation Day*			
W	Com. Religious *or* *also* 1 Cor. 13. 8–end Matt. 5. 13–16	Acts 17.15, 22 – 18.1 Ps. 148. 1–2, 11–end John 16. 12–15	Ps. *132*; 133 *alt.* Ps. 119. 105–128 Num. 17. 1–11 Luke 7. 1–10	*First EP of Ascension* *Day* Ps. 15; 24 2 Sam. 23. 1–5 Col. 2.20 – 3.4 **𝖂 ct**
9 Thursday	**ASCENSION DAY**			
𝖜	*The reading from* *Acts must be used* *as either the first or* *second reading at the* *Eucharist.*	Acts 1. 1–11 *or* Dan. 7. 9–14 Ps. 47 *or* Ps. 93 Eph. 1. 15–end *or* Acts 1. 1–11 Luke 24. 44–end	*MP:* Ps. 110; 150 Isa. 52. 7–end Heb. 7. [11–25] 26–end	*EP:* Ps. 8 Song of the Three 29–37 *or* 2 Kings 2. 1–15 Rev. ch. 5 *Gospel:* Matt. 28. 16–end
10 Friday				
W		Acts 18. 9–18 Ps. 47. 1–6 John 16. 20–23	Ps. 20; *81* *alt.* Ps. *88*; (95) Num. 20. 1–13 Luke 7. 11–17 [Exod. 35.30 – 36.1 Gal. 5. 13–end]**	Ps. 145 *alt.* Ps. 102 Deut. 29. 2–15 1 John 1.1 – 2.6

*For Rogation Day provision, see p. 11.
**The alternative readings in square brackets may be used at one of the offices, in preparation for the Day of Pentecost.

	Calendar and Holy Communion	Morning Prayer	Evening Prayer	NOTES
W		Num. 14. 26–end Luke 6. 12–26	Deut. 24. 5–end 1 Pet. 3. 13–end	
			ct	

THE FIFTH SUNDAY AFTER EASTER
Rogation Sunday

	Calendar and Holy Communion	Morning Prayer	Evening Prayer	NOTES
W	Joel 2. 21–26 Ps. 66. 1–8 Jas. 1. 22–end John 16. 23b–end	Ps. 104. 26–32 Ezek. 47. 1–12 John 21. 1–19	Ps. 45 Song of Sol. 4.16 – 5.2; 8. 6–7 Rev. 3. 14–end	

John the Evangelist, ante Portam Latinam
Rogation Day

	Calendar and Holy Communion	Morning Prayer	Evening Prayer	NOTES
W	CEG of 27 December or Job 28. 1–11 Ps. 107. 1–9 Jas. 5. 7–11 Luke 6. 36–42	Num. 16. 1–35 Luke 6. 27–38	Deut. ch. 26 1 Pet. 4. 1–11	

Rogation Day

	Calendar and Holy Communion	Morning Prayer	Evening Prayer	NOTES
W	Deut. 8. 1–10 Ps. 121 Jas. 5. 16–end Luke 11. 5–13	Num. 16. 36–end Luke 6. 39–end	Deut. 28. 1–14 1 Pet. 4. 12–end	

Rogation Day

	Calendar and Holy Communion	Morning Prayer	Evening Prayer	NOTES
W	Deut. 34. 1–7 Ps. 108. 1–6 Eph. 4. 7–13 John 17. 1–11	Num. 17. 1–11 Luke 7. 1–10	*First EP of Ascension Day* Ps. 15; 24 2 Sam. 23. 1–5 Col. 2.20 – 3.4 𝖜 **ct**	

ASCENSION DAY

	Calendar and Holy Communion	Morning Prayer	Evening Prayer	NOTES
𝖜	Dan. 7. 13–14 Ps. 68. 1–6 Acts 1. 1–11 Mark 16. 14–end *or* Luke 24. 44–end	Ps. 110; 150 Isa. 52. 7–end Heb. 7. [11–25] 26–end	Ps. 8 Song of the Three 29–37 *or* 2 Kings 2. 1–15 Rev. ch. 5	

	Calendar and Holy Communion	Morning Prayer	Evening Prayer	NOTES
W	Ascension CEG	Num. 20. 1–13 Luke 7. 11–17 [Exod. 35.30 – 36.1 Gal. 5. 13–end]**	Deut. 29. 2–15 1 John 1.1 – 2.6	

		Sunday Principal Service Weekday Eucharist	Third Service Morning Prayer	Second Service Evening Prayer
11 Saturday				
W		Acts 18. 22–end Ps. 47. 1–2, 7–end John 16. 23–28	Ps. 21; *47* *alt.* Ps. 96; *97*; 100 Num. 21. 4–9 Luke 7. 18–35 [Num. 11. 16–17, 24–29 1 Cor. ch. 2]*	Ps. 84; *85* *alt.* Ps. 104 Deut. ch. 30 1 John 2. 7–17 **ct**
12 Sunday	**THE SEVENTH SUNDAY OF EASTER (SUNDAY AFTER ASCENSION DAY)**			
W	*The reading from Acts must be used as either the first or second reading at the Principal Service.*	Acts 1. 15–17, 21–end [Ezek. 36. 24–28] Ps. 1 1 John 5. 9–13 John 17. 6–19	Ps. 76 Isa. 14. 3–15 Rev. 14. 1–13	Ps. 147. 1–12 Isa. ch. 61 Luke 4. 14–21
13 Monday				
W		Acts 19. 1–8 Ps. 68. 1–6 John 16. 29–end	Ps. *93*; 96; 97 *alt.* Ps. *98*; 99; 101 Num. 22. 1–35 Luke 7. 36–end [Num. 27. 15–end 1 Cor. ch. 3]*	Ps. 18 *alt.* Ps. *105*† (*or* 103) Deut. 31. 1–13 1 John 2. 18–end *or First EP of Matthias* Ps. 147 Isa. 22. 15–22 Phil. 3.13b – 4.1 **R ct**
14 Tuesday	**MATTHIAS THE APOSTLE****			
R		Isa. 22. 15–end *or* Acts 1. 15–end Ps. 15 Acts 1. 15–end *or* 1 Cor. 4. 1–7 John 15. 9–17	*MP*: Ps. 16; 147. 1–12 1 Sam. 2. 27–35 Acts 2. 37–end	*EP*: Ps. 80 1 Sam. 16. 1–13a Matt. 7. 15–27
W	*or, if Matthias is celebrated on 24 February:*	Acts 20. 17–27 Ps. 68. 9–10, 18–19 John 17. 1–11	Ps. 98; *99*; 100 *alt.* Ps. *106*† (*or* 103) Num. 22.36 – 23.12 Luke 8. 1–15 [1 Sam. 10. 1–10 1 Cor. 12. 1–13]*	Ps. 68 *alt.* Ps. 107† Deut. 31. 14–29 1 John 3. 1–10
15 Wednesday				
W		Acts 20. 28–end Ps. 68. 27–28, 32–end John 17. 11–19	Ps. 2; *29* *alt.* Ps. 110; *111*; 112 Num. 23. 13–end Luke 8. 16–25 [1 Kings 19. 1–18 Matt. 3. 13–end]*	Ps. 36; *46* *alt.* Ps. 119. 129–152 Deut. 31.30 – 32.14 1 John 3. 11–end
16 Thursday	*Caroline Chisholm, Social Reformer, 1877*			
W		Acts 22. 30; 23. 6–11 Ps. 16. 1, 5–end John 17. 20–end	Ps. *24*; 72 *alt.* Ps. 113; *115* Num. ch. 24 Luke 8. 26–39 [Ezek. 11. 14–20 Matt. 9.35 – 10.20]*	Ps. 139 *alt.* Ps. 114; *116*; 117 Deut. 32. 15–47 1 John 4. 1–6

*The alternative readings in square brackets may be used at one of the offices, in preparation for the Day of Pentecost.
**Matthias may be celebrated on 24 February instead of 14 May.

	Calendar and Holy Communion	Morning Prayer	Evening Prayer	NOTES
W	Ascension CEG	Num. 21. 4–9 Luke 7. 18–35 [Num. 11. 16–17, 24–29 1 Cor. ch. 2]*	Deut. ch. 30 1 John 2. 7–17	
			ct	
	THE SUNDAY AFTER ASCENSION DAY			
W	2 Kings 2. 9–15 Ps. 68. 32–end 1 Pet. 4. 7–11 John 15.26 – 16.4a	Ps. 76 Isa. 14. 3–15 Rev. 14. 1–13	Ps. 147. 1–12 Isa. ch. 61 Luke 4. 14–21	
W		Num. 22. 1–35 Luke 7. 36–end [Num. 27. 15–end 1 Cor. ch. 3]*	Deut. 31. 1–13 1 John 2. 18–end	
W		Num. 22.36 – 23.12 Luke 8. 1–15 [1 Sam. 10. 1–10 1 Cor. 12. 1–13]*	Deut. 31. 14–29 1 John 3. 1–10	
W		Num. 23. 13–end Luke 8. 16–25 [1 Kings 19. 1–18 Matt. 3. 13–end]*	Deut. 31.30 – 32.14 1 John 3. 11–end	
W		Num. ch. 24 Luke 8. 26–39 [Ezek. 11. 14–20 Matt. 9.35 – 10.20]*	Deut. 32. 15–47 1 John 4. 1–6	

	Sunday Principal Service Weekday Eucharist	Third Service Morning Prayer	Second Service Evening Prayer
17 Friday			
W	Acts 25. 13–21 Ps. 103. 1–2, 11–12, 19–20 John 21. 15–19	Ps. *28*; 30 *alt.* Ps. 139 Num. 27. 12–end Luke 8. 40–end [Ezek. 36. 22–28 Matt. 12. 22–32]*	Ps. 147 *alt.* Ps. *130*; 131; 137 Deut. ch. 33 1 John 4. 7–end
18 Saturday			
W	Acts 28. 16–20, 30–end Ps. 11. 4–end John 21. 20–end	Ps. 42; *43* *alt.* Ps. 120; *121*; 122 Num. 32. 1–27 Luke 9. 1–17 [Mic. 3. 1–8 Eph. 6. 10–20]*	*First EP of Pentecost* Ps. 48 Deut. 16. 9–15 John 7. 37–39 **R ct**
19 Sunday	**DAY OF PENTECOST** (Whit Sunday)		
R	*The reading from Acts must be used as either the first or second reading at the Principal Service.*	Acts 2. 1–21 *or* Ezek. 37. 1–14 Ps. 104. 26–36, 37b (or 26–end) Rom. 8. 22–27 *or* Acts 2. 1–21 John 15. 26–27; 16. 4b–15	*MP*: Ps. 145 Isa. 11. 1–9 *or* Wisd. 7. 15–23 [24–27] 1 Cor. 12. 4–13	*EP*: Ps. 139. 1–11, 13–18, 23–24 (or 139. 1–11) Ezek. 36. 22–28 Acts 2. 22–38 *Gospel*: John 20. 19–23
20 Monday	**Alcuin of York, Deacon, Abbot of Tours, 804** Ordinary Time resumes today		
Gw **DEL 7**	Com. Religious *or* *also* Col. 3. 12–16 John 4. 19–24	Jas. 3. 13–end Ps. 19. 7–end Mark 9. 14–29	Ps. 123; 124; 125; *126* Josh. ch. 1 Luke 9. 18–27	Ps. *127*; 128; 129 Job ch. 1 Rom. 1. 1–17
21 Tuesday	*Helena, Protector of the Holy Places, 330*		
G		Jas. 4. 1–10 Ps. 55. 7–9, 24 Mark 9. 30–37	Ps. *132*; 133 Josh. ch. 2 Luke 9. 28–36	Ps. (134); *135* Job ch. 2 Rom. 1. 18–end
22 Wednesday			
G		Jas. 4. 13–end Ps. 49. 1–2, 5–10 Mark 9. 38–40	Ps. 119. 153–end Josh. ch. 3 Luke 9. 37–50	Ps. 136 Job ch. 3 Rom. 2. 1–16
23 Thursday			
G		Jas. 5. 1–6 Ps. 49. 12–20 Mark 9. 41–end	Ps. *143*; 146 Josh. 4.1 – 5.1 Luke 9. 51–end	Ps. *138*; 140; 141 Job ch. 4 Rom. 2. 17–end
24 Friday	**John and Charles Wesley, Evangelists, Hymn Writers, 1791 and 1788**		
Gw	Com. Pastor *or* *also* Eph. 5. 15–20	Jas. 5. 9–12 Ps. 103. 1–4, 8–13 Mark 10. 1–12	Ps. *142*; 144 Josh. 5. 2–end Luke 10. 1–16	Ps. 145 Job ch. 5 Rom. 3. 1–20
25 Saturday	**The Venerable Bede, Monk at Jarrow, Scholar, Historian, 735** *Aldhelm, Bishop of Sherborne, 709*		
Gw	Com. Religious *or* *also* Ecclus. 39. 1–10	Jas. 5. 13–end Ps. 141. 1–4 Mark 10. 13–16	Ps. 147 Josh. 6. 1–20 Luke 10. 17–24	*First EP of Trinity Sunday* Ps. 97; 98 Isa. 40. 12–end Mark 1. 1–13 **ẘ ct**

*The alternative readings in square brackets may be used at one of the offices, in preparation for the Day of Pentecost.

	Calendar and Holy Communion	Morning Prayer	Evening Prayer	NOTES
W		Num. 27. 12–end Luke 8. 40–end [Ezek. 36. 22–28 Matt. 12. 22–32]*	Deut. ch. 33 1 John 4. 7–end	
W		Num. 32. 1–27 Luke 9. 1–17 [Mic. 3. 1–8 Eph. 6. 10–20]*	*First EP of Whit Sunday* Ps. 48 Deut. 16. 9–15 John 7. 37–39 **R ct**	

WHIT SUNDAY

	Calendar and Holy Communion	Morning Prayer	Evening Prayer	NOTES
R	Deut. 16. 9–12 Ps. 122 Acts 2. 1–11 John 14. 15–31a	Ps. 145 Isa. 11. 1–9 *or* Wisd. 7. 15–23 [24–27] 1 Cor. 12. 4–13	Ps. 139. 1–11, 13–18, 23–24 (or 139. 1–11) Ezek. 36. 22–28 Acts 2. 22–38	

Monday in Whitsun Week

R	Acts 10. 34–end John 3. 16–21	Ezek. 11. 14–20 Acts 2. 12–36	Exod. 35.30 – 36.1 Acts 2. 37–end	

Tuesday in Whitsun Week

R	Acts 8. 14–17 John 10. 1–10	Ezek. 37. 1–14 1 Cor. 12. 1–13	2 Sam. 23. 1–5 1 Cor. 12.27 – 13.end	

Ember Day

R	Ember CEG *or* Acts 2. 14–21 John 6. 44–51	Josh. ch. 3 Luke 9. 37–50	Job ch. 3 Rom. 2. 1–16	
R	Acts 2. 22–28 Luke 9. 1–6	Josh. 4.1 – 5.1 Luke 9. 51–end	Job ch. 4 Rom. 2. 17–end	

Ember Day

R	Ember CEG *or* Acts 8. 5–8 Luke 5. 17–26	Josh. 5. 2–end Luke 10. 1–16	Job ch. 5 Rom. 3. 1–20	

Ember Day

R	Ember CEG *or* Acts 13. 44–end Matt. 20. 29–end	Josh. 6. 1–20 Luke 10. 17–24	*First EP of Trinity Sunday* Ps. 97; 98 Isa. 40. 12–end Mark 1. 1–13 𝔚 **ct**	

	Sunday Principal Service Weekday Eucharist	Third Service Morning Prayer	Second Service Evening Prayer
26 Sunday	**TRINITY SUNDAY**		
ʍ	Isa. 6. 1–8 Ps. 29 Rom. 8. 12–17 John 3. 1–17	*MP*: Ps. 33. 1–12 Prov. 8. 1–4, 22–31 2 Cor. 13. [5–10] 11–end	*EP*: Ps. 104. 1–10 Ezek. 1. 4–10, 22–28a Rev. ch. 4 *Gospel*: Mark 1. 1–13
27 Monday			
G **DEL 8**	1 Pet. 1. 3–9 Ps. 111 Mark 10. 17–27	Ps. *1*; 2; 3 Josh. 7. 1–15 Luke 10. 25–37	Ps. *4*; 7 Job ch. 7 Rom. 4. 1–12
28 Tuesday	*Lanfranc, Prior of Le Bec, Archbishop of Canterbury, Scholar, 1089*		
G	1 Pet. 1. 10–16 Ps. 98. 1–5 Mark 10. 28–31	Ps. *5*; 6; (8) Josh. 7. 16–end Luke 10. 38–end	Ps. *9*; 10† Job ch. 8 Rom. 4. 13–end
29 Wednesday			
G	1 Pet. 1. 18–end Ps. 147. 13–end Mark 10. 32–45	Ps. 119. 1–32 Josh. 8. 1–29 Luke 11. 1–13	Ps. *11*; 12; 13 Job ch. 9 Rom. 5. 1–11 *or First EP of Corpus Christi* Ps. 110; 111 Exod. 16. 2–15 John 6. 22–35 **W ct**
30 Thursday	**DAY OF THANKSGIVING FOR HOLY COMMUNION (CORPUS CHRISTI)** Josephine Butler, Social Reformer, 1906 *Joan of Arc, Visionary, 1431; Apolo Kivebulaya, Evangelist in Central Africa, 1933*		
W	Gen. 14. 18–20 Ps. 116. 10–end 1 Cor. 11. 23–26 John 6. 51–58	*MP*: Ps. 147 Deut. 8. 2–16 1 Cor. 10. 1–17	*EP*: Ps. 23; 42; 43 Prov. 9. 1–5 Luke 9. 11–17
Gw	*or, if Corpus Christi is not observed:* Com. Saint *or* *esp.* Isa. 58. 6–11 *also* 1 John 3. 18–23 Matt. 9. 10–13	1 Pet. 2. 2–5, 9–12 Ps. 100 Mark 10. 46–end	Ps. 14; *15*; 16 Josh. 8. 30–end Luke 11. 14–28	Ps. 18† Job ch. 10 Rom. 5. 12–end *or First EP of the Visit of Mary to Elizabeth* Ps. 45 Song of Sol. 2. 8–14 Luke 1. 26–38 **W ct**
31 Friday	**THE VISIT OF THE BLESSED VIRGIN MARY TO ELIZABETH***		
W	Zeph. 3. 14–18 Ps. 113 Rom. 12. 9–16 Luke 1. 39–49 [50–56]	*MP*: Ps. 85; 150 1 Sam. 2. 1–10 Mark 3. 31–end	*EP*: Ps. 122; 127; 128 Zech. 2. 10–end John 3. 25–30
G	*or, if The Visitation is celebrated on 2 July:* 1 Pet. 4. 7–13 Ps. 96. 10–end Mark 11. 11–26	Ps. 17; *19* Josh. 9. 3–26 Luke 11. 29–36	Ps. 22 Job ch. 11 Rom. 6. 1–14

*The Visit of the Blessed Virgin Mary to Elizabeth may be celebrated on 2 July instead of 31 May.

	Calendar and Holy Communion	Morning Prayer	Evening Prayer	NOTES

TRINITY SUNDAY

w	Isa. 6. 1–8 Ps. 8 Rev. 4. 1–11 John 3. 1–15	Ps. 33. 1–12 Prov. 8. 1–4, 22–31 2 Cor. 13. [5–10] 11–end	Ps. 104. 1–10 Ezek. 1. 4–10, 22–28a Mark 1. 1–13

The Venerable Bede, Monk at Jarrow, Scholar, Historian, 735

Gw	Com. Religious	Josh. 7. 1–15 Luke 10. 25–37	Job ch. 7 Rom. 4. 1–12

G		Josh. 7. 16–end Luke 10. 38–end	Job ch. 8 Rom. 4. 13–end

G		Josh. 8. 1–29 Luke 11. 1–13	Job ch. 9 Rom. 5. 1–11

To celebrate Corpus Christi, see *Common Worship* provision.

G		Josh. 8. 30–end Luke 11. 14–28	Job ch. 10 Rom. 5. 12–end

G		Josh. 9. 3–26 Luke 11. 29–36	Job ch. 11 Rom. 6. 1–14

		Sunday Principal Service Weekday Eucharist	Third Service Morning Prayer	Second Service Evening Prayer

June 2024

1 Saturday — Justin, Martyr at Rome, c. 165

Gr	Com. Martyr *or* Jude 17, 20–end *esp.* John 15. 18–21 Ps. 63. 1–6 *also* 1 Macc. 2. 15–22 Mark 11. 27–end 1 Cor. 1. 18–25	Ps. 20; 21; **23** Josh. 10. 1–15 Luke 11. 37–end	Ps. **24**; 25 Job ch. 12 Rom. 6. 15–end ct

2 Sunday — THE FIRST SUNDAY AFTER TRINITY (Proper 4)

G	*Track 1* *Track 2* 1 Sam. 3. 1–10 [11–20] Deut. 5. 12–15 Ps. 139. 1–5, 12–18 Ps. 81. 1–10 2 Cor. 4. 5–12 2 Cor. 4. 5–12 Mark 2.23 – 3.6 Mark 2.23 – 3.6	Ps. 28; 32 Deut. 5. 1–21 Acts 21. 17–39a	Ps. 35 (*or* 35. 1–10) Jer. 5. 1–19 Rom. 7. 7–end *Gospel*: Luke 7. 1–10

3 Monday — *The Martyrs of Uganda, 1885–87 and 1977*

G DEL 9	2 Pet. 1. 2–7 Ps. 91. 1–2, 14–end Mark 12. 1–12	Ps. 27; **30** Josh. ch. 14 Luke 12. 1–12	Ps. 26; **28**; 29 Job ch. 13 Rom. 7. 1–6

4 Tuesday — *Petroc, Abbot of Padstow, 6th century*

G	2 Pet. 3. 11–15a, 17–end Ps. 90. 1–4, 10, 14, 16 Mark 12. 13–17	Ps. 32; **36** Josh. 21.43 – 22.8 Luke 12. 13–21	Ps. 33 Job ch. 14 Rom. 7. 7–end

5 Wednesday — Boniface (Wynfrith) of Crediton, Bishop, Apostle of Germany, Martyr, 754

Gr	Com. Martyr *or* 2 Tim. 1. 1–3, 6–12 *also* Acts 20. 24–28 Ps. 123 Mark 12. 18–27	Ps. 34 Josh. 22. 9–end Luke 12. 22–31	Ps. 119. 33–56 Job ch. 15 Rom. 8. 1–11

6 Thursday — *Ini Kopuria, Founder of the Melanesian Brotherhood, 1945*

G	2 Tim. 2. 8–15 Ps. 25. 4–12 Mark 12. 28–34	Ps. 37† Josh. ch. 23 Luke 12. 32–40	Ps. 39; **40** Job 16.1 - 17.2 Rom. 8. 12–17

7 Friday

G	2 Tim. 3. 10–end Ps. 119. 161–168 Mark 12. 35–37	Ps. 31 Josh. 24. 1–28 Luke 12. 41–48	Ps. 35 Job 17. 3–end Rom. 8. 18–30

8 Saturday — Thomas Ken, Bishop of Bath and Wells, Nonjuror, Hymn Writer, 1711

Gw	Com. Bishop *or* 2 Tim. 4. 1–8 *esp.* 2 Cor. 4. 1–10 Ps. 71. 7–16 Matt. 24. 42–46 Mark 12. 38–end	Ps. 41; **42**; 43 Josh. 24. 29–end Luke 12. 49–end	Ps. 45; **46** Job ch. 18 Rom. 8. 31–end ct

9 Sunday — THE SECOND SUNDAY AFTER TRINITY (Proper 5)

G	*Track 1* *Track 2* 1 Sam. 8. 4–11 [12–15] Gen. 3. 8–15 16–20; [11. 14–end] Ps. 130 Ps. 138 2 Cor. 4.13 – 5.1 2 Cor. 4.13 – 5.1 Mark 3. 20–end Mark 3. 20–end	Ps. 36 Deut. 6. 10–end Acts 22.22 – 23.11	Ps. 37. 1–17 (*or* 37. 1–11) Jer. 6. 16–21 Rom. 9. 1–13 *Gospel*: Luke 7. 11–17

	Calendar and Holy Communion	Morning Prayer	Evening Prayer	NOTES

Nicomede, Priest and Martyr at Rome (date unknown)

Gr	Com. Martyr	Josh. 10. 1–15 Luke 11. 37–end	Job ch. 12 Rom. 6. 15–end	
			ct	

THE FIRST SUNDAY AFTER TRINITY

G	2 Sam. 9. 6–end Ps. 41. 1–4 1 John 4. 7–end Luke 16. 19–31	Ps. 28; 32 Deut. 5. 1–21 Acts 21. 17–39a	Ps. 35 (or 35. 1–10) Jer. 5. 1–19 Rom. 7. 7–end	
G		Josh. ch. 14 Luke 12. 1–12	Job ch. 13 Rom. 7. 1–6	
G		Josh. 21.43 – 22.8 Luke 12. 13–21	Job ch. 14 Rom. 7. 7–end	

Boniface (Wynfrith) of Crediton, Bishop, Apostle of Germany, Martyr, 754

Gr	Com. Martyr	Josh. 22. 9–end Luke 12. 22–31	Job ch. 15 Rom. 8. 1–11	
G		Josh. ch. 23 Luke 12. 32–40	Job 16.1 – 17.2 Rom. 8. 12–17	
G		Josh. 24. 1–28 Luke 12. 41–48	Job 17. 3–end Rom. 8. 18–30	
G		Josh. 24. 29–end Luke 12. 49–end	Job ch. 18 Rom. 8. 31–end	
			ct	

THE SECOND SUNDAY AFTER TRINITY

G	Gen. 12. 1–4 Ps. 120 1 John 3. 13–end Luke 14. 16–24	Ps. 36 Deut. 6. 10–end Acts 22.22 – 23.11	Ps. 37. 1–17 (or 37. 1–11) Jer. 6. 16–21 Rom. 9. 1–13	

	Sunday Principal Service Weekday Eucharist	Third Service Morning Prayer	Second Service Evening Prayer

10 Monday

G **DEL 10**	1 Kings 17. 1–6 Ps. 121 Matt. 5. 1–12	Ps. 44 Judg. ch. 2 Luke 13. 1–9	Ps. *47*; 49 Job ch. 19 Rom. 9. 1–18 *or First EP of Barnabas* Ps. 1; 15 Isa. 42. 5–12 Acts 14. 8–end **R ct**

11 Tuesday   BARNABAS THE APOSTLE

R	Job 29. 11–16 *or* Acts 11. 19–end Ps. 112 Acts 11. 19–end *or* Gal. 2. 1–10 John 15. 12–17	*MP*: Ps. 100; 101; 117 Jer. 9. 23–24 Acts 4. 32–end	*EP*: Ps. 147 Eccles. 12. 9–end *or* Tobit 4. 5–11 Acts 9. 26–31

12 Wednesday

G	1 Kings 18. 20–39 Ps. 16. 1, 6–end Matt. 5. 17–19	Ps. 119. 57–80 Judg. ch. 5 Luke 13. 22–end	Ps. *59*; 60; (67) Job ch. 22 Rom. 10. 1–10

13 Thursday

G	1 Kings 18. 41–end Ps. 65. 8–end Matt. 5. 20–26	Ps. 56; *57*; (63†) Judg. 6. 1–24 Luke 14. 1–11	Ps. 61; *62*; 64 Job ch. 23 Rom. 10. 11–end

14 Friday   *Richard Baxter, Puritan Divine, 1691*

G	1 Kings 19. 9, 11–16 Ps. 27. 8–16 Matt. 5. 27–32	Ps. *51*; 54 Judg. 6. 25–end Luke 14. 12–24	Ps. 38 Job ch. 24 Rom. 11. 1–12

15 Saturday   *Evelyn Underhill, Spiritual Writer, 1941*

G	1 Kings 19. 19–end Ps. 16. 1–7 Matt. 5. 33–37	Ps. 68 Judg. ch. 7 Luke 14. 25–end	Ps. 65; *66* Job chs 25 & 26 Rom. 11. 13–24 **ct**

16 Sunday   THE THIRD SUNDAY AFTER TRINITY (Proper 6)

G	*Track 1* 1 Sam. 15.34 – 16.13 Ps. 20 2 Cor. 5. 6–10 [11–13] 14–17 Mark 4. 26–34 *Track 2* Ezek. 17. 22–end Ps. 92. 1–4, 12–end (*or* 1–8) 2 Cor. 5. 6–10 [11–13] 14–17 Mark 4. 26–34	Ps. 42; 43 Deut. 10.12 – 11.1 Acts 23. 12–35	Ps. 39 Jer. 7. 1–16 Rom. 9. 14–26 *Gospel:* Luke 7.36 – 8.3

17 Monday   *Samuel and Henrietta Barnett, Social Reformers, 1913 and 1936*

G **DEL 11**	1 Kings 21. 1–16 Ps. 5. 1–5 Matt. 5. 38–42	Ps. 71 Judg. 8. 22–end Luke 15. 1–10	Ps. *72*; 75 Job ch. 27 Rom. 11. 25–end

18 Tuesday   *Bernard Mizeki, Apostle of the MaShona, Martyr, 1896*

G	1 Kings 21. 17–end Ps. 51. 1–9 Matt. 5. 43–end	Ps. 73 Judg. 9. 1–21 Luke 15. 11–end	Ps. 74 Job ch. 28 Rom. 12. 1–8

	Calendar and Holy Communion	Morning Prayer	Evening Prayer	NOTES
G		Judg. ch. 2 Luke 13. 1–9	Job ch. 19 Rom. 9. 1–18 *or First EP of Barnabas* (Ps. 1; 15) Isa. 42. 5–12 Acts 14. 8–end	
			R ct	

BARNABAS THE APOSTLE

	Calendar and Holy Communion	Morning Prayer	Evening Prayer	NOTES
R	Job 29. 11–16 Ps. 112 Acts 11. 22–end John 15. 12–16	(Ps. 100; 101; 117) Jer. 9. 23–24 Acts 4. 32–end	(Ps. 147) Eccles. 12. 9–end *or Tobit 4. 5–11* Acts 9. 26–31	
G		Judg. ch. 5 Luke 13. 22–end	Job ch. 22 Rom. 10. 1–10	
G		Judg. 6. 1–24 Luke 14. 1–11	Job ch. 23 Rom. 10. 11–end	
G		Judg. 6. 25–end Luke 14. 12–24	Job ch. 24 Rom. 11. 1–12	
G		Judg. ch. 7 Luke 14. 25–end	Job chs 25 & 26 Rom. 11. 13–24	
			ct	

THE THIRD SUNDAY AFTER TRINITY

	Calendar and Holy Communion	Morning Prayer	Evening Prayer	NOTES
G	2 Chron. 33. 9–13 Ps. 55. 17–23 1 Pet. 5. 5b–11 Luke 15. 1–10	Ps. 42; 43 Deut. 10.12 – 11.1 Acts 23. 12–35	Ps. 39 Jer. 7. 1–16 Rom. 9. 14–26	

Alban, first Martyr of Britain, c. 250

	Calendar and Holy Communion	Morning Prayer	Evening Prayer	NOTES
Gr	Com. Martyr	Judg. 8. 22–end Luke 15. 1–10	Job ch. 27 Rom. 11. 25–end	
G		Judg. 9. 1–21 Luke 15. 11–end	Job ch. 28 Rom. 12. 1–8	

	Sunday Principal Service Weekday Eucharist	Third Service Morning Prayer	Second Service Evening Prayer

19 Wednesday *Sundar Singh of India, Sadhu (holy man), Evangelist, Teacher, 1929*

G	2 Kings 2. 1, 6–14 Ps. 31. 21–end Matt. 6. 1–6, 16–18	Ps. 77 Judg. 9. 22–end Luke 16. 1–18	Ps. 119. 81–104 Job ch. 29 Rom. 12. 9–end

20 Thursday

G	Ecclus. 48. 1–14 *or* Isa. 63. 7–9 Ps. 97. 1–8 Matt. 6. 7–15	Ps. 78. 1–39† Judg. 11. 1–11 Luke 16. 19–end	Ps. 78. 40–end† Job ch. 30 Rom. 13. 1–7

21 Friday

G	2 Kings 11. 1–4, 9–18, 20 Ps. 132. 1–5, 11–13 Matt. 6. 19–23	Ps. 55 Judg. 11. 29–end Luke 17. 1–10	Ps. 69 Job ch. 31 Rom. 13. 8–end

22 Saturday **Alban, first Martyr of Britain, c. 250**

Gr	Com. Martyr *or* *esp.* 2 Tim. 2. 3–13 John 12. 24–26	2 Chron. 24. 17–25 Ps. 89. 25–33 Matt. 6. 24–end	Ps. *76*; 79 Judg. 12. 1–7 Luke 17. 11–19	Ps. 81; *84* Job ch. 32 Rom. 14. 1–12 **ct**

23 Sunday **THE FOURTH SUNDAY AFTER TRINITY (Proper 7)**

G	*Track 1* 1 Sam. 17. [1a, 4–11, 19–23] 32–49 *and* Ps. 9. 9–end *or* 1 Sam. 17.57 – 18.5, 10–16 *and* Ps. 133 2 Cor. 6. 1–13 Mark 4. 35–end	*Track 2* Job 38. 1–11 Ps. 107. 1–3, 23–32 (or 23–32) 2 Cor. 6. 1–13 Mark 4. 35–end	Ps. 48 Deut. 11. 1–15 Acts 27. 1–12	Ps. 49 Jer. 10. 1–16 Rom. 11. 25–end *Gospel:* Luke 8. 26–39 *or First EP of The Birth of John the Baptist* Ps. 71 Judg. 13. 2–7, 24–end Luke 1. 5–25 **W ct**

24 Monday **THE BIRTH OF JOHN THE BAPTIST**

W **DEL 12**	Isa. 40. 1–11 Ps. 85. 7–end Acts 13. 14b–26 *or* Gal. 3. 23–end Luke 1. 57–66, 80	*MP:* Ps. 50; 149 Ecclus. 48. 1–10 *or* Mal. 3. 1–6 Luke 3. 1–17	*EP:* Ps. 80; 82 Mal. ch. 4 Matt. 11. 2–19

25 Tuesday

G	2 Kings 19. 9b–11, 14–21, 31–36 Ps. 48. 1–2, 8–end Matt. 7. 6, 12–14	Ps. 87; *89. 1–18* Judg. ch. 14 Luke 18. 1–14	Ps. 89. 19–end Job ch. 38 Rom. 15. 1–13

26 Wednesday Ember Day*

G *or* R	2 Kings 22. 8–13; 23. 1–3 Ps. 119. 33–40 Matt. 7. 15–20	Ps. 119. 105–128 Judg. 15.1 – 16.3 Luke 18. 15–30	Ps. *91*; 93 Job ch. 39 Rom. 15. 14–21

27 Thursday *Cyril, Bishop of Alexandria, Teacher, 444*

G	2 Kings 24. 8–17 Ps. 79. 1–9, 12 Matt. 7. 21–end	Ps. 90; *92* Judg. 16. 4–end Luke 18. 31–end	Ps. 94 Job ch. 40 Rom. 15. 22–end

*For Ember Day provision, see p. 11.

	Calendar and Holy Communion	Morning Prayer	Evening Prayer	NOTES
G		Judg. 9. 22–end Luke 16. 1–18	Job ch. 29 Rom. 12. 9–end	

Translation of Edward, King of the West Saxons, 979

Gr	Com. Martyr	Judg. 11. 1–11 Luke 16. 19–end	Job ch. 30 Rom. 13. 1–7	
G		Judg. 11. 29–end Luke 17. 1–10	Job ch. 31 Rom. 13. 8–end	
G		Judg. 12. 1–7 Luke 17. 11–19	Job ch. 32 Rom. 14. 1–12 **ct**	

THE FOURTH SUNDAY AFTER TRINITY

G	Gen. 3. 17–19 Ps. 79. 8–10 Rom. 8. 18–23 Luke 6. 36–42	Ps. 48 Deut. 11. 1–15 Acts 27. 1–12	Ps. 49 Jer. 10. 1–16 Rom. 11. 25–end *or First EP of The Nativity of John the Baptist* Ps. 71 Judg. 13. 2–7, 24–end Luke 1. 5–25 **W ct**	

THE NATIVITY OF JOHN THE BAPTIST

W	Isa. 40. 1–11 Ps. 80. 1–7 Acts 13. 22–26 Luke 1. 57–80	(Ps. 50; 149) Ecclus. 48. 1–10 *or* Mal. 3. 1–6 Luke 3. 1–17	(Ps. 82) Mal. ch. 4 Matt. 11. 2–19	
G		Judg. ch. 14 Luke 18. 1–14	Job ch. 38 Rom. 15. 1–13	
G		Judg. 15.1 – 16.3 Luke 18. 15–30	Job ch. 39 Rom. 15. 14–21	
G		Judg. 16. 4–end Luke 18. 31–end	Job ch. 40 Rom. 15. 22–end	

	Sunday Principal Service / Weekday Eucharist	Third Service / Morning Prayer	Second Service / Evening Prayer

28 Friday — **Irenaeus, Bishop of Lyons, Teacher, c. 200**
Ember Day*

Gw *or* **Rw**	Com. Teacher *or* **2 Kings 25. 1–12**	Ps. *88*; (95)	Ps. 102
	also 2 Pet. 1. 16–21 Ps. 137. 1–6	Judg. ch. 17	Job ch. 41
	Matt. 8. 1–4	Luke 19. 1–10	Rom. 16. 1–16
			or First EP of Peter and Paul
			Ps. 66; 67
			Ezek. 3. 4–11
			Gal. 1.13 – 2.8
			or, for Peter alone:
			Acts 9. 32–end
			R ct

29 Saturday — **PETER AND PAUL, APOSTLES**
Ember Day*

R	Zech. 4. 1–6a, 10b–end	*MP*: Ps. 71; 113	*EP*: Ps. 124; 138
	or Acts 12. 1–11	Isa. 49. 1–6	Ezek. 34. 11–16
	Ps. 125	Acts 11. 1–18	John 21. 15–22
	Acts 12. 1–11		
	or 2 Tim. 4. 6–8, 17–18		
	Matt. 16. 13–19		
	or, if Peter is commemorated alone:		
R	Ezek. 3. 22–end	*MP*: Ps. 71; 113	*EP*: Ps. 124; 138
	or Acts 12. 1–11	Isa. 49. 1–6	Ezek. 34. 11–16
	Ps. 125	Acts 11. 1–18	John 21. 15–22
	Acts 12. 1–11		
	or 1 Pet. 2. 19–end		
	Matt. 16. 13–19		

30 Sunday — **THE FIFTH SUNDAY AFTER TRINITY (Proper 8)**

G	*Track 1*	Ps. 56	Ps. [52]; 53
	2 Sam. 1. 1, 17–end	Deut. 15. 1–11	Jer. 11. 1–14
	Ps. 130	Acts 27. [13–32] 33–end	Rom. 13. 1–10
	2 Cor. 8. 7–end		*Gospel:* Luke 9. 51–end
	Mark 5. 21–end		
	Track 2		
	Wisd. of Sol. 1. 13–15;		
	2. 23–24		
	Canticle: Lam. 3. 22–33		
	or Ps. 30		
	2 Cor. 8. 7–end		
	Mark 5. 21–end		

July 2024

1 Monday — *Henry, John and Henry Venn the Younger, Priests, Evangelical Divines, 1797, 1813 and 1873*

G	Amos 2. 6–10, 13–end	Ps. *98*; 99; 101	Ps. *105*† (or 103)
DEL 13	Ps. 50. 16–23	1 Sam. 1. 1–20	Ezek. 1. 1–14
	Matt. 8. 18–22	Luke 19. 28–40	2 Cor. 1. 1–14

2 Tuesday**

G	Amos 3. 1–8; 4. 11–12	Ps. *106*† (or 103)	Ps. 107†
	Ps. 5. 8–end	1 Sam. 1.21 – 2.11	Ezek. 1.15 – 2.2
	Matt. 8. 23–27	Luke 19. 41–end	2 Cor. 1.15 – 2.4
			or First EP of Thomas
			Ps. 27
			Isa. ch. 35
			Heb. 10.35 – 11.1
			R ct

*For Ember Day provision, see p. 11.
**The Visit of the Blessed Virgin Mary to Elizabeth may be celebrated on 2 July instead of 31 May.
***Common Worship* Morning and Evening Prayer provision for 31 May may be used.

	Calendar and Holy Communion	Morning Prayer	Evening Prayer	NOTES
G		Judg. ch. 17 Luke 19. 1–10	Job ch. 41 Rom. 16. 1–16 or *First EP of Peter* (Ps. 66; 67) Ezek. 3. 4–11 Acts 9. 32–end	
			R ct	

PETER THE APOSTLE

R	Ezek. 3. 4–11 Ps. 125 Acts 12. 1–11 Matt. 16. 13–19	(Ps. 71; 113) Isa. 49. 1–6 Acts 11. 1–18	(Ps. 124; 138) Ezek. 34. 11–16 John 21. 15–22	

THE FIFTH SUNDAY AFTER TRINITY

G	1 Kings 19. 19–21 Ps. 84. 8–end 1 Pet. 3. 8–15a Luke 5. 1–11	Ps. 56 Deut. 15. 1–11 Acts 27. [13–32] 33–end	Ps. [52]; 53 Jer. 11. 1–14 Rom. 13. 1–10	

G		1 Sam. 1. 1–20 Luke 19. 28–40	Ezek. 1. 1–14 2 Cor. 1. 1–14	

The Visitation of the Blessed Virgin Mary***

Gw	1 Sam. 2. 1–3 Ps. 113 Gal. 4. 1–5 Luke 1. 39–45	1 Sam. 1.21 – 2.11 Luke 19. 41–end	Ezek. 1.15 – 2.2 2 Cor. 1.15 – 2.4	

		Sunday Principal Service Weekday Eucharist	Third Service Morning Prayer	Second Service Evening Prayer

3 Wednesday   **THOMAS THE APOSTLE***

R		Hab. 2. 1–4 Ps. 31. 1–6 Eph. 2. 19–end John 20. 24–29	*MP*: Ps. 92; 146 2 Sam. 15. 17–21 *or* Ecclus. ch. 2 John 11. 1–16	*EP*: Ps. 139 Job 42. 1–6 1 Pet. 1. 3–12
		or, if Thomas is not celebrated:		
G		Amos 5. 14–15, 21–24 Ps. 50. 7–14 Matt. 8. 28–end	Ps. 110; *111*; 112 1 Sam. 2. 12–26 Luke 20. 1–8	Ps. 119. 129–152 Ezek. 2.3 – 3.11 2 Cor. 2. 5–end

4 Thursday

G		Amos 7. 10–end Ps. 19. 7–10 Matt. 9. 1–8	Ps. 113; *115* 1 Sam. 2. 27–end Luke 20. 9–19	Ps. 114; *116*; 117 Ezek. 3. 12–end 2 Cor. ch. 3

5 Friday

G		Amos 8. 4–6, 9–12 Ps. 119. 1–8 Matt. 9. 9–13	Ps. 139 1 Sam. 3.1 – 4.1a Luke 20. 20–26	Ps. *130*; 131; 137 Ezek. ch. 8 2 Cor. ch. 4

6 Saturday   *Thomas More, Scholar, and John Fisher, Bishop of Rochester, Reformation Martyrs, 1535*

G		Amos 9. 11–end Ps. 85. 8–end Matt. 9. 14–17	Ps. 120; *121*; 122 1 Sam. 4. 1b–end Luke 20. 27–40	Ps. 118 Ezek. ch. 9 2 Cor. ch. 5 **ct**

7 **Sunday**   **THE SIXTH SUNDAY AFTER TRINITY (Proper 9)**

G		*Track 1* 2 Sam. 5. 1–5, 9–10 Ps. 48 2 Cor. 12. 2–10 Mark 6. 1–13	*Track 2* Ezek. 2. 1–5 Ps. 123 2 Cor. 12. 2–10 Mark 6. 1–13	Ps. 57 Deut. 24. 10–end Acts 28. 1–16

Second Service (Sunday 7): Ps. [63]; 64
Jer. 20. 1–11a
Rom. 14. 1–17
Gospel: Luke 10. 1–11, 16–20

8 Monday

G **DEL 14**		Hos. 2. 14–16, 19–20 Ps. 145. 2–9 Matt. 9. 18–26	Ps. 123; 124; 125; *126* 1 Sam. ch. 5 Luke 20.41 – 21.4	Ps. *127*; 128; 129 Ezek. 10. 1–19 2 Cor. 6.1 – 7.1

9 Tuesday

G		Hos. 8. 4–7, 11–13 Ps. 103. 8–12 Matt. 9. 32–end	Ps. *132*; 133 1 Sam. 6. 1–16 Luke 21. 5–19	Ps. (134); *135* Ezek. 11. 14–end 2 Cor. 7. 2–end

10 Wednesday

G		Hos. 10. 1–3, 7–8, 12 Ps. 115. 3–10 Matt. 10. 1–7	Ps. 119. 153–end 1 Sam. ch. 7 Luke 21. 20–28	Ps. 136 Ezek. 12. 1–16 2 Cor. 8. 1–15

11 Thursday   **Benedict of Nursia, Abbot of Monte Cassino, Father of Western Monasticism, c. 550**

Gw		Com. Religious *or* *also* 1 Cor. 3. 10–11 Luke 18. 18–22	Hos. 11. 1, 3–4, 8–9 Ps. 105. 1–7 Matt. 10. 7–15	Ps. *143*; 146 1 Sam. ch. 8 Luke 21. 29–end

Second Service (11): Ps. *138*; 140; 141
Ezek. 12. 17–end
2 Cor. 8.16 – 9.5

12 Friday

G		Hos. 14. 2–end Ps. 80. 1–7 Matt. 10. 16–23	Ps. 142; *144* 1 Sam. 9. 1–14 Luke 22. 1–13	Ps. 145 Ezek. 13. 1–16 2 Cor. 9. 6–end

*Thomas the Apostle may be celebrated on 21 December instead of 3 July.

	Calendar and Holy Communion	Morning Prayer	Evening Prayer	NOTES
G		1 Sam. 2. 12–26 Luke 20. 1–8	Ezek. 2.3 – 3.11 2 Cor. 2. 5–end	

Translation of Martin, Bishop of Tours, c. 397

	Calendar and Holy Communion	Morning Prayer	Evening Prayer	NOTES
Gw	Com. Bishop	1 Sam. 2. 27–end Luke 20. 9–19	Ezek. 3. 12–end 2 Cor. ch. 3	
G		1 Sam. 3.1 – 4.1a Luke 20. 20–26	Ezek. ch. 8 2 Cor. ch. 4	
G		1 Sam. 4. 1b–end Luke 20. 27–40	Ezek. ch. 9 2 Cor. ch. 5 ct	

THE SIXTH SUNDAY AFTER TRINITY

	Calendar and Holy Communion	Morning Prayer	Evening Prayer	NOTES
G	Gen. 4. 2b–15 Ps. 90. 12–end Rom. 6. 3–11 Matt. 5. 20–26	Ps. 57 Deut. 24. 10–end Acts 28. 1–16	Ps. [63]; 64 Jer. 20. 1–11a Rom. 14. 1–17	
G		1 Sam. ch. 5 Luke 20.41 – 21.4	Ezek. 10. 1–19 2 Cor. 6.1 – 7.1	
G		1 Sam. 6. 1–16 Luke 21. 5–19	Ezek. 11. 14–end 2 Cor. 7. 2–end	
G		1 Sam. ch. 7 Luke 21. 20–28	Ezek. 12. 1–16 2 Cor. 8. 1–15	
G		1 Sam. ch. 8 Luke 21. 29–end	Ezek. 12. 17–end 2 Cor. 8.16 – 9.5	
G		1 Sam. 9. 1–14 Luke 22. 1–13	Ezek. 13. 1–16 2 Cor. 9. 6–end	

		Sunday Principal Service Weekday Eucharist	Third Service Morning Prayer	Second Service Evening Prayer
13 Saturday				
G		Isa. 6. 1–8 Ps. 51. 1–7 Matt. 10. 24–33	Ps. 147 1 Sam. 9.15 – 10.1 Luke 22. 14–23	Ps. *148*; 149; 150 Ezek. 14. 1–11 2 Cor. ch. 10 ct
14 Sunday	**THE SEVENTH SUNDAY AFTER TRINITY (Proper 10)**			
G		*Track 1* 2 Sam. 6. 1–5, 12b–19 Ps. 24 Eph. 1. 3–14 Mark 6. 14–29	*Track 2* Amos 7. 7–15 Ps. 85. 8–end Eph. 1. 3–14 Mark 6. 14–29	Ps. 65 Deut. 28. 1–14 Acts 28. 17–end	Ps. 66 (or 66. 1–8) Job 4. 1; 5. 6–end *or* Ecclus. 4. 11–end Rom. 15. 14–29 *Gospel:* Luke 10. 25–37
15 Monday	*Swithun, Bishop of Winchester, c. 862* *Bonaventure, Friar, Bishop, Teacher, 1274*			
Gw **DEL 15**	Com. Bishop *or* *also* Jas. 5. 7–11, 13–18	Isa. 1. 11–17 Ps. 50. 7–15 Matt. 10.34 – 11.1	Ps. *1*; 2; 3 1 Sam. 10. 1–16 Luke 22. 24–30	Ps. *4*; 7 Ezek. 14. 12–end 2 Cor. 11. 1–15
16 Tuesday	*Osmund, Bishop of Salisbury, 1099*			
G		Isa. 7. 1–9 Ps. 48. 1–7 Matt. 11. 20–24	Ps. *5*; 6; (8) 1 Sam. 10. 17–end Luke 22. 31–38	Ps. *9*; 10† Ezek. 18. 1–20 2 Cor. 11. 16–end
17 Wednesday				
G		Isa. 10. 5–7, 13–16 Ps. 94. 5–11 Matt. 11. 25–27	Ps. 119. 1–32 1 Sam. ch. 11 Luke 22. 39–46	Ps. *11*; 12; 13 Ezek. 18. 21–32 2 Cor. ch. 12
18 Thursday	*Elizabeth Ferard, first Deaconess of the Church of England, Founder of the Community of St Andrew,* *1883*			
G		Isa. 26. 7–9, 16–19 Ps. 102. 14–21 Matt. 11. 28–end	Ps. 14; *15*; 16 1 Sam. ch. 12 Luke 22. 47–62	Ps. 18† Ezek. 20. 1–20 2 Cor. ch. 13
19 Friday	*Gregory, Bishop of Nyssa, and his sister Macrina, Deaconess, Teachers, c. 394 and c. 379*			
Gw	Com. Teacher *or* *esp.* 1 Cor. 2. 9–13 *also* Wisd. 9. 13–17	Isa. 38. 1–6, 21–22, 7–8 *Canticle:* Isa. 38. 10–16 *or* Ps. 32. 1–8 Matt. 12. 1–8	Ps. 17; *19* 1 Sam. 13. 5–18 Luke 22. 63–end	Ps. 22 Ezek. 20. 21–38 Jas. 1. 1–11
20 Saturday	*Margaret of Antioch, Martyr, 4th century; Bartolomé de las Casas, Apostle to the Indies, 1566*			
G		Mic. 2. 1–5 Ps. 10. 1–5a, 12 Matt. 12. 14–21	Ps. 20; 21; *23* 1 Sam. 13.19 – 14.15 Luke 23. 1–12	Ps. *24*; 25 Ezek. 24. 15–end Jas. 1. 12–end ct
21 Sunday	**THE EIGHTH SUNDAY AFTER TRINITY (Proper 11)**			
G		*Track 1* 2 Sam. 7. 1–14a Ps. 89. 20–37 Eph. 2. 11–end Mark 6. 30–34, 53–end	*Track 2* Jer. 23. 1–6 Ps. 23 Eph. 2. 11–end Mark 6. 30–34, 53–end	Ps. 67; 70 Deut. 30. 1–10 1 Pet. 3. 8–18	Ps. 73 (or 73. 21–end) Job 13.13 – 14.6 *or* Ecclus. 18. 1–14 Heb. 2. 5–end *Gospel:* Luke 10. 38–end *or First EP of Mary* *Magdalene* Ps. 139 Isa. 25. 1–9 2 Cor. 1. 3–7 **W** ct

	Calendar and Holy Communion	Morning Prayer	Evening Prayer	NOTES
G		1 Sam. 9.15 – 10.1 Luke 22. 14–23	Ezek. 14. 1–11 2 Cor. ch. 10	
			ct	
	THE SEVENTH SUNDAY AFTER TRINITY			
G	1 Kings 17. 8–16 Ps. 34. 11–end Rom. 6. 19–end Mark 8. 1–10a	Ps. 65 Deut. 28. 1–14 Acts 28. 17–end	Ps. 66 (or 66. 1–8) Job 4. 1; 5. 6–end or Ecclus. 4. 11–end Luke 10. 21–24	
	Swithun, Bishop of Winchester, c. 862			
Gw	Com. Bishop	1 Sam. 10. 1–16 Luke 22. 24–30	Ezek. 14. 12–end 2 Cor. 11. 1–15	
G		1 Sam. 10. 17–end Luke 22. 31–38	Ezek. 18. 1–20 2 Cor. 11. 16–end	
G		1 Sam. ch. 11 Luke 22. 39–46	Ezek. 18. 21–32 2 Cor. ch. 12	
G		1 Sam. ch. 12 Luke 22. 47–62	Ezek. 20. 1–20 2 Cor. ch. 13	
G		1 Sam. 13. 5–18 Luke 22. 63–end	Ezek. 20. 21–38 Jas. 1. 1–11	
	Margaret of Antioch, Martyr, 4th century			
Gr	Com. Virgin Martyr	1 Sam. 13.19 – 14.15 Luke 23. 1–12	Ezek. 24. 15–end Jas. 1. 12–end	
			ct	
	THE EIGHTH SUNDAY AFTER TRINITY			
G	Jer. 23. 16–24 Ps. 31. 1–6 Rom. 8. 12–17 Matt. 7. 15–21	Ps. 67; 70 Deut. 30. 1–10 1 Pet. 3. 13–22	Ps. 73 (or 73. 21–end) Job 13.13 – 14.6 or Ecclus. 18. 1–14 Heb. 2. 5–end or First EP of Mary Magdalene Ps. 139 Isa. 25. 1–9 2 Cor. 1. 3–7	
			W ct	

		Sunday Principal Service Weekday Eucharist	Third Service Morning Prayer	Second Service Evening Prayer
22 Monday	**MARY MAGDALENE**			
W **DEL 16**		Song of Sol. 3. 1–4 Ps. 42. 1–10 2 Cor. 5. 14–17 John 20. 1–2, 11–18	*MP*: Ps. 30; 32; 150 1 Sam. 16. 14–end Luke 8. 1–3	*EP*: Ps. 63 Zeph. 3. 14–end Mark 15.40 – 16.7
23 Tuesday	*Bridget of Sweden, Abbess of Vadstena, 1373*			
G		Mic. 7. 14–15, 18–20 Ps. 85. 1–7 Matt. 12. 46–end	Ps. 32; *36* 1 Sam. 15. 1–23 Luke 23. 26–43	Ps. 33 Ezek. 33. 1–20 Jas. 2. 14–end
24 Wednesday				
G		Jer. 1. 1, 4–10 Ps. 70 Matt. 13. 1–9	Ps. 34 1 Sam. ch. 16 Luke 23. 44–56a	Ps. 119. 33–56 Ezek. 33. 21–end Jas. ch. 3 or *First EP of James* Ps. 144 Deut. 30. 11–end Mark 5. 21–end **R ct**
25 Thursday	**JAMES THE APOSTLE**			
R		Jer. 45. 1–5 or Acts 11.27 – 12.2 Ps. 126 Acts 11.27 – 12.2 or 2 Cor. 4. 7–15 Matt. 20. 20–28	*MP*: Ps. 7; 29; 117 2 Kings 1. 9–15 Luke 9. 46–56	*EP*: Ps. 94 Jer. 26. 1–15 Mark 1. 14–20
26 Friday	Anne and Joachim, Parents of the Blessed Virgin Mary			
Gw		Zeph. 3. 14–18a *or* Ps. 127 Rom. 8. 28–30 Matt. 13. 16–17	Jer. 3. 14–17 Ps. 23 or *Canticle*: Jer. 31. 10–13 Matt. 13. 18–23	Ps. 31 1 Sam. 17. 31–54 Luke 24. 13–35
				Ps. 35 Ezek. 34. 17–end Jas. 4.13 – 5.6
27 Saturday	*Brooke Foss Westcott, Bishop of Durham, Teacher, 1901*			
G		Jer. 7. 1–11 Ps. 84. 1–6 Matt. 13. 24–30	Ps. 41; *42*; 43 1 Sam. 17.55 – 18.16 Luke 24. 36–end	Ps. 45; *46* Ezek. 36. 16–36 Jas. 5. 7–end **ct**
28 Sunday	**THE NINTH SUNDAY AFTER TRINITY (Proper 12)**			
G		*Track 1* 2 Sam. 11. 1–15 Ps. 14 Eph. 3. 14–end John 6. 1–21	*Track 2* 2 Kings 4. 42–end Ps. 145. 10–19 Eph. 3. 14–end John 6. 1–21	Ps. 75 Song of Sol. ch. 2 or 1 Macc. 2. [1–14] 15–22 1 Pet. 4. 7–14
				Ps. 74 (or 74. 11–16) Job 19. 1–27a or Ecclus. 38. 24–end Heb. ch. 8 *Gospel*: Luke 11. 1–13
29 Monday	Mary, Martha and Lazarus, Companions of Our Lord			
Gw **DEL 17**		Isa. 25. 6–9 *or* Ps. 49. 5–10, 16 Heb. 2. 10–15 John 12. 1–8	Jer. 13. 1–11 Ps. 82 or Deut. 32. 18–21 Matt. 13. 31–35	Ps. 44 1 Sam. 19. 1–18 Acts 1. 1–14
				Ps. *47*; 49 Ezek. 37. 1–14 Mark 1. 1–13

	Calendar and Holy Communion	Morning Prayer	Evening Prayer	NOTES
	MARY MAGDALENE			
W	Zeph. 3. 14–end Ps. 30. 1–5 2 Cor. 5. 14–17 John 20. 11–18	(Ps. 30; 32; 150) 1 Sam. 16. 14–end Luke 8. 1–3	(Ps. 63) Song of Sol. 3. 1–4 Mark 15.40 – 16.7	
G		1 Sam. 15. 1–23 Luke 23. 26–43	Ezek. 33. 1–20 Jas. 2. 14–end	
G		1 Sam. ch. 16 Luke 23. 44–56a	Ezek. 33. 21–end Jas. ch. 3 *or First EP of James* (Ps. 144) Deut. 30. 11–end Mark 5. 21–end **R ct**	
	JAMES THE APOSTLE			
R	2 Kings 1. 9–15 Ps. 15 Acts 11.27 – 12.3a Matt. 20. 20–28	(Ps. 7; 29; 117) Jer. 45. 1–5 Luke 9. 46–56	(Ps. 94) Jer. 26. 1–15 Mark 1. 14–20	
	Anne, Mother of the Blessed Virgin Mary			
Gw	Com. Saint	1 Sam. 17. 31–54 Luke 24. 13–35	Ezek. 34. 17–end Jas. 4.13 – 5.6	
G		1 Sam. 17.55 – 18.16 Luke 24. 36–end	Ezek. 36. 16–36 Jas. 5. 7–end **ct**	
	THE NINTH SUNDAY AFTER TRINITY			
G	Num. 10.35 – 11.3 Ps. 95 1 Cor. 10. 1–13 Luke 16. 1–9 *or Luke 15. 11–end*	Ps. 75 Song of Sol. ch. 2 *or 1 Macc. 2. [1–14]* 15–22 1 Pet. 4. 7–14	Ps. 74 (or 74. 11–16) Job 19. 1–27a *or Ecclus. 38. 24–end* Heb. ch. 8	
G		1 Sam. 19. 1–18 Acts 1. 1–14	Ezek. 37. 1–14 Mark 1. 1–13	

		Sunday Principal Service Weekday Eucharist	Third Service Morning Prayer	Second Service Evening Prayer

30 Tuesday — William Wilberforce, Social Reformer, Olaudah Equiano and Thomas Clarkson, Anti-Slavery Campaigners, 1833, 1797 and 1846

Gw	Com. Saint *or* *also* Job 31. 16–23 Gal. 3. 26–end; 4. 6–7 Luke 4. 16–21	Jer. 14. 17–end Ps. 79. 8–end Matt. 13. 36–43	Ps. **48**; 52 1 Sam. 20. 1–17 Acts 1. 15–end	Ps. 50 Ezek. 37. 15–end Mark 1. 14–20

31 Wednesday — *Ignatius of Loyola, Founder of the Society of Jesus, 1556*

G		Jer. 15. 10, 16–end Ps. 59. 1–4, 18–end Matt. 13. 44–46	Ps. 119. 57–80 1 Sam. 20. 18–end Acts 2. 1–21	Ps. **59**; 60; (67) Ezek. 39. 21–end Mark 1. 21–28

August 2024

1 Thursday

G		Jer. 18. 1–6 Ps. 146. 1–5 Matt. 13. 47–53	Ps. 56; **57**; (63†) 1 Sam. 21.1 – 22.5 Acts 2. 22–36	Ps. 61; **62**; 64 Ezek. 43. 1–12 Mark 1. 29–end

2 Friday

G		Jer. 26. 1–9 Ps. 69. 4–10 Matt. 13. 54–end	Ps. **51**; 54 1 Sam. 22. 6–end Acts 2. 37–end	Ps. 38 Ezek. 44. 4–16 Mark 2. 1–12

3 Saturday

G		Jer. 26. 11–16, 24 Ps. 69. 14–20 Matt. 14. 1–12	Ps. 68 1 Sam. ch. 23 Acts 3. 1–10	Ps. 65; **66** Ezek. 47. 1–12 Mark 2. 13–22 **ct**

4 Sunday — **THE TENTH SUNDAY AFTER TRINITY (Proper 13)**

G	*Track 1* 2 Sam. 11.26 – 12.13a Ps. 51. 1–13 Eph. 4. 1–16 John 6. 24–35	*Track 2* Exod. 16. 2–4, 9–15 Ps. 78. 23–29 Eph. 4. 1–16 John 6. 24–35	Ps. 86 Song of Sol. 5. 2–end *or* 1 Macc. 3. 1–12 2 Pet. 1. 1–15	Ps. 88 (*or* 88. 1–10) Job ch. 28 *or* Ecclus. 42. 15–end Heb. 11. 17–31 *Gospel:* Luke 12. 13–21

5 Monday — Oswald, King of Northumbria, Martyr, 642

Gr **DEL 18**	Com. Martyr *or* *esp.* 1 Pet. 4. 12–end John 16. 29–end	Jer. ch. 28 Ps. 119. 89–96 Matt. 14. 13–21 *or* 14. 22–end	Ps. 71 1 Sam. ch. 24 Acts 3. 11–end	Ps. **72**; 75 Prov. 1. 1–19 Mark 2.23 – 3.6 *or First EP of The* *Transfiguration* Ps. 99; 110 Exod. 24. 12–end John 12. 27–36a **𝔚 ct**

6 Tuesday — **THE TRANSFIGURATION OF OUR LORD**

𝔚		Dan. 7. 9–10, 13–14 Ps. 97 2 Pet. 1. 16–19 Luke 9. 28–36	*MP:* Ps. 27; 150 Ecclus. 48. 1–10 *or* 1 Kings 19. 1–16 1 John 3. 1–3	*EP:* Ps. 72 Exod. 34. 29–end 2 Cor. ch. 3

	Calendar and Holy Communion	Morning Prayer	Evening Prayer	NOTES
G		1 Sam. 20. 1–17 Acts 1. 15–end	Ezek. 37. 15–end Mark 1. 14–20	
G		1 Sam. 20. 18–end Acts 2. 1–21	Ezek. 39. 21–end Mark 1. 21–28	

	Calendar and Holy Communion	Morning Prayer	Evening Prayer	NOTES
	Lammas Day			
G		1 Sam. 21.1 – 22.5 Acts 2. 22–36	Ezek. 43. 1–12 Mark 1. 29–end	
G		1 Sam. 22. 6–end Acts 2. 37–end	Ezek. 44. 4–16 Mark 2. 1–12	
G		1 Sam. ch. 23 Acts 3. 1–10	Ezek. 47. 1–12 Mark 2. 13–22 **ct**	
	THE TENTH SUNDAY AFTER TRINITY			
G	Jer. 7. 9–15 Ps. 17. 1–8 1 Cor. 12. 1–11 Luke 19. 41–47a	Ps. 86 Song of Sol. 5. 2–end *or* 1 Macc. 3. 1–12 2 Pet. 1. 1–15	Ps. 88 (*or* 88. 1–10) Job ch. 28 *or* Ecclus. 42. 15–end Heb. 11. 17–31	
G		1 Sam. ch. 24 Acts 3. 11–end	Prov. 1. 1–19 Mark 2.23 – 3.6 *or First EP of The* *Transfiguration* (Ps. 99; 110) Exod. 24. 12–end John 12. 27–36a **𝔴 ct**	
	THE TRANSFIGURATION OF OUR LORD			
𝔴	Exod. 24. 12–end Ps. 84. 1–7 1 John 3. 1–3 Mark 9. 2–7	(Ps. 27; 150) Ecclus. 48. 1–10 *or* 1 Kings 19. 1–16 2 Pet. 1. 16–19	(Ps. 72) Exod. 34. 29–end 2 Cor. ch. 3	

	Sunday Principal Service / Weekday Eucharist	Third Service / Morning Prayer	Second Service / Evening Prayer
7 Wednesday *John Mason Neale, Priest, Hymn Writer, 1866*			
G	Jer. 31. 1–7 Ps. 121 Matt. 15. 21–28	Ps. 77 1 Sam. 28. 3–end Acts 4. 13–31	Ps. 119. 81–104 Prov. ch. 2 Mark 3. 19b–end
8 Thursday **Dominic, Priest, Founder of the Order of Preachers, 1221**			
Gw	Com. Religious *or* Jer. 31. 31–34 *also* Ecclus. 39. 1–10 Ps. 51. 11–18 Matt. 16. 13–23	Ps. 78. 1–39† 1 Sam. ch. 31 Acts 4.32 – 5.11	Ps. 78. 40–end† Prov. 3. 1–26 Mark 4. 1–20
9 Friday **Mary Sumner, Founder of the Mothers' Union, 1921**			
Gw	Com. Saint *or* Nahum 2. 1, 3; 3. 1–3, *also* Heb. 13. 1–5 6–7 Ps. 137. 1–6 *or* Deut. 32. 35–36, 39, 41 Matt. 16. 24–28	Ps. 55 2 Sam. ch. 1 Acts 5. 12–26	Ps. 69 Prov. 3.27 – 4.19 Mark 4. 21–34
10 Saturday **Laurence, Deacon at Rome, Martyr, 258**			
Gr	Com. Martyr *or* Hab. 1.12 – 2.4 *also* 2 Cor. 9. 6–10 Ps. 9. 7–11 Matt. 17. 14–20	Ps. *76*; 79 2 Sam. 2. 1–11 Acts 5. 27–end	Ps. 81; *84* Prov. 6. 1–19 Mark 4. 35–end **ct**
11 **Sunday** **THE ELEVENTH SUNDAY AFTER TRINITY (Proper 14)**			
G	*Track 1* *Track 2* 2 Sam. 18. 5–9, 15, 1 Kings 19. 4–8 31–33 Ps. 34. 1–8 Ps. 130 Eph. 4.25 – 5.2 Eph. 4.25 – 5.2 John 6. 35, 41–51 John 6. 35, 41–51	Ps. 90 Song of Sol. 8. 5–7 *or* 1 Macc. 14. 4–15 2 Pet. 3. 8–13	Ps. 91 (*or* 91. 1–12) Job 39.1 – 40.4 *or* Ecclus. 43. 13–end Heb. 12. 1–17 *Gospel:* Luke 12. 32–40
12 Monday			
G **DEL 19**	Ezek. 1. 2–5, 24–end Ps. 148. 1–4, 12–13 Matt. 17. 22–end	Ps. *80*; 82 2 Sam. 3. 12–end Acts ch. 6	Ps. *85*; 86 Prov. 8. 1–21 Mark 5. 1–20
13 Tuesday **Jeremy Taylor, Bishop of Down and Connor, Teacher, 1667** *Florence Nightingale, Nurse, Social Reformer, 1910; Octavia Hill, Social Reformer, 1912*			
Gw	Com. Teacher *or* Ezek. 2.8 – 3.4 *also* Titus 2. 7–8, Ps. 119. 65–72 11–14 Matt. 18. 1–5, 10, 12–14	Ps. 87; *89. 1–18* 2 Sam. 5. 1–12 Acts 7. 1–16	Ps. 89. 19–end Prov. 8. 22–end Mark 5. 21–34
14 Wednesday *Maximilian Kolbe, Friar, Martyr, 1941*			
G	Ezek. 9. 1–7; 10. 18–22 Ps. 113 Matt. 18. 15–20	Ps. 119. 105–128 2 Sam. 6. 1–19 Acts 7. 17–43	Ps. *91*; 93 Prov. ch. 9 Mark 5. 35–end *or First EP of The* *Blessed Virgin Mary* Ps. 72 Prov. 8. 22–31 John 19. 23–27 **W ct**

	Calendar and Holy Communion	Morning Prayer	Evening Prayer	NOTES
	The Name of Jesus			
Gw	Jer. 14. 7–9 Ps. 8 Acts 4. 8–12 Matt. 1. 20–23	1 Sam. 28. 3–end Acts 4. 13–31	Prov. ch. 2 Mark 3. 19b–end	
G		1 Sam. ch. 31 Acts 4.32 – 5.11	Prov. 3. 1–26 Mark 4. 1–20	
G		2 Sam. ch. 1 Acts 5. 12–26	Prov. 3.27 – 4.19 Mark 4. 21–34	
	Laurence, Deacon at Rome, Martyr, 258			
Gr	Com. Martyr	2 Sam. 2. 1–11 Acts 5. 27–end	Prov. 6. 1–19 Mark 4. 35–end	
			ct	
	THE ELEVENTH SUNDAY AFTER TRINITY			
G	1 Kings 3. 5–15 Ps. 28 1 Cor. 15. 1–11 Luke 18. 9–14	Ps. 89. 1–18 Song of Sol. 8. 5–7 or 1 Macc. 14. 4–15 2 Pet. 3. 8–13	Ps. 91 (or 91. 1–12) Job 39.1 – 40.4 or Ecclus. 43. 13–end Heb. 12. 1–17	
G		2 Sam. 3. 12–end Acts ch. 6	Prov. 8. 1–21 Mark 5. 1–20	
G		2 Sam. 5. 1–12 Acts 7. 1–16	Prov. 8. 22–end Mark 5. 21–34	
G		2 Sam. 6. 1–19 Acts 7. 17–43	Prov. ch. 9 Mark 5. 35–end	

	Sunday Principal Service Weekday Eucharist	Third Service Morning Prayer	Second Service Evening Prayer

15 Thursday — **THE BLESSED VIRGIN MARY***

W	Isa. 61. 10–end or Rev. 11.19 – 12.6, 10 Ps. 45. 10–end Gal. 4. 4–7 Luke 1. 46–55	*MP*: Ps. 98; 138; 147. 1–12 Isa. 7. 10–15 Luke 11. 27–28	*EP*: Ps. 132 Song of Sol. 2. 1–7 Acts 1. 6–14
	or, if The Blessed Virgin Mary is celebrated on 8 September:		
G	Ezek. 12. 1–12 Ps. 78. 58–64 Matt. 18.21 – 19.1	Ps. 90; **92** 2 Sam. 7. 1–17 Acts 7. 44–53	Ps. 94 Prov. 10. 1–12 Mark 6. 1–13

16 Friday

G	Ezek. 16. 1–15, 60–end Ps. 118. 14–18 or *Canticle*: Song of Deliverance Matt. 19. 3–12	Ps. **88**; (95) 2 Sam. 7. 18–end Acts 7.54 – 8.3	Ps. 102 Prov. 11. 1–12 Mark 6. 14–29

17 Saturday

G	Ezek. 18. 1–11a, 13b, 30, 32 Ps. 51. 1–3, 15–17 Matt. 19. 13–15	Ps. 96; **97**; 100 2 Sam. ch. 9 Acts 8. 4–25	Ps. 104 Prov. 12. 10–end Mark 6. 30–44 **ct**

18 Sunday — **THE TWELFTH SUNDAY AFTER TRINITY (Proper 15)**

G	*Track 1* 1 Kings 2. 10–12; 3. 3–14 Ps. 111 Eph. 5. 15–20 John 6. 51–58	*Track 2* Prov. 9. 1–6 Ps. 34. 9–14 Eph. 5. 15–20 John 6. 51–58	Ps. 106. 1–10 Jonah ch. 1 or Ecclus. 3. 1–15 2 Pet. 3. 14–end	Ps. [92]; 100 Exod. 2.23 – 3.10 Heb. 13. 1–15 *Gospel*: Luke 12. 49–56

19 Monday

G **DEL 20**	Ezek. 24. 15–24 Ps. 78. 1–8 Matt. 19. 16–22	Ps. **98**; 99; 101 2 Sam. ch. 11 Acts 8. 26–end	Ps. **105**† (or 103) Prov. 14.31 – 15.17 Mark 6. 45–end

20 Tuesday — Bernard, Abbot of Clairvaux, Teacher, 1153
William and Catherine Booth, Founders of the Salvation Army, 1912 and 1890

Gw	Com. Religious esp. Rev. 19. 5–9	*or* Ezek. 28. 1–10 Ps. 107. 1–3, 40, 43 Matt. 19. 23–end	Ps. **106**† (or 103) 2 Sam. 12. 1–25 Acts 9. 1–19a	Ps. 107† Prov. 15. 18–end Mark 7. 1–13

21 Wednesday

G	Ezek. 34. 1–11 Ps. 23 Matt. 20. 1–16	Ps. 110; **111**; 112 2 Sam. 15. 1–12 Acts 9. 19b–31	Ps. 119. 129–152 Prov. 18. 10–end Mark 7. 14–23

22 Thursday

G	Ezek. 36. 23–28 Ps. 51. 7–12 Matt. 22. 1–14	Ps. 113; **115** 2 Sam. 15. 13–end Acts 9. 32–end	Ps. 114; **116**; 117 Prov. 20. 1–22 Mark 7. 24–30

*The Blessed Virgin Mary may be celebrated on 8 September instead of 15 August.

Calendar and Holy Communion	Morning Prayer	Evening Prayer	NOTES
To celebrate The Blessed Virgin Mary, see *Common Worship* provision.			
G	2 Sam. 7. 1–17 Acts 7. 44–53	Prov. 10. 1–12 Mark 6. 1–13	
G	2 Sam. 7. 18–end Acts 7.54 – 8.3	Prov. 11. 1–12 Mark 6. 14–29	
G	2 Sam. ch. 9 Acts 8. 4–25	Prov. 12. 10–end Mark 6. 30–44 **ct**	
THE TWELFTH SUNDAY AFTER TRINITY			
G	Exod. 34. 29–end Ps. 34. 1–10 2 Cor. 3. 4–9 Mark 7. 31–37	Ps. 106. 1–10 Jonah ch. 1 *or* Ecclus. 3. 1–15 2 Pet. 3. 14–end	Ps. [92]; 100 Exod. 2.23 – 3.10 Heb. 13. 1–15
G	2 Sam. ch. 11 Acts 8. 26–end	Prov. 14.31 – 15.17 Mark 6. 45–end	
G	2 Sam. 12. 1–25 Acts 9. 1–19a	Prov. 15. 18–end Mark 7. 1–13	
G	2 Sam. 15. 1–12 Acts 9. 19b–31	Prov. 18. 10–end Mark 7. 14–23	
G	2 Sam. 15. 13–end Acts 9. 32–end	Prov. 20. 1–22 Mark 7. 24–30	

		Sunday Principal Service Weekday Eucharist	Third Service Morning Prayer	Second Service Evening Prayer
23 Friday				
G		Ezek. 37. 1–14 Ps. 107. 1–8 Matt. 22. 34–40	Ps. 139 2 Sam. 16. 1–14 Acts 10. 1–16	Ps. ***130***; 131; 137 Prov. 22. 1–16 Mark 7. 31–end *or First EP of Bartholomew* Ps. 97 Isa. 61. 1–9 2 Cor. 6. 1–10 **R ct**
24 Saturday	**BARTHOLOMEW THE APOSTLE**			
R		Isa. 43. 8–13 *or* Acts 5. 12–16 Ps. 145. 1–7 Acts 5. 12–16 *or* 1 Cor. 4. 9–15 Luke 22. 24–30	*MP*: Ps. 86; 117 Gen. 28. 10–17 John 1. 43–end	*EP*: Ps. 91; 116 Ecclus. 39. 1–10 *or* Deut. 18. 15–19 Matt. 10. 1–22
25 Sunday	**THE THIRTEENTH SUNDAY AFTER TRINITY (Proper 16)**			
G	*Track 1* 1 Kings 8. [1, 6, 10–11] 22–30, 41–43 Ps. 84 Eph. 6. 10–20 John 6. 56–69	*Track 2* Josh. 24. 1–2a, 14–18 Ps. 34. 15–end Eph. 6. 10–20 John 6. 56–69	Ps. 115 Jonah ch. 2 *or* Ecclus. 3. 17–29 Rev. ch. 1	Ps. 116 (*or* 116. 10–end) Exod. 4.27 – 5.1 Heb. 13. 16–21 *Gospel*: Luke 13. 10–17
26 Monday				
G **DEL 21**		2 Thess. 1. 1–5, 11–end Ps. 39. 1–9 Matt. 23. 13–22	Ps. 123; 124; 125; ***126*** 2 Sam. 18. 1–18 Acts 10. 34–end	Ps. ***127***; 128; 129 Prov. 25. 1–14 Mark 8. 11–21
27 Tuesday	**Monica, Mother of Augustine of Hippo, 387**			
Gw	Com. Saint *or* *also* Ecclus. 26. 1–3, 13–16	2 Thess. 2. 1–3a, 14–end Ps. 98 Matt. 23. 23–26	Ps. ***132***; 133 2 Sam. 18.19 – 19.8a Acts 11. 1–18	Ps. (134); ***135*** Prov. 25. 15–end Mark 8. 22–26
28 Wednesday	**Augustine, Bishop of Hippo, Teacher, 430**			
Gw	Com. Teacher *or* *esp.* Ecclus. 39. 1–10 *also* Rom. 13. 11–13	2 Thess. 3. 6–10, 16–end Ps. 128 Matt. 23. 27–32	Ps. 119. 153–end 2 Sam. 19. 8b–23 Acts 11. 19–end	Ps. 136 Prov. 26. 12–end Mark 8.27 – 9.1
29 Thursday	**The Beheading of John the Baptist**			
Gr	Jer. 1. 4–10 *or* Ps. 11 Heb. 11.32 – 12.2 Matt. 14. 1–12	1 Cor. 1. 1–9 Ps. 145. 1–7 Matt. 24. 42–end	Ps. ***143***; 146 2 Sam. 19. 24–end Acts 12. 1–17	Ps. ***138***; 140; 141 Prov. 27. 1–22 Mark 9. 2–13
30 Friday	**John Bunyan, Spiritual Writer, 1688**			
Gw	Com. Teacher *or* *also* Heb. 12. 1–2 Luke 21. 21, 34–36	1 Cor. 1. 17–25 Ps. 33. 6–12 Matt. 25. 1–13	Ps. 142; ***144*** 2 Sam. 23. 1–7 Acts 12. 18–end	Ps. 145 Prov. 30. 1–9, 24–31 Mark 9. 14–29

	Calendar and Holy Communion	Morning Prayer	Evening Prayer	NOTES
G		2 Sam. 16. 1–14 Acts 10. 1–16	Prov. 22. 1–16 Mark 7. 31–end *or First EP of* *Bartholomew* (Ps. 97) Isa. 61. 1–9 2 Cor. 6. 1–10 **R** ct	

BARTHOLOMEW THE APOSTLE

	Calendar and Holy Communion	Morning Prayer	Evening Prayer	NOTES
R	Gen. 28. 10–17 Ps. 15 Acts 5. 12–16 Luke 22. 24–30	(Ps. 86; 117) Isa. 43. 8–13 John 1. 43–end	(Ps. 91; 116) Ecclus. 39. 1–10 *or* Deut. 18. 15–19 Matt. 10. 1–22	

THE THIRTEENTH SUNDAY AFTER TRINITY

	Calendar and Holy Communion	Morning Prayer	Evening Prayer	NOTES
G	Lev. 19. 13–18 Ps. 74. 20–end Gal. 3. 16–22 *or* Heb. 13. 1–6 Luke 10. 23b–37	Ps. 115 Jonah ch. 2 *or* Ecclus. 3. 17–29 Rev. ch. 1	Ps. 116 (*or* 116. 10–end) Exod. 4.27 – 5.1 Heb. 13. 16–21	
G		2 Sam. 18. 1–18 Acts 10. 34–end	Prov. 25. 1–14 Mark 8. 11–21	
G		2 Sam. 18.19 – 19.8a Acts 11. 1–18	Prov. 25. 15–end Mark 8. 22–26	

Augustine, Bishop of Hippo, Teacher, 430

	Calendar and Holy Communion	Morning Prayer	Evening Prayer	NOTES
Gw	Com. Doctor	2 Sam. 19. 8b–23 Acts 11. 19–end	Prov. 26. 12–end Mark 8.27 – 9.1	

The Beheading of John the Baptist

	Calendar and Holy Communion	Morning Prayer	Evening Prayer	NOTES
Gr	2 Chron. 24. 17–21 Ps. 92. 11–end Heb. 11.32 – 12.2 Matt. 14. 1–12	2 Sam. 19. 24–end Acts 12. 1–17	Prov. 27. 1–22 Mark 9. 2–13	
G		2 Sam. 23. 1–7 Acts 12. 18–end	Prov. 30. 1–9, 24–31 Mark 9. 14–29	

		Sunday Principal Service Weekday Eucharist	Third Service Morning Prayer	Second Service Evening Prayer
31 Saturday	**Aidan, Bishop of Lindisfarne, Missionary, 651**			
Gw	Com. Missionary *or* *also* 1 Cor. 9. 16–19	1 Cor. 1. 26–end Ps. 33. 12–15, 20–end Matt. 25. 14–30	Ps. 147 2 Sam. ch. 24 Acts 13. 1–12	Ps. *148*; 149; 150 Prov. 31. 10–end Mark 9. 30–37 **ct**

September 2024

1 Sunday	**THE FOURTEENTH SUNDAY AFTER TRINITY (Proper 17)**			
G	*Track 1* Song of Sol. 2. 8–13 Ps. 45. 1–2, 6–9 (or 1–7) Jas. 1. 17–end Mark 7. 1–8, 14–15, 21–23	*Track 2* Deut. 4. 1–2, 6–9 Ps. 15 Jas. 1. 17–end Mark 7. 1–8, 14–15, 21–23	Ps. 119. 17–40 Jonah 3. 1–9 or Ecclus. 11. 7–28 (or 19–28) Rev. 3. 14–end	Ps. 119. 1–16 (or 9–16) Exod. 12. 21–27 Matt. 4.23 – 5.20
2 Monday	*The Martyrs of Papua New Guinea, 1901 and 1942*			
G **DEL 22**		1 Cor. 2. 1–5 Ps. 33. 12–21 Luke 4. 16–30	Ps. *1*; 2; 3 1 Kings 1. 5–31 Acts 13. 13–43	Ps. *4*; 7 Wisd. ch. 1 or 1 Chron. 10.1 – 11.9 Mark 9. 38–end
3 Tuesday	**Gregory the Great, Bishop of Rome, Teacher, 604**			
Gw	Com. Teacher *or* *also* 1 Thess. 2. 3–8	1 Cor. 2. 10b–end Ps. 145. 10–17 Luke 4. 31–37	Ps. *5*; 6; (8) 1 Kings 1.32 – 2.4, 10–12 Acts 13.44 – 14.7	Ps. *9*; 10† Wisd. ch. 2 or 1 Chron. ch. 13 Mark 10. 1–16
4 Wednesday	*Birinus, Bishop of Dorchester (Oxon), Apostle of Wessex, 650**			
G		1 Cor. 3. 1–9 Ps. 62 Luke 4. 38–end	Ps. 119. 1–32 1 Kings ch. 3 Acts 14. 8–end	Ps. *11*; 12; 13 Wisd. 3. 1–9 or 1 Chron. 15.1 – 16.3 Mark 10. 17–31
5 Thursday				
G		1 Cor. 3. 18–end Ps. 24. 1–6 Luke 5. 1–11	Ps. 14; *15*; 16 1 Kings 4.29 – 5.12 Acts 15. 1–21	Ps. 18† Wisd. 4. 7–end or 1 Chron. ch. 17 Mark 10. 32–34
6 Friday	*Allen Gardiner, Founder of the South American Mission Society, 1851*			
G		1 Cor. 4. 1–5 Ps. 37. 3–8 Luke 5. 33–end	Ps. 17; *19* 1 Kings 6. 1, 11–28 Acts 15. 22–35	Ps. 22 Wisd. 5. 1–16 or 1 Chron. 21.1 – 22.1 Mark 10. 35–45
7 Saturday				
G		1 Cor. 4. 6–15 Ps. 145. 18–end Luke 6. 1–5	Ps. 20; 21; *23* 1 Kings 8. 1–30 Acts 15.36 – 16.5	Ps. *24*; 25 Wisd. 5.17 – 6.11 or 1 Chron. 22. 2–end Mark 10. 46–end **ct**

*Cuthbert may be celebrated on 4 September instead of 20 March.

	Calendar and Holy Communion	Morning Prayer	Evening Prayer	NOTES
G		2 Sam. ch. 24 Acts 13. 1–12	Prov. 31. 10–end Mark 9. 30–37	
			ct	

<table>
<tr><td colspan="5">THE FOURTEENTH SUNDAY AFTER TRINITY</td></tr>
<tr><td>G</td><td>2 Kings 5. 9–16
Ps. 118. 1–9
Gal. 5. 16–24
Luke 17. 11–19</td><td>Ps. 119. 17–40
Jonah 3. 1–9
or Ecclus. 11. 7–28
(or 19–28)
Rev. 3. 14–end</td><td>Ps. 119. 1–16 (or 9–16)
Exod. 12. 21–27
Matt. 4.23 – 5.20</td><td></td></tr>
<tr><td>G</td><td></td><td>1 Kings 1. 5–31
Acts 13. 13–43</td><td>Wisd. ch. 1
or 1 Chron. 10.1 – 11.9
Mark 9. 38–end</td><td></td></tr>
<tr><td>G</td><td></td><td>1 Kings 1.32 – 2.4,
10–12
Acts 13.44 – 14.7</td><td>Wisd. ch. 2
or 1 Chron. ch. 13
Mark 10. 1–16</td><td></td></tr>
<tr><td>G</td><td></td><td>1 Kings ch. 3
Acts 14. 8–end</td><td>Wisd. 3. 1–9
or 1 Chron. 15.1 – 16.3
Mark 10. 17–31</td><td></td></tr>
<tr><td>G</td><td></td><td>1 Kings 4.29 – 5.12
Acts 15. 1–21</td><td>Wisd. 4. 7–end
or 1 Chron. ch. 17
Mark 10. 32–34</td><td></td></tr>
<tr><td>G</td><td></td><td>1 Kings 6. 1, 11–28
Acts 15. 22–35</td><td>Wisd. 5. 1–16
or 1 Chron. 21.1 – 22.1
Mark 10. 35–45</td><td></td></tr>
<tr><td colspan="5">Evurtius, Bishop of Orleans, 4th century</td></tr>
<tr><td>Gw</td><td>Com. Bishop</td><td>1 Kings 8. 1–30
Acts 15.36 – 16.5</td><td>Wisd. 5.17 – 6.11
or 1 Chron. 22. 2–end
Mark 10. 46–end</td><td></td></tr>
<tr><td></td><td></td><td></td><td>ct</td><td></td></tr>
</table>

		Sunday Principal Service Weekday Eucharist	Third Service Morning Prayer	Second Service Evening Prayer
8 **Sunday**		**THE FIFTEENTH SUNDAY AFTER TRINITY (Proper 18)*** (The Accession of King Charles III may be observed on 8 September, and Collect, Readings and Post-Communion for the sovereign used.)		

G	*Track 1* Prov. 22. 1–2, 8–9, 22–23 Ps. 125 Jas. 2. 1–10 [11–13] 14–17 Mark 7. 24–end	*Track 2* Isa. 35. 4–7a Ps. 146 Jas. 2. 1–10 [11–13] 14–17 Mark 7. 24–end	Ps. 119. 57–72 Jonah 3.10 – 4.11 *or* Ecclus. 27.30 – 28.9 Rev. 8. 1–5	Ps. 119. 41–56 (*or* 49–56) Exod. 14. 5–end Matt. 6. 1–18

9 Monday	*Charles Fuge Lowder, Priest, 1880*			
G **DEL 23**		1 Cor. 5. 1–8 Ps. 5. 5–9a Luke 6. 6–11	Ps. 27; **30** 1 Kings 8. 31–62 Acts 16. 6–24	Ps. 26; **28**; 29 Wisd. 6. 12–23 *or* 1 Chron. 28. 1–10 Mark 11. 1–11

10 Tuesday				
G		1 Cor. 6. 1–11 Ps. 149. 1–5 Luke 6. 12–19	Ps. 32; **36** 1 Kings 8.63 – 9.9 Acts 16. 25–end	Ps. 33 Wisd. 7. 1–14 *or* 1 Chron. 28. 11–end Mark 11. 12–26

11 Wednesday				
G		1 Cor. 7. 25–31 Ps. 45. 11–end Luke 6. 20–26	Ps. 34 1 Kings 10. 1–25 Acts 17. 1–15	Ps. 119. 33–56 Wisd. 7.15 – 8.4 *or* 1 Chron. 29. 1–9 Mark 11. 27–end

12 Thursday				
G		1 Cor. 8. 1–7, 11–end Ps. 139. 1–9 Luke 6. 27–38	Ps. 37† 1 Kings 11. 1–13 Acts 17. 16–end	Ps. 39; **40** Wisd. 8. 5–18 *or* 1 Chron. 29. 10–20 Mark 12. 1–12

13 Friday	*John Chrysostom, Bishop of Constantinople, Teacher, 407*			
Gw	Com. Teacher *esp.* Matt. 5. 13–19 *also* Jer. 1. 4–10	*or* 1 Cor. 9. 16–19, 22–end Ps. 84. 1–6 Luke 6. 39–42	Ps. 31 1 Kings 11. 26–end Acts 18. 1–21	Ps. 35 Wisd. 8.21 – 9.end *or* 1 Chron. 29. 21–end Mark 12. 13–17 *or First EP of Holy* *Cross Day* Ps. 66 Isa, 52.13 – 53.end Eph. 2. 11–end **R ct**

14 Saturday	**HOLY CROSS DAY**			
R		Num. 21. 4–9 Ps. 22. 23–28 Phil. 2. 6–11 John 3. 13–17	*MP*: Ps. 2; 8; 146 Gen. 3. 1–15 John 12. 27–36a	*EP*: Ps. 110; 150 Isa. 63. 1–16 1 Cor. 1. 18–25

*The Blessed Virgin Mary may be celebrated on 8 September instead of 15 August.

	Calendar and Holy Communion	Morning Prayer	Evening Prayer	NOTES
	THE FIFTEENTH SUNDAY AFTER TRINITY The Accession of King Charles III, 2022			
G	Josh. 24. 14–25 Ps. 92. 1–6 Gal. 6. 11–end Matt. 6. 24–end	Ps. 119. 57–72 Jonah 3.10 – 4.11 or Ecclus. 27.30 – 28.9 Rev. 8. 1–5	Ps. 119. 41–56 (or 49–56) Exod. 14. 5–end Matt. 6. 1–18	
G		1 Kings 8. 31–62 Acts 16. 6–24	Wisd. 6. 12–23 or 1 Chron. 28. 1–10 Mark 11. 1–11	
G		1 Kings 8.63 – 9.9 Acts 16. 25–end	Wisd. 7. 1–14 or 1 Chron. 28. 11–end Mark 11. 12–26	
G		1 Kings 10. 1–25 Acts 17. 1–15	Wisd. 7.15 – 8.4 or 1 Chron. 29. 1–9 Mark 11. 27–end	
G		1 Kings 11. 1–13 Acts 17. 16–end	Wisd. 8. 5–18 or 1 Chron. 29. 10–20 Mark 12. 1–12	
G		1 Kings 11. 26–end Acts 18. 1–21	Wisd. 8.21 – 9.end or 1 Chron. 29. 21–end Mark 12. 13–17	
	Holy Cross Day To celebrate Holy Cross as a festival, see *Common Worship* provision.			
Gr	Num. 21. 4–9 Ps. 67 1 Cor. 1. 17–25 John 12. 27–33	1 Kings 12. 1–24 Acts 18.22 – 19.7	Wisd. 10.15 – 11.10 or 2 Chron. 1. 1–13 Mark 12. 18–27 **ct**	

		Sunday Principal Service / Weekday Eucharist	Third Service / Morning Prayer	Second Service / Evening Prayer
15 Sunday	**THE SIXTEENTH SUNDAY AFTER TRINITY (Proper 19)**			
G	*Track 1* Prov. 1. 20–33 Ps. 19 (or 19. 1–6) *or Canticle:* Wisd. 7.26 – 8.1 Jas. 3. 1–12 Mark 8. 27–end	*Track 2* Isa. 50. 4–9a Ps. 116. 1–8 Jas. 3. 1–12 Mark 8. 27–end	Ps. 119. 105–120 Isa. 44.24 – 45.8 Rev. 12. 1–12	Ps. 119. 73–88 (or 73–80) Exod. 18. 13–26 Matt. 7. 1–14
16 Monday	**Ninian, Bishop of Galloway, Apostle of the Picts, *c.* 432** *Edward Bouverie Pusey, Priest, Tractarian, 1882*			
Gw **DEL 24**	Com. Missionary *or* *esp.* Acts 13. 46–49 Mark 16. 15–end	1 Cor. 11. 17–26, 33 Ps. 40. 7–11 Luke 7. 1–10	Ps. 44 1 Kings 12.25 – 13.10 Acts 19. 8–20	Ps. *47*; 49 Wisd. 11.21 – 12.2 *or* 2 Chron. 2. 1–16 Mark 12. 28–34
17 Tuesday	**Hildegard, Abbess of Bingen, Visionary, 1179**			
Gw	Com. Religious *or* *also* 1 Cor. 2. 9–13 Luke 10. 21–24	1 Cor. 12. 12–14, 27–end Ps. 100 Luke 7. 11–17	Ps. *48*; 52 1 Kings 13. 11–end Acts 19. 21–end	Ps. 50 Wisd. 12. 12–21 *or* 2 Chron. ch. 3 Mark 12. 35–end
18 Wednesday				
G		1 Cor. 12.13b – 13.end Ps. 33. 1–12 Luke 7. 31–35	Ps. 119. 57–80 1 Kings ch. 17 Acts 20. 1–16	Ps. *59*; 60; (67) Wisd. 13. 1–9 *or* 2 Chron. ch. 5 Mark 13. 1–13
19 Thursday	*Theodore of Tarsus, Archbishop of Canterbury, 690*			
G		1 Cor. 15. 1–11 Ps. 118. 1–2, 17–20 Luke 7. 36–end	Ps. 56; *57*; (63†) 1 Kings 18. 1–20 Acts 20. 17–end	Ps. 61; *62*; 64 Wisd. 16.15 – 17.1 *or* 2 Chron. 6. 1–21 Mark 13. 14–23
20 Friday	**John Coleridge Patteson, first Bishop of Melanesia, and his Companions, Martyrs, 1871**			
Gr	Com. Martyr *or* *esp.* 2 Chron. 24. 17–21 *also* Acts 7. 55–end	1 Cor. 15. 12–20 Ps. 17. 1–8 Luke 8. 1–3	Ps. *51*; 54 1 Kings 18. 21–end Acts 21. 1–16	Ps. 38 Wisd. 18. 6–19 *or* 2 Chron. 6. 22–end Mark 13. 24–31 *or First EP of Matthew* Ps. 34 Isa. 33. 13–17 Matt. 6. 19–end **R ct**
21 Saturday	**MATTHEW, APOSTLE AND EVANGELIST**			
R		Prov. 3. 13–18 Ps. 119. 65–72 2 Cor. 4. 1–6 Matt. 9. 9–13	*MP*: Ps. 49; 117 1 Kings 19. 15–end 2 Tim. 3. 14–end	*EP*: Ps. 119. 33–40, 89–96 Eccles. 5. 4–12 Matt. 19. 16–end
22 Sunday	**THE SEVENTEENTH SUNDAY AFTER TRINITY (Proper 20)**			
G	*Track 1* Prov. 31. 10–end Ps. 1 Jas. 3.13 – 4.3, 7–8a Mark 9. 30–37	*Track 2* Wisd. 1.16 – 2.1, 12–22 *or* Jer. 11. 18–20 Ps. 54 Jas. 3.13 – 4.3, 7–8a Mark 9. 30–37	Ps. 119. 153–end Isa. 45. 9–22 Rev. 14. 1–5	Ps. 119. 137–152 (or 137–144) Exod. 19. 10–end Matt. 8. 23–end

	Calendar and Holy Communion	Morning Prayer	Evening Prayer	NOTES
	THE SIXTEENTH SUNDAY AFTER TRINITY			
G	1 Kings 17. 17–end Ps. 102. 12–17 Eph. 3. 13–end Luke 7. 11–17	Ps. 119. 105–120 Isa. 44.24 – 45.8 Rev. 12. 1–12	Ps. 119. 73–88 (or 73–80) Exod. 18. 13–26 Matt. 7. 1–14	
G		1 Kings 12.25 – 13.10 Acts 19. 8–20	Wisd. 11.21 – 12.2 or 2 Chron. 2. 1–16 Mark 12. 28–34	
	Lambert, Bishop of Maastricht, Martyr, 709			
Gr	Com. Martyr	1 Kings 13. 11–end Acts 19. 21–end	Wisd. 12. 12–21 or 2 Chron. ch. 3 Mark 12. 35–end	
	Ember Day			
G	Ember CEG	1 Kings ch. 17 Acts 20. 1–16	Wisd. 13. 1–9 or 2 Chron. ch. 5 Mark 13. 1–13	
G		1 Kings 18. 1–20 Acts 20. 17–end	Wisd. 16.15 – 17.1 or 2 Chron. 6. 1–21 Mark 13. 14–23	
	Ember Day			
G	Ember CEG	1 Kings 18. 21–end Acts 21. 1–16	Wisd. 18. 6–19 or 2 Chron. 6. 22–end Mark 13. 24–31 or First EP of Matthew (Ps. 34) Prov. 3. 3–18 Matt. 6. 19–end	
			R ct	
	MATTHEW, APOSTLE AND EVANGELIST Ember Day			
R	Isa. 33. 13–17 Ps. 119. 65–72 2 Cor. 4. 1–6 Matt. 9. 9–13	(Ps. 49; 117) 1 Kings 19. 15–end 2 Tim. 3. 14–end	(Ps. 119. 33–40, 89–96) Eccles. 5. 4–12 Matt. 19. 16–end	
	THE SEVENTEENTH SUNDAY AFTER TRINITY			
G	Prov. 25. 6–14 Ps. 33. 6–12 Eph. 4. 1–6 Luke 14. 1–11	Ps. 119. 153–end Isa. 45. 9–22 Rev. 14. 1–5	Ps. 119. 137–152 (or 137–144) Exod. 19. 10–end Matt. 8. 23–end	

		Sunday Principal Service Weekday Eucharist	Third Service Morning Prayer	Second Service Evening Prayer
23 Monday				
G **DEL 25**		Prov. 3. 27–34 Ps. 15 Luke 8. 16–18	Ps. 71 1 Kings ch. 21 Acts 21.37 – 22.21	Ps. *72*; 75 1 Macc. 1. 1–19 *or* 2 Chron. 9. 1–12 Mark 14. 1–11
24 Tuesday				
G		Prov. 21. 1–6, 10–13 Ps. 119. 1–8 Luke 8. 19–21	Ps. 73 1 Kings 22. 1–28 Acts 22.22 – 23.11	Ps. 74 1 Macc. 1. 20–40 *or* 2 Chron. 10.1 – 11.4 Mark 14. 12–25
25 Wednesday	**Lancelot Andrewes, Bishop of Winchester, Spiritual Writer, 1626** Ember Day* *Sergei of Radonezh, Russian Monastic Reformer, Teacher, 1392*			
Gw *or* **Rw**	Com. Bishop *or* *esp.* Isa. 6. 1–8	Prov. 30. 5–9 Ps. 119. 105–112 Luke 9. 1–6	Ps. 77 1 Kings 22. 29–45 Acts 23. 12–end	Ps. 119. 81–104 1 Macc. 1. 41–end *or* 2 Chron. ch. 12 Mark 14. 26–42
26 Thursday	*Wilson Carlile, Founder of the Church Army, 1942*			
G		Eccles. 1. 2–11 Ps. 90. 1–6 Luke 9. 7–9	Ps. 78. 1–39† 2 Kings 1. 2–17 Acts 24. 1–23	Ps. 78. 40–end† 1 Macc. 2. 1–28 *or* 2 Chron. 13.1 – 14.1 Mark 14. 43–52
27 Friday	**Vincent de Paul, Founder of the Congregation of the Mission (Lazarists), 1660** Ember Day*			
Gw *or* **Rw**	Com. Religious *or* *also* 1 Cor. 1. 25–end Matt. 25. 34–40	Eccles. 3. 1–11 Ps. 144. 1–4 Luke 9. 18–22	Ps. 55 2 Kings 2. 1–18 Acts 24.24 – 25.12	Ps. 69 1 Macc. 2. 29–48 *or* 2 Chron. 14. 2–end Mark 14. 53–65
28 Saturday	Ember Day*			
G *or* **R**		Eccles. 11.9 – 12.8 Ps. 90. 1–2, 12–end Luke 9. 43b–45	Ps. *76*; 79 2 Kings 4. 1–37 Acts 25. 13–end	Ps. 81; *84* 1 Macc. 2. 49–end *or* 2 Chron. 15. 1–15 Mark 14. 66–end *or First EP of Michael and All Angels* Ps. 91 2 Kings 6. 8–17 Matt. 18. 1–6, 10 **W ct**
29 Sunday	**MICHAEL AND ALL ANGELS** (*or transferred to 30 September*) **OR THE EIGHTEENTH SUNDAY AFTER TRINITY (Proper 21)**			
W		Gen. 28. 10–17 *or* Rev. 12. 7–12 Ps. 103. 19–end Rev. 12. 7–12 *or* Heb. 1. 5–end John 1. 47–end	*MP*: Ps. 34; 150 Tobit 12. 6–end *or* Dan. 12. 1–4 Acts 12. 1–11	*EP*: Ps. 138; 148 Dan. 10. 4–end Rev. ch. 5
	or, for The Eighteenth Sunday after Trinity (Proper 21):			
G	*Track 1* Esth. 7. 1–6, 9–10; 9. 20–22 Ps. 124 Jas. 5. 13–end Mark 9. 38–end	*Track 2* Num. 11. 4–6, 10–16, 24–29 Ps. 19. 7–end Jas. 5. 13–end Mark 9. 38–end	Ps. 122 Isa. 48. 12–end Luke 11. 37–end	Ps. 120; 121 Exod. ch. 24 Matt. 9. 1–8

*For Ember Day provision, see p. 11.

	Calendar and Holy Communion	Morning Prayer	Evening Prayer	NOTES
G		1 Kings ch. 21 Acts 21.37 – 22.21	1 Macc. 1. 1–19 or 2 Chron. 9. 1–12 Mark 14. 1–11	
G		1 Kings 22. 1–28 Acts 22.22 – 23.11	1 Macc. 1. 20–40 or 2 Chron. 10.1 – 11.4 Mark 14. 12–25	
G		1 Kings 22. 29–45 Acts 23. 12–end	1 Macc. 1. 41–end or 2 Chron. ch. 12 Mark 14. 26–42	
	Cyprian, Bishop of Carthage, Martyr, 258			
Gr	Com. Martyr	2 Kings 1. 2–17 Acts 24. 1–23	1 Macc. 2. 1–28 or 2 Chron. 13.1 – 14.1 Mark 14. 43–52	
G		2 Kings 2. 1–18 Acts 24.24 – 25.12	1 Macc. 2. 29–48 or 2 Chron. 14. 2–end Mark 14. 53–65	
G		2 Kings 4. 1–37 Acts 25. 13–end	1 Macc. 2. 49–end or 2 Chron. 15. 1–15 Mark 14. 66–end or First EP of Michael and All Angels (Ps. 91) 2 Kings 6. 8–17 John 1. 47–51	
			W ct	
	MICHAEL AND ALL ANGELS			
W	Dan. 10. 10–19a Ps. 103. 17–22 Rev. 12. 7–12 Matt. 18. 1–10	Ps. 34; 150 Tobit 12. 6–end or Dan. 12. 1–4 Acts 12. 1–11	Ps. 138; 148 Gen. 28. 10–17 Rev. ch. 5	
	or, for The Eighteenth Sunday after Trinity:			
G	Deut. 6. 4–9 Ps. 122 1 Cor. 1. 4–8 Matt. 22. 34–end	Ps. 132 Isa. 48. 12–end Luke 11. 37–end	Ps. 120; 121 Exod. ch. 24 Matt. 9. 1–8	

		Sunday Principal Service Weekday Eucharist	Third Service Morning Prayer	Second Service Evening Prayer
30 Monday	*Jerome, Translator of the Scriptures, Teacher, 420*			
G **DEL 26**		Job 1. 6–end Ps. 17. 1–11 Luke 9. 46–50	Ps. *80*; 82 2 Kings ch. 5 Acts 26. 1–23	Ps. *85*; 86 1 Macc. 3. 1–26 *or* 2 Chron. 17. 1–12 Mark 15. 1–15

October 2024

1 Tuesday	*Remigius, Bishop of Rheims, Apostle of the Franks, 533; Anthony Ashley Cooper, Earl of Shaftesbury, Social Reformer, 1885*			
G		Job 3. 1–3, 11–17, 20–23 Ps. 88. 14–19 Luke 9. 51–56	Ps. 87; *89. 1–18* 2 Kings 6. 1–23 Acts 26. 24–end	Ps. 89. 19–end 1 Macc. 3. 27–41 *or* 2 Chron. 18. 1–27 Mark 15. 16–32
2 Wednesday				
G		Job 9. 1–12, 14–16 Ps. 88. 1–6, 11 Luke 9. 57–end	Ps. 119. 105–128 2 Kings 9. 1–16 Acts 27. 1–26	Ps. *91*; 93 1 Macc. 3. 42–end *or* 2 Chron. 18.28 – 19.end Mark 15. 33–41
3 Thursday	*George Bell, Bishop of Chichester, Ecumenist, Peacemaker, 1958*			
G		Job 19. 21–27a Ps. 27. 13–16 Luke 10. 1–12	Ps. 90; *92* 2 Kings 9. 17–end Acts 27. 27–end	Ps. 94 1 Macc. 4. 1–25 *or* 2 Chron. 20. 1–23 Mark 15. 42–end
4 Friday	**Francis of Assisi, Friar, Founder of the Friars Minor, 1226**			
Gw	Com. Religious *or* *also* Gal. 6. 14–end Luke 12. 22–34	Job 38. 1, 12–21; 40. 3–5 Ps. 139. 6–11 Luke 10. 13–16	Ps. *88*; (95) 2 Kings 12. 1–19 Acts 28. 1–16	Ps. 102 1 Macc. 4. 26–35 *or* 2 Chron. 22.10 – 23.end Mark 16. 1–8
5 Saturday				
G		Job 42. 1–3, 6, 12–end Ps. 119. 169–end Luke 10. 17–24	Ps. 96; *97*; 100 2 Kings 17. 1–23 Acts 28. 17–end	Ps. 104 1 Macc. 4. 36–end *or* 2 Chron. 24. 1–22 Mark 16. 9–end **ct** *or First EP of Dedication Festival:* Ps. 24 2 Chron. 7. 11–16 John 4. 19–29 **𝕨 ct**
6 Sunday	**THE NINETEENTH SUNDAY AFTER TRINITY (Proper 22)**			
G	*Track 1* Job 1. 1; 2. 1–10 Ps. 26 Heb. 1. 1–4; 2. 5–12 Mark 10. 2–16	*Track 2* Gen. 2. 18–24 Ps. 8 Heb. 1. 1–4; 2. 5–12 Mark 10. 2–16	Ps. 123; 124 Isa. 49. 13–23 Luke 12. 1–12	Ps. 125; 126 Josh. 3. 7–end Matt. 10. 1–22
𝕨		*or, if observed as Dedication Festival:* Gen. 28. 11–18 *or* Rev. 21. 9–14 Ps. 122 1 Pet. 2. 1–10 John 10. 22–29	*MP*: Ps. 48; 150 Hag. 2. 6–9 Heb. 10. 19–25	*EP*: Ps. 132 Jer. 7. 1–11 Luke 19. 1–10

	Calendar and Holy Communion	Morning Prayer	Evening Prayer	NOTES
	Jerome, Translator of the Scriptures, Teacher, 420			
Gw	Com. Doctor	2 Kings ch. 5 Acts 26. 1–23	1 Macc. 3. 1–26 *or* 2 Chron. 17. 1–12 Mark 15. 1–15	
	Remigius, Bishop of Rheims, Apostle of the Franks, 533			
Gw	Com. Bishop	2 Kings 6. 1–23 Acts 26. 24–end	1 Macc. 3. 27–41 *or* 2 Chron. 18. 1–27 Mark 15. 16–32	
G		2 Kings 9. 1–16 Acts 27. 1–26	1 Macc. 3. 42–end *or* 2 Chron. 18.28 – 19.end Mark 15. 33–41	
G		2 Kings 9. 17–end Acts 27. 27–end	1 Macc. 4. 1–25 *or* 2 Chron. 20. 1–23 Mark 15. 42–end	
G		2 Kings 12. 1–19 Acts 28. 1–16	1 Macc. 4. 26–35 *or* 2 Chron. 22.10 – 23.end Mark 16. 1–8	
G		2 Kings 17. 1–23 Acts 28. 17–end	1 Macc. 4. 36–end *or* 2 Chron. 24. 1–22 Mark 16. 9–end **ct** *or First EP of Dedication Festival:* Ps. 24 2 Chron. 7. 11–16 John 4. 19–29 **𝖂 ct**	
	THE NINETEENTH SUNDAY AFTER TRINITY			
G	Gen. 18. 23–32 Ps. 141. 1–9 Eph. 4. 17–end Matt. 9. 1–8	Ps. 123; 124 Isa. 49. 13–23 Luke 12. 1–12	Ps. 125; 126 Josh. 3. 7–end Matt. 10. 1–22	
𝖂	*or, if observed as Dedication Festival:* 2 Chron. 7. 11–16 Ps. 122 1 Cor. 3. 9–17 *or* 1 Pet. 2. 1–5 Matt. 21. 12–16 *or* John 10. 22–29	Ps. 48; 150 Hag. 2. 6–9 Heb. 10. 19–25	Ps. 132 Jer. 7. 1–11 Luke 19. 1–10	

	Sunday Principal Service Weekday Eucharist	Third Service Morning Prayer	Second Service Evening Prayer
7 Monday			
G **DEL 27**	Gal. 1. 6–12 Ps. 111. 1–6 Luke 10. 25–37	Ps. *98*; 99; 101 2 Kings 17. 24–end Phil. 1. 1–11	Ps. 105† (or 103) 1 Macc. 6. 1–17 *or* 2 Chron. 26. 1–21 John 13. 1–11
8 Tuesday			
G	Gal. 1. 13–end Ps. 139. 1–9 Luke 10. 38–end	Ps. *106*† (or 103) 2 Kings 18. 1–12 Phil. 1. 12–end	Ps. 107† 1 Macc. 6. 18–47 *or* 2 Chron. ch. 28 John 13. 12–20
9 Wednesday *Denys, Bishop of Paris, and his Companions, Martyrs, c. 250; Robert Grosseteste, Bishop of Lincoln, Philosopher, Scientist, 1253*			
G	Gal. 2. 1–2, 7–14 Ps. 117 Luke 11. 1–4	Ps. 110; *111*; 112 2 Kings 18. 13–end Phil. 2. 1–13	Ps. 119. 129–152 1 Macc. 7. 1–20 *or* 2 Chron. 29. 1–19 John 13. 21–30
10 Thursday **Paulinus, Bishop of York, Missionary, 644** *Thomas Traherne, Poet, Spiritual Writer, 1674*			
Gw	Com. Missionary *or* Gal. 3. 1–5 *esp.* Matt. 28. 16–end *Canticle:* Benedictus Luke 11. 5–13	Ps. 113; *115* 2 Kings 19. 1–19 Phil. 2. 14–end	Ps. 114; *116*; 117 1 Macc. 7. 21–end *or* 2 Chron. 29. 20–end John 13. 31–end
11 Friday *Ethelburga, Abbess of Barking, 675; James the Deacon, Companion of Paulinus, 7th century*			
G	Gal. 3. 7–14 Ps. 111. 4–end Luke 11. 15–26	Ps. 139 2 Kings 19. 20–36 Phil. 3.1 – 4.1	Ps. *130*; 131; 137 1 Macc. 9. 1–22 *or* 2 Chron. ch. 30 John 14. 1–14
12 Saturday **Wilfrid of Ripon, Bishop, Missionary, 709** *Elizabeth Fry, Prison Reformer, 1845; Edith Cavell, Nurse, 1915*			
Gw	Com. Missionary *or* Gal. 3. 22–end *esp.* Luke 5. 1–11 Ps. 105. 1–7 *also* 1 Cor. 1. 18–25 Luke 11. 27–28	Ps. 120; *121*; 122 2 Kings ch. 20 Phil. 4. 2–end	Ps. 118 1 Macc. 13. 41–end; 14. 4–15 *or* 2 Chron. 32. 1–22 John 14. 15–end **ct**
13 **Sunday** **THE TWENTIETH SUNDAY AFTER TRINITY (Proper 23)**			
G	*Track 1* *Track 2* Job 23. 1–9, 16–end Amos 5. 6–7, 10–15 Ps. 22. 1–15 Ps. 90. 12–end Heb. 4. 12–end Heb. 4. 12–end Mark 10. 17–31 Mark 10. 17–31	Ps. 129; 130 Isa. 50. 4–10 Luke 13. 22–30	Ps. 127; [128] Josh. 5.13 – 6.20 Matt. 11. 20–end
14 Monday			
G **DEL 28**	Gal. 4. 21–24, 26–27, 31; 5. 1 Ps. 113 Luke 11. 29–32	Ps. 123; 124; 125; *126* 2 Kings 21. 1–18 1 Tim. 1. 1–17	Ps. *127*; 128; 129 2 Macc. 4. 7–17 *or* 2 Chron. 33. 1–13 John 15. 1–11
15 Tuesday **Teresa of Avila, Teacher, 1582**			
Gw	Com. Teacher *or* Gal. 5. 1–6 *also* Rom. 8. 22–27 Ps. 119. 41–48 Luke 11. 37–41	Ps. *132*; 133 2 Kings 22.1 – 23.3 1 Tim. 1.18 – 2.end	Ps. (134); *135* 2 Macc. 6. 12–end *or* 2 Chron. 34. 1–18 John 15. 12–17

	Calendar and Holy Communion	Morning Prayer	Evening Prayer	NOTES
G		2 Kings 17. 24–end Phil. 1. 1–11	1 Macc. 6. 1–17 *or* 2 Chron. 26. 1–21 John 13. 1–11	
G		2 Kings 18. 1–12 Phil. 1. 12–end	1 Macc. 6. 18–47 *or* 2 Chron. ch. 28 John 13. 12–20	

Denys, Bishop of Paris, Martyr, c. 250

	Calendar and Holy Communion	Morning Prayer	Evening Prayer	NOTES
Gr	Com. Martyr	2 Kings 18. 13–end Phil. 2. 1–13	1 Macc. 7. 1–20 *or* 2 Chron. 29. 1–19 John 13. 21–30	
G		2 Kings 19. 1–19 Phil. 2. 14–end	1 Macc. 7. 21–end *or* 2 Chron. 29. 20–end John 13. 31–end	
G		2 Kings 19. 20–36 Phil. 3.1 – 4.1	1 Macc. 9. 1–22 *or* 2 Chron. ch. 30 John 14. 1–14	
G		2 Kings ch. 20 Phil. 4. 2–end	1 Macc. 13. 41 end; 14. 4–15 *or* 2 Chron. 32. 1–22 John 14. 15–end	

ct

THE TWENTIETH SUNDAY AFTER TRINITY

	Calendar and Holy Communion	Morning Prayer	Evening Prayer	NOTES
G	Prov. 9. 1–6 Ps. 145. 15–end Eph. 5. 15–21 Matt. 22. 1–14	Ps. 129; 130 Isa. 50. 4–10 Luke 13. 22–30	Ps. 127; [128] Josh. 5.13 – 6.20 Matt. 11. 20–end	
G		2 Kings 21. 1–18 1 Tim. 1. 1–17	2 Macc. 4. 7–17 *or* 2 Chron. 33. 1–13 John 15. 1–11	
G		2 Kings 22.1 – 23.3 1 Tim. 1.18 – 2.end	2 Macc. 6. 12–end *or* 2 Chron. 34. 1–18 John 15. 12–17	

		Sunday Principal Service Weekday Eucharist	Third Service Morning Prayer	Second Service Evening Prayer

16 Wednesday *Nicholas Ridley, Bishop of London, and Hugh Latimer, Bishop of Worcester, Reformation Martyrs, 1555*

G		Gal. 5. 18–end Ps. 1 Luke 11. 42–46	Ps. 119. 153–end 2 Kings 23. 4–25 1 Tim. ch. 3	Ps. 136 2 Mac. 7. 1–19 *or* 2 Chron. 34. 19–end John 15. 18–end

17 Thursday **Ignatius, Bishop of Antioch, Martyr, c. 107**

Gr	Com. Martyr *or* *also* Phil. 3. 7–12 John 6. 52–58	Eph. 1. 1–10 Ps. 98. 1–4 Luke 11. 47–end	Ps. *143*; 146 2 Kings 23.36 – 24.17 1 Tim. ch. 4	Ps. *138*; 140; 141 2 Macc. 7. 20–41 *or* 2 Chron. 35. 1–19 John 16. 1–15 *or First EP of Luke* Ps. 33 Hos. 6. 1–3 2 Tim. 3. 10–end **R ct**

18 Friday **LUKE THE EVANGELIST**

R		Isa. 35. 3–6 *or* Acts 16. 6–12a Ps. 147. 1–7 2 Tim. 4. 5–17 Luke 10. 1–9	*MP*: Ps. 145; 146 Isa. ch. 55 Luke 1. 1–4	*EP*: Ps. 103 Ecclus. 38. 1–14 *or* Isa. 61. 1–6 Col. 4. 7–end

19 Saturday **Henry Martyn, Translator of the Scriptures, Missionary in India and Persia, 1812**

Gw	Com. Missionary *or* *esp.* Mark 16. 15–end *also* Isa. 55. 6–11	Eph. 1. 15–end Ps. 8 Luke 12. 8–12	Ps. 147 2 Kings 25. 22–end 1 Tim. 5. 17–end	Ps. *148*; 149; 150 Tobit ch. 2 *or* 2 Chron. 36. 11–end John 16. 23–end **ct**

20 Sunday **THE TWENTY-FIRST SUNDAY AFTER TRINITY (Proper 24)**

G	*Track 1* Job 38. 1–7 [34–end] Ps. 104. 1–10, 26, 35c (*or* 1–10) Heb. 5. 1–10 Mark 10. 35–45	*Track 2* Isa. 53. 4–end Ps. 91. 9–end Heb. 5. 1–10 Mark 10. 35–45	Ps. 133; 134; 137. 1–6 Isa. 54. 1–14 Luke 13. 31–end	Ps. 141 Josh. 14. 6–14 Matt. 12. 1–21

21 Monday

G **DEL 29**		Eph. 2. 1–10 Ps. 100 Luke 12. 13–21	Ps. *1*; 2; 3 Judith ch. 4 *or* Exod. 22. 21–27; 23. 1–17 1 Tim. 6. 1–10	Ps. *4*; 7 Tobit ch. 3 *or* Mic. 1. 1–9 John 17. 1–5

22 Tuesday

G		Eph. 2. 12–end Ps. 85. 7–end Luke 12. 35–38	Ps. *5*; 6; (8) Judith 5.1 – 6.4 *or* Exod. 29.38 – 30.16 1 Tim. 6. 11–end	Ps. *9*; 10† Tobit ch. 4 *or* Mic. ch. 2 John 17. 6–19

23 Wednesday

G		Eph. 3. 2–12 Ps. 98 Luke 12. 39–48	Ps. 119. 1–32 Judith 6.10 – 7.7 *or* Lev. ch. 8 2 Tim. 1. 1–14	Ps. *11*; 12; 13 Tobit 5.1 – 6.1a *or* Mic. ch. 3 John 17. 20–end

	Calendar and Holy Communion	Morning Prayer	Evening Prayer	NOTES
G		2 Kings 23. 4–25 1 Tim. ch. 3	2 Mac. 7. 1–19 or 2 Chron. 34. 19–end John 15. 18–end	
	Etheldreda, Abbess of Ely, 679			
Gw	Com. Abbess	2 Kings 23.36 – 24.17 1 Tim. ch. 4	2 Macc. 7. 20–41 or 2 Chron. 35. 1–19 John 16. 1–15 or First EP of Luke (Ps. 33) Hos. 6. 1–3 2 Tim. 3. 10–end	
			R ct	
	LUKE THE EVANGELIST			
R	Isa. 35. 3–6 Ps. 147. 1–6 2 Tim. 4. 5–15 Luke 10. 1–9 or Luke 7. 36–end	(Ps. 145; 146) Isa. ch. 55 Luke 1. 1–4	(Ps. 103) Ecclus. 38. 1–14 or Isa. 61. 1–6 Col. 4. 7–end	
G		2 Kings 25. 22–end 1 Tim. 5. 17–end	Tobit ch. 2 or 2 Chron. 36. 11–end John 16. 23–end	
			ct	
	THE TWENTY-FIRST SUNDAY AFTER TRINITY			
G	Gen. 32. 24–29 Ps. 90. 1–12 Eph. 6. 10–20 John 4. 46b–end	Ps. 133; 134; 137. 1–6 Isa. 54. 1–14 Luke 13. 31–end	Ps. 142 Josh. 14. 6–14 Matt. 12. 1–21	
G		Judith ch. 4 or Exod. 22. 21–27; 23. 1–17 1 Tim. 6. 1–10	Tobit ch. 3 or Mic. 1. 1–9 John 17. 1–5	
G		Judith 5.1 – 6.4 or Exod. 29.38 – 30.16 1 Tim. 6. 11–end	Tobit ch. 4 or Mic. ch. 4 John 17. 6–19	
G		Judith 6.10 – 7.7 or Lev. ch. 8 2 Tim. 1. 1–14	Tobit 5.1 – 6.1a or Mic. ch. 3 John 17. 20–end	

	Sunday Principal Service Weekday Eucharist	Third Service Morning Prayer	Second Service Evening Prayer
24 Thursday			
G	Eph. 3. 14–end Ps. 33. 1–6 Luke 12. 49–53	Ps. 14; *15*; 16 Judith 7. 19–end *or* Lev. ch. 9 2 Tim. 1.15 – 2.13	Ps. 18† Tobit 6. 1b–end *or* Mic. 4.1 – 5.1 John 18. 1–11
25 Friday	*Crispin and Crispinian, Martyrs at Rome, c. 287*		
G	Eph. 4. 1–6 Ps. 24. 1–6 Luke 12. 54–end	Ps. 17; *19* Judith 8. 9–end *or* Lev. 16. 2–24 2 Tim. 2. 14–end	Ps. 22 Tobit ch. 7 *or* Mic. 5. 2–end John 18. 12–27
26 Saturday	**Alfred the Great, King of the West Saxons, Scholar, 899** *Cedd, Abbot of Lastingham, Bishop of the East Saxons, 664**		
Gw	Com. Saint *or* *also* 2 Sam. 23. 1–5 John 18. 33–37	Eph. 4. 7–16 Ps. 122 Luke 13. 1–9	Ps. 20; 21; *23* Judith ch. 9 *or* Lev. ch. 17 2 Tim. ch. 3	Ps. *24*; 25 Tobit ch. 8 *or* Mic. ch. 6 John 18. 28–end **ct**
27 Sunday	**THE LAST SUNDAY AFTER TRINITY****		
G	*Track 1* Job 42. 1–6, 10–end Ps. 34. 1–8, 19–end (*or* 1–8) Heb. 7. 23–end Mark 10. 46–end	*Track 2* Jer. 31. 7–9 Ps. 126 Heb. 7. 23–end Mark 10. 46–end	Ps. 119. 89–104 Isa. 59. 9–20 Luke 14. 1–14	Ps. 119. 121–136 Eccles. chs 11 and 12 2 Tim. 2. 1–7 *Gospel:* Luke 18. 9–14 *or First EP of Simon* *and Jude* Ps. 124; 125; 126 Deut. 32. 1–4 John 14. 15–26 **R ct**
G	*or, if being observed as Bible Sunday:*	Isa. 55. 1–11 Ps. 19. 7–end 2 Tim. 3.14 – 4.5 John 5. 36b–end	Ps. 119. 89–104 Isa. 45. 22–end Matt. 24. 30–35 *or* Luke 14. 1–14	Ps. 119. 1–16 2 Kings ch. 22 Col. 3. 12–17 *Gospel:* Luke 4. 14–30 *or First EP of Simon* *and Jude* Ps. 124; 125; 126 Deut. 32. 1–4 John 14. 15–26 **R ct**
28 Monday	**SIMON AND JUDE, APOSTLES**		
R **DEL 30**	Isa. 28. 14–16 Ps. 119. 89–96 Eph. 2. 19–end John 15. 17–end	*MP:* Ps. 116; 117 Wisd. 5. 1–16 *or* Isa. 45. 18–end Luke 6. 12–16	*EP:* Ps. 119. 1–16 1 Macc. 2. 42–66 *or* Jer. 3. 11–18 Jude 1–4, 17–end
29 Tuesday	**James Hannington, Bishop of Eastern Equatorial Africa, Martyr in Uganda, 1885**		
Gr	Com. Martyr *or* *esp.* Matt. 10. 28–39	Eph. 5. 21–end Ps. 128 Luke 13. 18–21	Ps. 32; *36* Judith ch. 11 *or* Lev. 23. 1–22 2 Tim. 4. 9–end	Ps. 33 Tobit ch. 10 *or* Mic. 7. 8–end John 19. 17–30

*Chad may be celebrated with Cedd on 26 October instead of 2 March.
**If the Dedication Festival is kept on this Sunday, use the provision given on 5 and 6 October.

	Calendar and Holy Communion	Morning Prayer	Evening Prayer	NOTES
G		Judith 7. 19–end *or* Lev. ch. 9 2 Tim. 1.15 – 2.13	Tobit 6. 1b–end *or* Mic. 4.1 – 5.1 John 18. 1–11	

Crispin, Martyr at Rome, c. 287

	Calendar and Holy Communion	Morning Prayer	Evening Prayer	NOTES
Gr	Com. Martyr	Judith 8. 9–end *or* Lev. 16. 2–24 2 Tim. 2. 14–end	Tobit ch. 7 *or* Mic. 5. 2–end John 18. 12–27	
G		Judith ch. 9 *or* Lev. ch. 17 2 Tim. ch. 3	Tobit ch. 8 *or* Mic. ch. 6 John 18. 28–end	
			ct	

THE TWENTY-SECOND SUNDAY AFTER TRINITY

	Calendar and Holy Communion	Morning Prayer	Evening Prayer	NOTES
G	Gen. 45. 1–7, 15 Ps. 133 Phil. 1. 3–11 Matt. 18. 21–end	Ps. 119. 89–104 Isa. 59. 9–20 Luke 14. 1–14	Ps. 119. 121–136 Eccles. chs 11 and 12 2 Tim. 2. 1–7 *or First EP of Simon and Jude* Ps. 124; 125; 126 Deut. 32. 1–4 John 14. 15–26 **R ct**	

SIMON AND JUDE, APOSTLES

	Calendar and Holy Communion	Morning Prayer	Evening Prayer	NOTES
R	Isa. 28. 9–16 Ps. 116. 11–end Jude 1–8 *or* Rev. 21. 9–14 John 15. 17–end	(Ps. 119. 89–96) Wisd. 5. 1–16 *or* Isa. 45. 18–end Luke 6. 12–16	(Ps. 119. 1–16) 1 Macc. 2. 42–66 *or* Jer. 3. 11–18 Eph. 2. 19–end	
G		Judith ch. 11 *or* Lev. 23. 1–22 2 Tim. 4. 9–end	Tobit ch. 10 *or* Mic. 7. 8–end John 19. 17–30	

		Sunday Principal Service Weekday Eucharist	Third Service Morning Prayer	Second Service Evening Prayer
30 Wednesday				
	G	Eph. 6. 1–9 Ps. 145. 10–20 Luke 13. 22–30	Ps. 34 Judith ch. 12 or Lev. 23. 23–end Titus ch. 1	Ps. 119. 33–56 Tobit ch. 11 or Hab. 1. 1–11 John 19. 31–end
31 Thursday	*Martin Luther, Reformer, 1546*			
	G	Eph. 6. 10–20 Ps. 144. 1–2, 9–11 Luke 13. 31–end	Ps. 37† Judith ch. 13 or Lev. 24. 1–9 Titus ch. 2	*First EP of All Saints* Ps. 1; 5 Ecclus. 44. 1–15 or Isa. 40. 27–end Rev. 19. 6–10 𝖂 ct *or, if All Saints is observed on 3 November:* Tobit ch. 12 or Hab. 1.12 – 2.5 John 20. 1–10

November 2024

		Sunday Principal Service Weekday Eucharist	Third Service Morning Prayer	Second Service Evening Prayer
1 Friday	**ALL SAINTS' DAY**			
	𝖂	Wisd. 3. 1–9 or Isa. 25. 6–9 Ps. 24. 1–6 Rev. 21. 1–6a John 11. 32–44	MP: Ps. 15; 84; 149 Isa. ch. 35 Luke 9. 18–27	EP: Ps. 148; 150 Isa. 65. 17–end Heb. 11.32 – 12.2
		or, if the readings above are used on Sunday 3 November:		
	𝖂	Isa. 56. 3–8 or 2 Esdras 2. 42–end Ps. 33. 1–5 Heb. 12. 18–24 Matt. 5. 1–12	MP: 111; 112; 117 Wisd. 5. 1–16 or Jer. 31. 31–34 2 Cor. 4. 5–12	EP: Ps. 145 Isa. 66. 20–23 Col. 1. 9–14
		or, if kept as a feria:		
	G	Phil. 1. 1–11 Ps. 111 Luke 14. 1–6	Ps. 31 Judith 15. 1–13 or Lev. 25. 1–24 Titus ch. 3	Ps. 35 Tobit 13.1 – 14.1 or Hab. 2. 6–end John 20. 11–18
2 Saturday	**Commemoration of the Faithful Departed (All Souls' Day)**			
	Rp *or* Gp	Lam. 3. 17–26, 31–33 or or Wisd. 3. 1–9 Ps. 23 or Ps. 27. 1–6, 16–end Rom. 5. 5–11 or 1 Pet. 1. 3–9 John 5. 19–25 or John 6. 37–40	Phil. 1. 18–26 Ps. 42. 1–7 Luke 14. 1, 7–11	Ps. 41; *42*; 43 Judith 15.14 – 16.end or Num. 6. 1–5, 21–end Philem.	Ps. 45; *46* Tobit 14. 2–end or Hab. 3. 2–19a John 20. 19–end ct
3 Sunday	**THE FOURTH SUNDAY BEFORE ADVENT**			
	R *or* G	Deut. 6. 1–9 Ps. 119. 1–8 Heb. 9. 11–14 Mark 12. 28–34	Ps. 112; 149 Jer. 31. 31–34 1 John 3. 1–3	Ps. 145 (or 145. 1–9) Dan. 2. 1–48 (or 2. 1–11, 25–48) Rev. 7. 9–end *Gospel:* Matt. 5. 1–12
		or ALL SAINTS' SUNDAY (see readings for 1 November throughout the day)		
	𝖂			

	Calendar and Holy Communion	Morning Prayer	Evening Prayer	NOTES
G		Judith ch. 12 *or* Lev. 23. 23–end Titus ch. 1	Tobit ch. 11 *or* Hab. 1. 1–11 John 19. 31–end	
G		Judith ch. 13 *or* Lev. 24. 1–9 Titus ch. 2	*First EP of All Saints* Ps. 1; 5 Ecclus. 44. 1–15 *or* Isa. 40. 27–end Rev. 19. 6–10 𝖂 ct	

ALL SAINTS' DAY

| 𝖂 | Isa. 66. 20–23 Ps. 33. 1–5 Rev. 7. 2–4 [5–8] 9–12 Matt. 5. 1–12 | Ps. 15; 84; 149 Isa. ch. 35 Luke 9. 18–27 | Ps. 148; 150 Isa. 65. 17–end Heb. 11.32 – 12.2 | |

To celebrate All Souls' Day, see *Common Worship* provision.

| G | | Judith 15.14 – 16.end *or* Num. 6. 1–5, 21–end Philem. | Tobit 14. 2–end *or* Hab. 3. 2–19a John 20. 19–end | |

ct

THE TWENTY-THIRD SUNDAY AFTER TRINITY

| G | Isa. 11. 1–10 Ps. 44. 1–9 Phil. 3. 17–end Matt. 22. 15–22 | Ps. 112; 149 Jer. 31. 31–34 1 John 3. 1–3 | Ps. 145 (*or* 145. 1–9) Dan. 2. 1–48 (*or* 2. 1–11, 25–48) Rev. 7. 9–end | |

		Sunday Principal Service Weekday Eucharist	Third Service Morning Prayer	Second Service Evening Prayer
4 Monday				
R or **G** **DEL 31**		Phil. 2. 1–4 Ps. 131 Luke 14. 12–14	Ps. **2**; 146 *alt.* Ps. 44 Dan. ch. 1 Rev. ch. 1	Ps. **92**; 96; 97 *alt.* Ps. **47**; 49 Isa. 1. 1–20 Matt. 1. 18–end
5 Tuesday				
R or **G**		Phil. 2. 5–11 Ps. 22. 22–27 Luke 14. 15–24	Ps. **5**; 147. 1–12 *alt.* Ps. **48**; 52 Dan. 2. 1–24 Rev. 2. 1–11	Ps. 98; 99; **100** *alt.* Ps. 50 Isa. 1. 21–end Matt. 2. 1–15
6 Wednesday	*Leonard, Hermit, 6th century; William Temple, Archbishop of Canterbury, Teacher, 1944*			
R or **G**		Phil. 2. 12–18 Ps. 27. 1–5 Luke 14. 25–33	Ps. **9**; 147. 13–end *alt.* Ps. 119. 57–80 Dan. 2. 25–end Rev. 2. 12–end	Ps. 111; **112**; 116 *alt.* Ps. **59**; 60; (67) Isa. 2. 1–11 Matt. 2. 16–end
7 Thursday	**Willibrord of York, Bishop, Apostle of Frisia, 739**			
Rw or **Gw**	Com. Missionary or *esp.* Isa. 52. 7–10 Matt. 28. 16–end	Phil. 3. 3–8a Ps. 105. 1–7 Luke 15. 1–10	Ps. 11; **15**; 148 *alt.* Ps. 56; **57**; (63†) Dan. 3. 1–18 Rev. 3. 1–13	Ps. 118 *alt.* Ps. 61; **62**; 64 Isa. 2. 12–end Matt. ch. 3
8 Friday	**The Saints and Martyrs of England**			
Rw or **Gw**	Isa. 61. 4–9 or or Ecclus. 44. 1–15 Ps. 15 Rev. 19. 5–10 John 17. 18–23	Phil. 3.17 – 4.1 Ps. 122 Luke 16. 1–8	Ps. **16**; 149 *alt.* Ps. **51**; 54 Dan. 3. 19–end Rev. 3. 14–end	Ps. 137; 138; **143** *alt.* Ps. 38 Isa. 3. 1–15 Matt. 4. 1–11
9 Saturday	*Margery Kempe, Mystic, c. 1440*			
R or **G**		Phil. 4. 10–19 Ps. 112 Luke 16. 9–15	Ps. **18. 31–end**; 150 *alt.* Ps. 68 Dan. 4. 1–18 Rev. ch. 4	Ps. 145 *alt.* Ps. 65; **66** Isa. 4.2 – 5.7 Matt. 4. 12–22 **ct**
10 Sunday	**THE THIRD SUNDAY BEFORE ADVENT** (Remembrance Sunday)			
R or **G**		Jonah 3. 1–5, 10 Ps. 62. 5–end Heb. 9. 24–end Mark 1. 14–20	Ps. 136 Mic. 4. 1–5 Phil. 4. 6–9	Ps. 46; [82] Isa. 10.33 – 11.9 John 14. 1–29 (or 23–29)
11 Monday	**Martin, Bishop of Tours, c. 397**			
Rw or **Gw** **DEL 32**	Com. Bishop or *also* 1 Thess. 5. 1–11 Matt. 25. 34–40	Titus 1. 1–9 Ps. 24. 1–6 Luke 17. 1–6	Ps. 19; **20** *alt.* Ps. 71 Dan. 4. 19–end Rev. ch. 5	Ps. 34 *alt.* Ps. **72**; 75 Isa. 5. 8–24 Matt. 4.23 – 5.12
12 Tuesday				
R or **G**		Titus 2. 1–8, 11–14 Ps. 37. 3–5, 30–32 Luke 17. 7–10	Ps. **21**; 24 *alt.* Ps. 73 Dan. 5. 1–12 Rev. ch. 6	Ps. 36; **40** *alt.* Ps. 74 Isa. 5. 25–end Matt. 5. 13–20

	Calendar and Holy Communion	Morning Prayer	Evening Prayer	NOTES
G		Dan. ch. 1 Rev. ch. 1	Isa. 1. 1–20 Matt. 1. 18–end	
G		Dan. 2. 1–24 Rev. 2. 1–11	Isa. 1. 21–end Matt. 2. 1–15	
	Leonard, Hermit, 6th century			
Gw	Com. Abbot	Dan. 2. 25–end Rev. 2. 12–end	Isa. 2. 1–11 Matt. 2. 16–end	
G		Dan. 3. 1–18 Rev. 3. 1–13	Isa. 2. 12–end Matt. ch. 3	
G		Dan. 3. 19–end Rev. 3. 14–end	Isa. 3. 1–15 Matt. 4. 1–11	
G		Dan. 4. 1–18 Rev. ch. 4	Isa. 4.2 – 5.7 Matt. 4. 12–22	
			ct	
	THE TWENTY-FOURTH SUNDAY AFTER TRINITY			
G	Isa. 55. 6–11 Ps. 85. 1–7 Col. 1. 3–12 Matt. 9. 18–26	Ps. 136 Mic. 4. 1–5 Phil. 4. 6–9	Ps. 144 Isa. 10.33 – 11.9 John 14. 1–29 (or 23–29)	
	Martin, Bishop of Tours, c. 397			
Gw	Com. Bishop	Dan. 4. 19–end Rev. ch. 5	Isa. 5. 8–24 Matt. 4.23 – 5.12	
G		Dan. 5. 1–12 Rev. ch. 6	Isa. 5. 25–end Matt. 5. 13–20	

	Sunday Principal Service Weekday Eucharist	Third Service Morning Prayer	Second Service Evening Prayer

13 Wednesday **Charles Simeon, Priest, Evangelical Divine, 1836**

Rw *or* **Gw**	Com. Pastor *or* Titus 3. 1–7	Ps. **23**; 25	Ps. 37
	esp. Mal. 2. 5–7 Ps. 23	*alt.* Ps. 77	*alt.* Ps. 119. 81–104
	also Col. 1. 3–8 Luke 17. 11–19	Dan. 5. 13–end	Isa. ch. 6
	Luke 8. 4–8	Rev. 7. 1–4, 9–end	Matt. 5. 21–37

14 Thursday *Samuel Seabury, first Anglican Bishop in North America, 1796*

R *or* **G**	Philem. 7–20	Ps. **26**; 27	Ps. 42; **43**
	Ps. 146. 4–end	*alt.* Ps. 78. 1–39†	*alt.* Ps. 78. 40–end†
	Luke 17. 20–25	Dan. ch. 6	Isa. 7. 1–17
		Rev. ch. 8	Matt. 5. 38–end

15 Friday

R *or* **G**	2 John 4–9	Ps. 28; **32**	Ps. 31
	Ps. 119. 1–8	*alt.* Ps. 55	*alt.* Ps. 69
	Luke 17. 26–end	Dan. 7. 1–14	Isa. 8. 1–15
		Rev. 9. 1–12	Matt. 6. 1–18

16 Saturday **Margaret, Queen of Scotland, Philanthropist, Reformer of the Church, 1093**
Edmund Rich of Abingdon, Archbishop of Canterbury, 1240

Rw *or* **Gw**	Com. Saint *or* 3 John 5–8	Ps. 33	Ps. 84; **86**
	also Prov. 31. 10–12, Ps. 112	*alt.* Ps. **76**; 79	*alt.* Ps. 81; **84**
	20, 26–end Luke 18. 1–8	Dan. 7. 15–end	Isa. 8.16 – 9.7
	1 Cor. 12.13 – 13.3	Rev. 9. 13–end	Matt. 6. 19–end
	Matt. 25. 34–end		ct

17 Sunday **THE SECOND SUNDAY BEFORE ADVENT**

R *or* **G**	Dan. 12. 1–3	Ps. 96	Ps. 95
	Ps. 16	1 Sam. 9.27 – 10.2a;	Dan. ch. 3.
	Heb. 10. 11–14 [15–18]	10. 17–26	(*or* 3. 13–end)
	19–25	Matt. 13. 31–35	Matt. 13. 24–30, 36–43
	Mark 13. 1–8		

18 Monday **Elizabeth of Hungary, Princess of Thuringia, Philanthropist, 1231**

Rw *or* **Gw** **DEL 33**	Com. Saint *or* Rev. 1. 1–4; 2. 1–5	Ps. 46; **47**	Ps. 70; **71**
	esp. Matt. 25. 31–end Ps. 1	*alt.* Ps. **80**; 82	*alt.* Ps. **85**; 86
	also Prov. 31. 10–end Luke 18. 35–end	Dan. 8. 1–14	Isa. 9.8 – 10.4
		Rev. ch. 10	Matt. 7. 1–12

19 Tuesday **Hilda, Abbess of Whitby, 680**
Mechtild, Béguine of Magdeburg, Mystic, 1280

Rw *or* **Gw**	Com. Religious *or* Rev. 3. 1–6, 14–end	Ps. 48; **52**	Ps. **67**; 72
	esp. Isa. 61.10 – 62.5 Ps. 15	*alt.* Ps. 87; **89. 1–18**	*alt.* Ps. 89. 19–end
	Luke 19. 1–10	Dan. 8. 15–end	Isa. 10. 5–19
		Rev. 11. 1–14	Matt. 7. 13–end

20 Wednesday **Edmund, King of the East Angles, Martyr, 870**
Priscilla Lydia Sellon, a Restorer of the Religious Life in the Church of England, 1876

R *or* **Gr**	Com. Martyr *or* Rev. ch. 4	Ps. **56**; 57	Ps. 73
	also Prov. 20. 28; Ps. 150	*alt.* Ps. 119. 105–128	*alt.* Ps. **91**; 93
	21. 1–4, 7 Luke 19. 11–28	Dan. 9. 1–19	Isa. 10. 20–32
		Rev. 11. 15–end	Matt. 8. 1–13

	Calendar and Holy Communion	Morning Prayer	Evening Prayer	NOTES
	Britius, Bishop of Tours, 444			
Gw	Com. Bishop	Dan. 5. 13–end Rev. 7. 1–4, 9–end	Isa. ch. 6 Matt. 5. 21–37	
G		Dan. ch. 6 Rev. ch. 8	Isa. 7. 1–17 Matt. 5. 38–end	
	Machutus, Bishop, Apostle of Brittany, c. 564			
Gw	Com. Bishop	Dan. 7. 1–14 Rev. 9. 1–12	Isa. 8. 1–15 Matt. 6. 1–18	
G		Dan. 7. 15–end Rev. 9. 13–end	Isa. 8.16 – 9.7 Matt. 6. 19–end	
			ct	
	THE TWENTY-FIFTH SUNDAY AFTER TRINITY			
G	1 Sam. 10. 17–24 Ps. 97 Rom. 13. 1–7 Matt. 8. 23–34	Ps. 96 1 Sam. 9.27 – 10.2a; 10. 17–26 Matt. 13. 31–35	Ps. 95 Dan. ch. 3. (or 3. 13–end) Matt. 13. 24–30, 36–43	
G		Dan. 8. 1–14 Rev. ch. 10	Isa. 9.8 – 10.4 Matt. 7. 1–12	
G		Dan. 8. 15–end Rev. 11. 1–14	Isa. 10. 5–19 Matt. 7. 13–end	
	Edmund, King of the East Angles, Martyr, 870			
Gr	Com. Martyr	Dan. 9. 1–19 Rev. 11. 15–end	Isa. 10. 20–32 Matt. 8. 1–13	

	Sunday Principal Service Weekday Eucharist	Third Service Morning Prayer	Second Service Evening Prayer
21 Thursday			
R *or* **G**	Rev. 5. 1–10 Ps. 149. 1–5 Luke 19. 41–44	Ps. 61; *62* *alt.* Ps. 90; *92* Dan. 9. 20–end Rev. ch. 12	Ps. 74; *76* *alt.* Ps. 94 Isa. 10.33 – 11.9 Matt. 8. 14–22
22 Friday	*Cecilia, Martyr at Rome, c. 230*		
R *or* **G**	Rev. 10. 8–end Ps. 119. 65–72 Luke 19. 45–end	Ps. *63*; 65 *alt.* Ps. *88*; (95) Dan. 10.1 – 11.1 Rev. 13. 1–10	Ps. 77 *alt.* Ps. 102 Isa. 11.10 – 12.end Matt. 8. 23–end
23 Saturday	**Clement, Bishop of Rome, Martyr, c. 100**		
R *or* **Gr**	Com. Martyr *or* *also* Phil. 3.17 – 4.3 Matt. 16. 13–19 Rev. 11. 4–12 Ps. 144. 1–9 Luke 20. 27–40	Ps. 78. 1–39 *alt.* Ps. 96; *97*; 100 Dan. ch. 12 Rev. 13. 11–end	Ps. 78. 40–end *alt.* Ps. 104 Isa. 13. 1–13 Matt. 9. 1–17 **ct** *or First EP of Christ the King* Ps. 99; 100 Isa. 10.33 – 11.9 1 Tim. 6. 11–16 **R** *or* **W ct**
24 Sunday	**CHRIST THE KING** The Sunday Next Before Advent		
R *or* **W**	Dan. 7. 9–10, 13–14 Ps. 93 Rev. 1. 4b–8 John 18. 33–37	*MP*: Ps. 29; 110 Isa. 32. 1–8 Rev. 3. 7–end	*EP*: Ps. 72 (or 72. 1–7) Dan. ch. 5 John 6. 1–15
25 Monday	*Catherine of Alexandria, Martyr, 4th century; Isaac Watts, Hymn Writer, 1748*		
R *or* **G** **DEL 34**	Rev. 14. 1–5 Ps. 24. 1–6 Luke 21. 1–4	Ps. 92; *96* *alt.* Ps. *98*; 99; 101 Isa. 40. 1–11 Rev. 14. 1–13	Ps. *80*; 81 *alt.* Ps. 105† (or 103) Isa. 14. 3–20 Matt. 9. 18–34
26 Tuesday			
R *or* **G**	Rev. 14. 14–19 Ps. 96 Luke 21. 5–11	Ps. *97*; 98; 100 *alt.* Ps. *106*† (or 103) Isa. 40. 12–26 Rev. 14.14 – 15.end	Ps. 99; *101* *alt.* Ps. 107† Isa. ch. 17 Matt. 9.35 – 10.15
27 Wednesday			
R *or* **G**	Rev. 15. 1–4 Ps. 98 Luke 21. 12–19	Ps. 110; 111; *112* *alt.* Ps. 110; *111*; 112 Isa. 40.27 – 41.7 Rev. 16. 1–11	Ps. 121; *122*; 123; 124 *alt.* Ps. 119. 129–152 Isa. ch. 19 Matt. 10. 16–33
28 Thursday			
R *or* **G**	Rev. 18. 1–2, 21–23; 19. 1–3, 9 Ps. 100 Luke 21. 20–28	Ps. *125*; 126; 127; 128 *alt.* Ps. 113; *115* Isa. 41. 8–20 Rev. 16. 12–end	Ps. 131; 132; *133* *alt.* Ps. 114; *116*; 117 Isa. 21. 1–12 Matt. 10.34 – 11.1

	Calendar and Holy Communion	Morning Prayer	Evening Prayer	NOTES
G		Dan. 9. 20–end Rev. ch. 12	Isa. 10.33 – 11.9 Matt. 8. 14–22	

	Cecilia, Martyr at Rome, _c._ 230			
Gr	Com. Virgin Martyr	Dan. 10.1 – 11.1 Rev. 13. 1–10	Isa. 11.10 – 12.end Matt. 8. 23–end	

	Clement, Bishop of Rome, Martyr, _c._ 100			
Gr	Com. Martyr	Dan. ch. 12 Rev. 13. 11–end	Isa. 13. 1–13 Matt. 9. 1–17 **ct**	

THE SUNDAY NEXT BEFORE ADVENT
To celebrate Christ the King, see _Common Worship_ provision.

	Calendar and Holy Communion	Morning Prayer	Evening Prayer	NOTES
G	Jer. 23. 5–8 Ps. 85. 8–end Col. 1. 13–20 John 6. 5–14	Ps. 29; 110 Isa. 32. 1–8 Rev. 3. 7–end	Ps. 72 (_or_ 72. 1–7) Dan. ch. 5 Rev. 1. 4b–8	

	Catherine of Alexandria, Martyr, 4th century			
Gr	Com. Virgin Martyr	Isa. 40. 1–11 Rev. 14. 1–13	Isa. 14. 3–20 Matt. 9. 18–34	
G		Isa. 40. 12–26 Rev. 14.14 – 15.end	Isa. ch. 17 Matt. 9.35 – 10.15	
G		Isa. 40.27 – 41.7 Rev. 16. 1–11	Isa. ch. 19 Matt. 10. 16–33	
G		Isa. 41. 8–20 Rev. 16. 12–end	Isa. 21. 1–12 Matt. 10.34 – 11.1	

	Sunday Principal Service Weekday Eucharist	Third Service Morning Prayer	Second Service Evening Prayer

29 Friday

| **R or G** | Rev. 20.1–4, 11 – 21.2
Ps. 84. 1–6
Luke 21. 29–33 | Ps. 139
alt. Ps. 139
Isa. 41.21 – 42.9
Rev. ch. 17 | Ps. **146**; 147
alt. Ps. **130**; 131; 137
Isa. 22. 1–14
Matt. 11. 2–19
*or First EP of Andrew
the Apostle*
Ps. 48
Isa. 49. 1–9a
1 Cor. 4. 9–16
R ct |

Day of Intercession and Thanksgiving for the Missionary Work of the Church

Isa. 49. 1–6; Isa. 52. 7–10; Mic. 4. 1–5
Ps. 2; 46; 47
Acts 17. 12–end; 2 Cor. 5.14 – 6.2; Eph. 2. 13–end
Matt. 5. 13–16; Matt. 28. 16–end; John 17. 20–end

30 Saturday   **ANDREW THE APOSTLE**

| **R** | Isa. 52. 7–10
Ps. 19. 1–6
Rom. 10. 12–18
Matt. 4. 18–22 | *MP*: Ps. 47; 147. 1–12
Ezek. 47. 1–12
or Ecclus. 14. 20–end
John 12. 20–32 | *EP*: Ps. 87; 96
Zech. 8. 20–end
John 1. 35–42 |

December 2024

1 Sunday   **THE FIRST SUNDAY OF ADVENT**
Common Worship Year C begins

| **P** | Jer. 33. 14–16
Ps. 25. 1–9
1 Thess. 3. 9–end
Luke 21. 25–36 | Ps. 44
Isa. 51. 4–11
Rom. 13. 11–end | Ps. 9 (or 9. 1–8)
Joel 3. 9–end
Rev. 14.13 – 15.4
Gospel: John 3. 1–17 |

2 Monday   Daily Eucharistic Lectionary Year 1 begins

| **P** | Isa. 2. 1–5
Ps. 122
Matt. 8. 5–11 | Ps. **50**; 54
alt. Ps. **1**; 2; 3
Isa. 42. 18–end
Rev. ch. 19 | Ps. 70; **71**
alt. Ps. **4**; 7
Isa. 25. 1–9
Matt. 12. 1–21 |

3 Tuesday   *Francis Xavier, Missionary, Apostle of the Indies, 1552*

| **P** | Isa. 11. 1–10
Ps. 72. 1–4, 18–19
Luke 10. 21–24 | Ps. **80**; 82
alt. Ps. **5**; 6; (8)
Isa. 43. 1–13
Rev. ch. 20 | Ps. **74**; 75
alt. Ps. **9**; 10†
Isa. 26. 1–13
Matt. 12. 22–37 |

4 Wednesday   *John of Damascus, Monk, Teacher, c. 749; Nicholas Ferrar, Deacon, Founder of the Little Gidding
Community, 1637*

| **P** | Isa. 25. 6–10a
Ps. 23
Matt. 15. 29–37 | Ps. 5; **7**
alt. Ps. 119. 1–32
Isa. 43. 14–end
Rev. 21. 1–8 | Ps. 76; **77**
alt. Ps. **11**; 12; 13
Isa. 28. 1–13
Matt. 12. 38–end |

5 Thursday

| **P** | Isa. 26. 1–6
Ps. 118. 18–27a
Matt. 7. 21, 24–27 | Ps. **42**; 43
alt. Ps. 14; **15**; 16
Isa. 44. 1–8
Rev. 21. 9–21 | Ps. **40**; 46
alt. Ps. 18†
Isa. 28. 14–end
Matt. 13. 1–23 |

	Calendar and Holy Communion	Morning Prayer	Evening Prayer	NOTES
G		Isa. 41.21 – 42.9 Rev. ch. 17	Isa. 22. 1–14 Matt. 11. 2–19 *or First EP of Andrew the Apostle* (Ps. 48) Isa. 49. 1–9a 1 Cor. 4. 9–16	

R ct

To celebrate the Day of Intercession and Thanksgiving for the Missionary Work of the Church, see *Common Worship* provision.

ANDREW THE APOSTLE

R	Zech. 8. 20–end Ps. 92. 1–5 Rom. 10. 9–end Matt. 4. 18–22	(Ps. 47; 147. 1–12) Ezek. 47. 1–12 or Ecclus. 14. 20–end John 12. 20–32	(Ps. 87; 96) Isa. 52. 7–10 John 1. 35–42	

THE FIRST SUNDAY IN ADVENT
Advent 1 Collect until Christmas Eve

P	Mic. 4. 1–4, 6–7 Ps. 25. 1–9 Rom. 13. 8–14 Matt. 21. 1–13	Ps. 44 Isa. 51. 4–11 Rom. 13. 11–end	Ps. 9 (or 9. 1–8) Joel 3. 9–end Rev. 14.13 – 15.4	
P		Isa. 42. 18–end Rev. ch. 19	Isa. 25. 1–9 Matt. 12. 1–21	
P		Isa. 43. 1–13 Rev. ch. 20	Isa. 26. 1–13 Matt. 12. 22–37	
P		Isa. 43. 14–end Rev. 21. 1–8	Isa. 28. 1–13 Matt. 12. 38–end	
P		Isa. 44. 1–8 Rev. 21. 9–21	Isa. 28. 14–end Matt. 13. 1–23	

	Sunday Principal Service / Weekday Eucharist	Third Service / Morning Prayer	Second Service / Evening Prayer
6 Friday	Nicholas, Bishop of Myra, *c.* 326		
Pw	Com. Bishop *or* Isa. 29. 17–end / *also* Isa. 61. 1–3 / Ps. 27. 1–4, 16–17 / 1 Tim. 6. 6–11 / Matt. 9. 27–31 / Mark 10. 13–16	Ps. *25*; 26 / *alt.* Ps. 17; *19* / Isa. 44. 9–23 / Rev. 21.22 – 22.5	Ps. 16; *17* / *alt.* Ps. 22 / Isa. 29. 1–14 / Matt. 13. 24–43
7 Saturday	Ambrose, Bishop of Milan, Teacher, 397		
Pw	Com. Teacher *or* Isa. 30. 19–21, 23–26 / *also* Isa. 41. 9b–13 / Ps. 146. 4–9 / Luke 22. 24–30 / Matt. 9.35 – 10.1, 6–8	Ps. *9*; 10 / *alt.* Ps. 20; 21; *23* / Isa. 44.24 – 45.13 / Rev. 22. 6–end	Ps. *27*; 28 / *alt.* Ps. *24*; 25 / Isa. 29. 15–end / Matt. 13. 44–end / ct
8 Sunday	THE SECOND SUNDAY OF ADVENT		
P	Baruch ch. 5 / *or* Mal. 3. 1–4 / *Canticle*: Benedictus / Phil. 1. 3–11 / Luke 3. 1–6	Ps. 80 / Isa. 64. 1–7 / Matt. 11. 2–11	Ps. 75; [76] / Isa. 40. 1–11 / Luke 1. 1–25
9 Monday			
P	Isa. ch. 35 / Ps. 85. 7–end / Luke 5. 17–26	Ps. 44 / *alt.* Ps. 27; *30* / Isa. 45. 14–end / 1 Thess. ch. 1	Ps. *144*; 146 / *alt.* Ps. 26; *28*; 29 / Isa. 30. 1–18 / Matt. 14. 1–12
10 Tuesday			
P	Isa. 40. 1–11 / Ps. 96. 1, 10–end / Matt. 18. 12–14	Ps. *56*; 57 / *alt.* Ps. 32; *36* / Isa. ch. 46 / 1 Thess. 2. 1–12	Ps. *11*; 12; 13 / *alt.* Ps. 33 / Isa. 30. 19–end / Matt. 14. 13–end
11 Wednesday	Ember Day*		
P	Isa. 40. 25–end / Ps. 103. 8–13 / Matt. 11. 28–end	Ps. *62*; 63 / *alt.* Ps. 34 / Isa. ch. 47 / 1 Thess. 2. 13–end	Ps. *10*; 14 / *alt.* Ps. 119. 33–56 / Isa. ch. 31 / Matt. 15. 1–20
12 Thursday			
P	Isa. 41. 13–20 / Ps. 145. 1, 8–13 / Matt. 11. 11–15	Ps. 53; *54*; 60 / *alt.* Ps. 37† / Isa. 48. 1–11 / 1 Thess. ch. 3	Ps. 73 / *alt.* Ps. 39; *40* / Isa. ch. 32 / Matt. 15. 21–28
13 Friday	Lucy, Martyr at Syracuse, 304 / Ember Day* / *Samuel Johnson, Moralist, 1784*		
Pr	Com. Martyr *or* Isa. 48. 17–19 / *also* Wisd. 3. 1–7 / Ps. 1 / 2 Cor. 4. 6–15 / Matt. 11. 16–19	Ps. 85; *86* / *alt.* Ps. 31 / Isa. 48. 12–end / 1 Thess. 4. 1–12	Ps. 82; *90* / *alt.* Ps. 35 / Isa. 33. 1–22 / Matt. 15. 29–end

*For Ember Day provision, see p. 11.

	Calendar and Holy Communion	Morning Prayer	Evening Prayer	NOTES
	Nicholas, Bishop of Myra, c. 326			
Pw	Com. Bishop	Isa. 44. 9–23	Isa. 29. 1–14	
		Rev. 21.22 – 22.5	Matt. 13. 24–43	
P		Isa. 44.24 – 45.13	Isa. 29. 15–end	
		Rev. 22. 6–end	Matt. 13. 44–end	
			ct	
	THE SECOND SUNDAY IN ADVENT			
P	2 Kings 22. 8–10; 23. 1–3	Ps. 40	Ps. 75 [76]	
	Ps. 50. 1–6	Isa. 64. 1–7	Mal. 3. 1–4	
	Rom. 15. 4–13	Luke 3. 1–6	Luke 1. 1–25	
	Luke 21. 25–33			
P		Isa. 45. 14–end	Isa. 30. 1–18	
		1 Thess. ch. 1	Matt. 14. 1–12	
P		Isa. ch. 46	Isa. 30. 19–end	
		1 Thess. 2. 1–12	Matt. 14. 13–end	
P		Isa. ch. 47	Isa. ch. 31	
		1 Thess. 2. 13–end	Matt. 15. 1–20	
P		Isa. 48. 1–11	Isa. ch. 32	
		1 Thess. ch. 3	Matt. 15. 21–28	
	Lucy, Martyr at Syracuse, 304			
Pr	Com. Virgin Martyr	Isa. 48. 12–end	Isa. 33. 1–22	
		1 Thess. 4. 1–12	Matt. 15. 29–end	

		Sunday Principal Service Weekday Eucharist	Third Service Morning Prayer	Second Service Evening Prayer
14 Saturday		John of the Cross, Poet, Teacher, 1591 Ember Day*		
Pw	Com. Teacher *or* *esp.* 1 Cor. 2. 1–10 *also* John 14. 18–23	Ecclus. 48. 1–4, 9–11 or 2 Kings 2. 9–12 Ps. 80. 1–4, 18–19 Matt. 17. 10–13	Ps. 145 *alt.* Ps. 41; **42**; 43 Isa. 49. 1–13 1 Thess. 4. 13–end	Ps. 93; **94** *alt.* Ps. 45; **46** Isa. ch. 35 Matt. 16. 1–12 **ct**
15 Sunday		**THE THIRD SUNDAY OF ADVENT**		
P		Zeph. 3. 14–end *Canticle:* Isa. 12. 2–end or Ps. 146. 4–end Phil. 4. 4–7 Luke 3. 7–18	Ps. 12; 14 Isa. 25. 1–9 1 Cor. 4. 1–5	Ps. 50. 1–6; [62] Isa. ch. 35 Luke 1. 57–66 [67–end]
16 Monday				
P		Num. 24. 2–7, 15–17 Ps. 25. 3–8 Matt. 21. 23–27	Ps. 40 *alt.* Ps. 44 Isa. 49. 14–25 1 Thess. 5. 1–11	Ps. 25; **26** *alt.* Ps. **47**; 49 Isa. 38. 1–8, 21–22 Matt. 16. 13–end
17 Tuesday	O Sapientia *Eglantyne Jebb, Social Reformer, Founder of 'Save the Children', 1928*			
P		Gen. 49. 2, 8–10 Ps. 72. 1–5, 18–19 Matt. 1. 1–17	Ps. **70**; 74 *alt.* Ps. **48**; 52 Isa. ch. 50 1 Thess. 5. 12–end	Ps. **50**; 54 *alt.* Ps. 50 Isa. 38. 9–20 Matt. 17. 1–13
18 Wednesday				
P		Jer. 23. 5–8 Ps. 72. 1–2, 12–13, 18–end Matt. 1. 18–24	Ps. **75**; 96 *alt.* Ps. 119. 57–80 Isa. 51. 1–8 2 Thess. ch. 1	Ps. 25; **82** *alt.* Ps. **59**; 60; (67) Isa. ch. 39 Matt. 17. 14–21
19 Thursday				
P		Judg. 13. 2–7, 24–end Ps. 71. 3–8 Luke 1. 5–25	Ps. 144; **146** Isa. 51. 9–16 2 Thess. ch. 2	Ps. 10; **57** Zeph. 1.1 – 2.3 Matt. 17. 22–end
20 Friday				
P		Isa. 7. 10–14 Ps. 24. 1–6 Luke 1. 26–38	Ps. **46**; 95 Isa. 51. 17–end 2 Thess. ch. 3	Ps. **4**; 9 Zeph. 3. 1–13 Matt. 18. 1–20
21 Saturday**				
P		Zeph. 3. 14–18 Ps. 33. 1–4, 11–12, 20–end Luke 1. 39–45	Ps. **121**; 122; 123 Isa. 52. 1–12 Jude	Ps. 80; **84** Zeph. 3. 14–end Matt. 18. 21–end **ct**

*For Ember Day provision, see p. 11.
**Thomas the Apostle may be celebrated on 21 December instead of 3 July.

	Calendar and Holy Communion	Morning Prayer	Evening Prayer	NOTES
P		Isa. 49. 1–13 1 Thess. 4. 13–end	Isa. ch. 35 Matt. 16. 1–12	
			ct	
	THE THIRD SUNDAY IN ADVENT			
P	Isa. ch. 35 Ps. 80. 1–7 1 Cor. 4. 1–5 Matt. 11. 2–10	Ps. 12; 14 Isa. 25. 1–9 Luke 3. 7–18	Ps. 62 Zeph. 3. 14–end Luke 1. 57–66 [67–end]	
	O Sapientia			
P		Isa. 49. 14–25 1 Thess. 5. 1–11	Isa. 38. 1–8, 21–22 Matt. 16. 13–end	
P		Isa. ch. 50 1 Thess. 5. 12–end	Isa. 38. 9–20 Matt. 17. 1–13	
	Ember Day			
P	Ember CEG	Isa. 51. 1–8 2 Thess. ch. 1	Isa. ch. 39 Matt. 17. 14–21	
P		Isa. 51. 9–16 2 Thess. ch. 2	Zeph. 1.1 – 2.3 Matt. 17. 22–end	
	Ember Day			
P	Ember CEG	Isa. 51. 17–end 2 Thess. ch. 3	Zeph. 3. 1–13 Matt. 18. 1–20 *or First EP of Thomas* (Ps. 27) Isa. ch. 35 Heb. 10.35 – 11.1 **R ct**	
	THOMAS THE APOSTLE Ember Day			
R	Job 42. 1–6 Ps. 139. 1–11 Eph. 2. 19–end John 20. 24–end	(Ps. 92; 146) 2 Sam. 15. 17–21 *or* Ecclus. ch. 2 John 11. 1–16	(Ps. 139) Hab. 2. 1–4 1 Pet. 1. 3–12	

		Sunday Principal Service Weekday Eucharist	Third Service Morning Prayer	Second Service Evening Prayer
22 Sunday	**THE FOURTH SUNDAY OF ADVENT**			
P		Mic. 5. 2–5a *Canticle*: Magnificat or Ps. 80. 1–8 Heb. 10. 5–10 Luke 1. 39–45 [46–55]	Ps. 144 Isa. 32. 1–8 Rev. 22. 6–end	Ps. 123; [131] Isa. 10.33 – 11.10 Matt. 1. 18–end
23 Monday				
P		Mal. 3. 1–4; 4. 5–end Ps. 25. 3–9 Luke 1. 57–66	Ps. 128; 129; *130*; 131 Isa. 52.13 – 53.end 2 Pet. 1. 1–15	Ps. 89. 1–37 Mal. 1. 1, 6–end Matt. 19. 1–12
24 Tuesday	**CHRISTMAS EVE**			
P		*Morning Eucharist* 2 Sam. 7. 1–5, 8–11, 16 Ps. 89. 2, 19–27 Acts 13. 16–26 Luke 1. 67–79	Ps. *45*; 113 Isa. ch. 54 2 Pet. 1.16 – 2.3	Ps. 85 Zech. ch. 2 Rev. 1. 1–8
25 Wednesday	**CHRISTMAS DAY**			
w		*Any of the following sets of readings may be used on the evening of Christmas Eve and on Christmas Day. Set III should be used at some service during the celebration.* *I* Isa. 9. 2–7 Ps. 96 Titus 2. 11–14 Luke 2. 1–14 [15–20] *II* Isa. 62. 6–end Ps. 97 Titus 3. 4–7 Luke 2. [1–7] 8–20 *III* Isa. 52. 7–10 Ps. 98 Heb. 1. 1–4 [5–12] John 1. 1–14	*MP*: Ps. *110*; 117 Isa. 62. 1–5 Matt. 1. 18–end	*EP*: Ps. 8 Isa. 65. 17–25 Phil. 2. 5–11 or Luke 2. 1–20 *if it has not been used at the principal service of the day*
26 Thursday	**STEPHEN, DEACON, FIRST MARTYR**			
R		2 Chron. 24. 20–22 or Acts 7. 51–end Ps. 119. 161–168 Acts 7. 51–end or Gal. 2. 16b–20 Matt. 10. 17–22	*MP*: Ps. *13*; 31. 1–8; 150 Jer. 26. 12–15 Acts ch. 6	*EP*: Ps. 57; *86* Gen. 4. 1–10 Matt. 23. 34–end
27 Friday	**JOHN, APOSTLE AND EVANGELIST**			
W		Exod. 33. 7–11a Ps. 117 1 John ch. 1 John 21. 19b–end	*MP*: Ps. *21*; 147. 13–end Exod. 33. 12–end 1 John 2. 1–11	*EP*: Ps. 97 Isa. 6. 1–8 1 John 5. 1–12

	Calendar and Holy Communion	Morning Prayer	Evening Prayer

THE FOURTH SUNDAY IN ADVENT

P	Isa. 40. 1–9	Ps. 144	Ps. 123; [131]
	Ps. 145. 17–end	Isa. 32. 1–8	Isa. 10.33 – 11.10
	Phil. 4. 4–7	Rev. 22. 6–end	Matt. 1. 18–end
	John 1. 19–28		

P		Isa. 52.13 – 53.end	Mal. 1. 1, 6–end
		2 Pet. 1. 1–15	Matt. 19. 1–12

CHRISTMAS EVE

P	Collect	Isa. ch. 54	Zech. ch. 2
	(1) Christmas Eve	2 Pet. 1.16 – 2.3	Rev. 1. 1–8
	(2) Advent 1		
	Mic. 5. 2–5a		
	Ps. 24		
	Titus 3. 3–7		
	Luke 2. 1–14		

CHRISTMAS DAY

𝔴	Isa. 9. 2–7	Ps. 110; 117	Ps. 8
	Ps. 98	Isa. 62. 1–5	Isa. 65. 17–25
	Heb. 1. 1–12	Matt. 1. 18–end	Phil. 2. 5–11
	John 1. 1–14		or Luke 2. 1–20

STEPHEN, DEACON, FIRST MARTYR

R	Collect	(Ps. 13; 31. 1–8; 150)	(Ps. 57; 86)
	(1) Stephen	Jer. 26. 12–15	Gen. 4. 1–10
	(2) Christmas	Acts ch. 6	Matt. 10. 17–22
	2 Chron. 24. 20–22		
	Ps. 119. 161–168		
	Acts 7. 55–end		
	Matt. 23. 34–end		

JOHN, APOSTLE AND EVANGELIST

W	Collect	(Ps. 21; 147. 13–end)	(Ps. 97)
	(1) John	Exod. 33. 7–11a	Isa. 6. 1–8
	(2) Christmas	1 John 2. 1–11	1 John 5. 1–12
	Exod. 33. 18–end		
	Ps. 92. 11–end		
	1 John ch. 1		
	John 21. 19b–end		

NOTES

	Sunday Principal Service Weekday Eucharist	Third Service Morning Prayer	Second Service Evening Prayer
28 Saturday	**THE HOLY INNOCENTS**		
R	Jer. 31. 15–17 Ps. 124 1 Cor. 1. 26–29 Matt. 2. 13–18	*MP*: Ps. *36*; 146 Baruch 4. 21–27 *or* Gen. 37. 13–20 Matt. 18. 1–10	*EP*: Ps. 123; *128* Isa. 49. 14–25 Mark 10. 13–16
29 Sunday	**THE FIRST SUNDAY OF CHRISTMAS**		
W	1 Sam. 2. 18–20, 26 Ps. 148 (or 148. 1–6) Col. 3. 12–17 Luke 2. 41–end	Ps. 105. 1–11 Isa. 41.21 – 42.1 1 John 1. 1–7	Ps. 132 Isa. ch. 61 Gal. 3.27 – 4.7 *Gospel:* Luke 2. 15–21
30 Monday			
W	1 John 2. 12–17 Ps. 96. 7–10 Luke 2. 36–40	Ps. 111; 112; *113* Isa. 59. 1–15a John 1. 19–28	Ps. *65*; 84 Jonah ch. 2 Col. 1. 15–23
31 Tuesday	*John Wyclif, Reformer, 1384*		
W	1 John 2. 18–21 Ps. 96. 1, 11–end John 1. 1–18	Ps. 102 Isa. 59. 15b–end John 1. 29–34	Ps. *90*; 148 Jonah chs 3 & 4 Col. 1.24 – 2.7 *or First EP of The Naming of Jesus* Ps. 148 Jer. 23. 1–6 Col. 2. 8–15 **ct**

	Calendar and Holy Communion	Morning Prayer	Evening Prayer	NOTES
	THE HOLY INNOCENTS			
R	Collect (1) Innocents (2) Christmas Jer. 31. 10–17 Ps. 123 Rev. 14. 1–5 Matt. 2. 13–18	(Ps. 36; 146) Baruch 4. 21–27 *or* Gen. 37. 13–20 Matt. 18. 1–10	(Ps. 124; 128) Isa. 49. 14–25 Mark 10. 13–16	
	THE SUNDAY AFTER CHRISTMAS DAY			
W	Isa. 62. 10–12 Ps. 45. 1–7 Gal. 4. 1–7 Matt. 1. 18–end	Ps. 105. 1–11 Isa. 41.21 – 42.1 1 John 1. 1–7	Ps. 132 Isa. ch. 61 Luke 2. 15–21	
W		Isa. 59. 1–15a John 1. 19–28	Jonah ch. 2 Col. 1. 15–23	
	Silvester, Bishop of Rome, 335			
W	Com. Bishop	Isa. 59. 15b–end John 1. 29–34	Jonah chs 3 & 4 Col. 1.24 – 2.7 *or First EP of The Circumcision of Christ* (Ps. 148) Jer. 23. 1–6 Col. 2. 8–15 **ct**	

The *Common Worship* Additional Weekday Lectionary

The Additional Weekday Lectionary provides two readings on a one-year cycle for each day (except for Sundays, Principal Feasts and Holy Days, Festivals and Holy Week). They 'stand alone' and are intended particularly for use in those churches and cathedrals that attract occasional rather than regular congregations. The Additional Weekday Lectionary has been designed to complement rather than replace the existing Weekday Lectionary. Thus a church with a regular congregation in the morning and a congregation made up mainly of visitors in the evening would continue to use the Weekday Lectionary in the morning but might choose to use this Additional Weekday Lectionary for Evening Prayer.

Psalms are not provided, since the Weekday Lectionary already offers a variety of approaches with regard to psalmody. This Lectionary is not intended for use at the Eucharist; the Daily Eucharistic Lectionary is already authorized for that purpose.

On Sundays, Principal Feasts, other Principal Holy Days, Festivals, and in Holy Week, where no readings are provided in this table, the lectionary provision in the main part of this volume should be used.

Date	Old Testament	New Testament
December 2023		
3 S	THE FIRST SUNDAY OF ADVENT	
4 M	Mal. 3. 1–6	Matt. 3. 1–6
5 Tu	Zeph. 3. 14–end	1 Thess. 4. 13–end
6 W	Isa. 65.17 – 66.2	Matt. 24. 1–14
7 Th	Mic. 5. 2–5a	John 3. 16–21
8 F	Isa. 66. 18–end	Luke 13. 22–30
9 Sa	Mic. 7. 8–15	Rom. 15.30 – 16.7, 25–end
10 S	THE SECOND SUNDAY OF ADVENT	
11 M	Jer. 7. 1–11	Phil. 4. 4–9
12 Tu	Dan. 7. 9–14	Matt. 24. 15–28
13 W	Amos 9. 11–end	Rom. 13. 8–14
14 Th	Jer. 23. 5–8	Mark 11. 1–11
15 F	Jer. 33. 14–22	Luke 21. 25–36
16 Sa	Zech. 14. 4–11	Rev. 22. 1–7
17 S	THE THIRD SUNDAY OF ADVENT	
18 M	Exod. 3. 1–6	Acts 7. 20–36
19 Tu	Isa. 11. 1–9	Rom. 15. 7–13
20 W	Isa. 22. 21–23	Rev. 3. 7–13
21 Th	Num. 24. 15b–19	Rev. 22. 10–21
22 F	Jer. 30. 7–11a	Acts 4. 1–12
23 Sa	Isa. 7. 10–15	Matt. 1. 18–23
24 S	THE FOURTH SUNDAY OF ADVENT **(Christmas Eve)**	
25 M	**CHRISTMAS DAY**	
26 Tu	STEPHEN	
27 W	JOHN THE EVANGELIST	
28 Th	THE HOLY INNOCENTS	
29 F	Mic. 1. 1–4; 2. 12–13	Luke 2. 1–7
30 Sa	Isa. 9. 2–7	John 8. 12–20
31 S	THE FIRST SUNDAY OF CHRISTMAS	
January 2024		
1 M	**NAMING AND CIRCUMCISION OF JESUS**	
2 Tu	Isa. 66. 6–14	Matt. 12. 46–50
3 W	Deut. 6. 4–15	John 10. 31–end
4 Th	Isa. 63. 7–16	Gal. 3.23 – 4.7
5 F	At Evening prayer, the readings for the Eve of Epiphany are used. At other services, or where, for pastoral reasons, The Epiphany is celebrated on Sunday 8 January, the following readings are used:	
	Isa. ch. 12	2 Cor. 2. 12–end
6 Sa	**THE EPIPHANY**	
	Where The Epiphany is celebrated on Sunday 7 January, the readings for the Eve of The Epiphany are used at Evening Prayer. At other services, the following readings are used:	
	Gen. 25. 19–end	Eph. 1. 1–6
7 S	THE BAPTISM OF CHRIST (The First Sunday of Epiphany)	
8 M	Where The Epiphany is celebrated on Saturday 6 January and the Baptism of Christ on Sunday 7 January, these readings are used on Monday 8 January:	
	Isa. 41. 14–20	John 1. 29–34
	Where The Epiphany is celebrated on Sunday 7 January, The Baptism of Christ is transferred to	

Date	Old Testament	New Testament
	Monday 8 January.	
9 Tu	Exod. 17. 1–7	Acts 8. 26–end
10 W	Exod. 15. 1–19	Col. 2. 8–15
11 Th	Zech. 6. 9–15	1 Pet. 2. 4–10
12 F	Isa. 51. 7–16	Gal. 6. 14–18
13 Sa	Lev. 16. 11–22	Heb. 10. 19–25
14 S	THE SECOND SUNDAY OF EPIPHANY	
15 M	1 Kings 17. 8–16	Mark 8. 1–10
16 Tu	1 Kings 19. 1–9a	Mark 1. 9–15
17 W	1 Kings 19. 9b–18	Mark 9. 2–13
18 Th	Lev. 11. 1–8, 13–19, 41–45	Acts 10. 9–16
19 F	Isa. 49. 8–13	Acts 10. 34–43
20 Sa	Gen. 35. 1–15	Acts 10. 44–end
21 S	THE THIRD SUNDAY OF EPIPHANY	
22 M	Ezek. 37. 15–end	John 17. 1–19
23 Tu	Ezek. 20. 39–44	John 17. 20–end
24 W	Neh. 2. 1–10	Rom. 12. 1–8
25 Th	THE CONVERSION OF PAUL	
26 F	Lev. 19. 9–28	Rom. 15. 1–7
27 Sa	Jer. 33. 1–11	1 Pet. 5. 5b–end
	or, where The Presentation is celebrated on Sunday 28 January, First EP of Presentation of Christ	
28 S	THE FOURTH SUNDAY OF EPIPHANY (or The Presentation)	
29 M	Jonah ch. 3	2 Cor. 5. 11–21
30 Tu	Prov. 4. 10–end	Matt. 5. 13–20
31 W	Isa. 61. 1–9	Luke 7. 18–30
February 2024		
1 Th	Isa. 52. 1–12	Matt. 10. 1–15
2 F	**THE PRESENTATION** or	
	Isa. 56. 1–8	Matt. 28. 16–end
3 Sa	Hab. 2. 1–4	Rev. 14. 1–7
4 S	THE SECOND SUNDAY BEFORE LENT	
5 M	Isa. 61. 1–9	Mark 6. 1–13
6 Tu	Isa. 52. 1–10	Rom. 10. 5–21
7 W	Isa. 52.13 – 53.6	Rom. 15. 14–21
8 Th	Isa. 53. 4–12	2 Cor. 4. 1–10
9 F	Zech. 8. 16–end	Matt. 10. 1–15
10 Sa	Jer. 1. 4–10	Matt. 10. 16–22
11 S	THE SUNDAY NEXT BEFORE LENT	
12 M	2 Kings 2. 13–22	3 John
13 Tu	Judg. 14. 5–17	Rev. 10. 4–11
14 W	**ASH WEDNESDAY**	
15 Th	Gen. 2. 7–end	Heb. 2. 5–end
16 F	Gen. 4. 1–12	Heb. 4. 12–end
17 Sa	2 Kings 22. 11–end	Heb. 5. 1–10
18 S	THE FIRST SUNDAY OF LENT	
19 M	Gen. 6. 11–end; 7. 11–16	Luke 4. 14–21
20 Tu	Deut. 31. 7–13	1 John 3. 1–10
21 W	Gen. 11. 1–9	Matt. 24. 15–28
22 Th	Gen. 13. 1–13	1 Pet. 2. 13–end
23 F	Gen. 21. 1–8	Luke 9. 18–27
24 Sa	Gen. 32. 22–32	2 Pet. 1. 10–end
25 S	THE SECOND SUNDAY OF LENT	
26 M	1 Chron. 21. 1–17	1 John 2. 1–8
27 Tu	Zech. ch. 3	2 Pet. 2. 1–10a

| 28 | W | Job. 1. 1–22 | Luke 21.34 – 22.6 |
| 29 | Th | 2 Chron. 29. 1–11 | Mark 11. 15–19 |

March 2024

1	F	Exod. 19. 1–9a	1 Pet. 1. 1–9
2	Sa	Exod. 19. 9b–19	Acts 7. 44–50
3	S	THE THIRD SUNDAY OF LENT	
4	M	Josh. 4. 1–13	Luke 9. 1–11
5	Tu	Exod. 15. 22–27	Heb. 10. 32–end
6	W	Gen. 9. 8–17	1 Pet. 3. 18–end
7	Th	Dan. 12. 5–end	Mark 13. 21–end
8	F	Num. 20. 1–13	1 Cor. 10. 23–end
9	Sa	Isa. 43. 14–end	Heb. 3. 1–15
10	S	THE FOURTH SUNDAY OF LENT (Mothering Sunday)	
11	M	2 Kings 24.18 – 25.7	1 Cor. 15. 20–34
12	Tu	Jer. 13. 12–19	Acts 13. 26–35
13	W	Jer. 13. 20–27	1 Pet. 1.17 – 2.3
14	Th	Jer. 22. 11–19	Luke 11. 37–52
15	F	Jer. 17. 1–14	Luke 6. 17–26
16	Sa	Ezra ch. 1	2 Cor. 1. 12–19
17	S	THE FIFTH SUNDAY OF LENT (Passiontide begins)	
18	M	Joel 2. 12–17	2 John
19	Tu	JOSEPH OF NAZARETH	
20	W	Joel 36. 1–12	John 14. 1–14
21	Th	Jer. 9. 17–22	Luke 13. 31–35
22	F	Lam. 5. 1–3, 19–22	John 12. 20–26
23	Sa	Job 17. 6–end	John 12. 27–36
24	S	PALM SUNDAY	
		HOLY WEEK	
31	S	**EASTER DAY**	

April 2024

1	M	Isa. 54. 1–14	Rom. 1. 1–7
2	Tu	Isa. 51. 1–11	John 5. 19–29
3	W	Isa. 26. 1–19	John 20. 1–10
4	Th	Isa. 43. 14–21	Rev. 1. 4–end
5	F	Isa. 42. 10–17	1 Thess. 5. 1–11
6	Sa	Job 14. 1–14	John 21. 1–14
7	S	THE SECOND SUNDAY OF EASTER	
8	M	**THE ANNUNCIATION** (transferred from 25 March)	
9	Tu	Prov. 8. 1–11	Acts 16. 6–15
10	W	Hos. 5.15 – 6.6	1 Cor. 15. 1–11
11	Th	Jonah ch. 2	Mark 4. 35–end
12	F	Gen. 6. 9–end	1 Pet. 3. 8–end
13	Sa	1 Sam. 2. 1–8	Matt. 28. 8–15
14	S	THE THIRD SUNDAY OF EASTER	
15	M	Exod. 24. 1–11	Rev. ch. 5
16	Tu	Lev. 19. 9–18, 32–end	Matt. 5. 38–end
17	W	Gen. 3. 8–21	1 Cor. 15. 12–28
18	Th	Isa. 33. 13–22	Mark 6. 47–end
19	F	Neh. 9. 6–17	Rom. 5. 12–end
20	Sa	Isa. 61.10 – 62.5	Luke 24. 1–12
21	S	THE FOURTH SUNDAY OF EASTER	
22	M	Jer. 31. 10–17	Rev. 7. 9–end
23	Tu	GEORGE	
24	W	Gen. 2. 4b–9	1 Cor. 15. 35–49
25	Th	MARK	
26	F	Eccles. 12. 1–8	Rom. 6. 1–11
27	Sa	1 Chron. 29. 10–13	Luke 24. 13–35
28	S	THE FIFTH SUNDAY OF EASTER	
29	M	Gen. 15. 1–18	Rom. 4. 13–end
30	Tu	Deut. 8. 1–10	Matt. 6. 19–end

May 2024

1	W	PHILIP AND JAMES	
2	Th	Exod. 3. 1–15	Mark 12. 18–27
3	F	Ezek. 36. 33–end	Rom. 8. 1–11
4	Sa	Isa. 38. 9–20	Luke 24. 33–end
5	S	THE SIXTH SUNDAY OF EASTER	
6	M	Prov. 4. 1–13	Phil. 2. 1–11
7	Tu	Isa. 32. 12–end	Rom. 1. 1–11

8	W	At Evening Prayer, the readings for the Eve of Ascension Day are used. At other services, the following readings are used:	
		Isa. 43. 1–13	Titus 2.11 – 3.8
9	Th	**ASCENSION DAY**	
10	F	Exod. 35.30 – 36.1	Gal. 5. 13–end
11	Sa	Num. 11. 16–17, 24–29	1 Cor. ch. 2
12	S	THE SEVENTH SUNDAY OF EASTER (Sunday after Ascension Day)	
13	M	Num. 27. 15–end	1 Cor. ch. 3
14	Tu	MATTHIAS	
		Where Matthias is celebrated on Monday 25 February:	
		1 Sam. 10. 1–10	1 Cor. 12. 1–13
15	W	1 Kings 19. 1–18	Matt. 3. 13–end
16	Th	Ezek. 11. 14–20	Matt. 9.35 – 10.20
17	F	Ezek. 36. 22–28	Matt. 12. 22–32
18	Sa	At Evening Prayer, the readings for the Eve of Pentecost are used. At other services, the following readings are used:	
		Mic. 3. 1–8	Eph. 6. 10–20
19	S	**PENTECOST** (Whit Sunday)	
20	M	Gen. 12. 1–9	Rom. 4. 13–end
21	Tu	Gen. 13. 1–12	Rom. 12. 9–end
22	W	Gen. ch. 15	Rom. 4. 1–8
23	Th	Gen. 22. 1–18	Heb. 11. 8–19
24	F	Isa. 51. 1–8	John 8. 48–end
25	Sa	At Evening Prayer, the readings for the Eve of Trinity Sunday are used. At other services, the following readings are used:	
		Ecclus. 44. 19–23	Jas. 2. 14–26
		or Josh. 2. 1–15	
26	S	**TRINITY SUNDAY**	
27	M	Exod. 2. 1–10	Heb. 11. 23–31
28	Tu	Exod. 2. 11–end	Acts 7. 17–29
29	W	Exod. 3. 1–12	Acts 7. 30–38
30	Th	Day of Thanksgiving for the Institution of Holy Communion (Corpus Christi) or, where Corpus Christi is celebrated as a Lesser Festival:	
		Exod. 6. 1–13	John 9. 24–38
31	F	THE VISITATION	

June 2024

1	Sa	Exod. 34. 27–end	2 Cor. 3. 7–end
2	S	THE FIRST SUNDAY AFTER TRINITY	
3	M	Gen. 37. 1–11	Rom. 11. 9–21
4	Tu	Gen. 41. 15–40	Mark 13. 1–13
5	W	Gen. 42. 17–end	Matt. 18. 1–14
6	Th	Gen. 45. 1–15	Acts 7. 9–16
7	F	Gen. 47. 1–12	1 Thess. 5. 12–end
8	Sa	Gen. 50. 4–21	Luke 15. 11–end
9	S	THE SECOND SUNDAY AFTER TRINITY	
10	M	Isa. ch. 32	Jas. 3. 13–end
11	Tu	BARNABAS	
12	W	Judg. 6. 1–16	Matt. 5. 13–24
13	Th	Jer. 6. 9–15	1 Tim. 2. 1–6
14	F	1 Sam. 16. 14–end	John 14. 15–end
15	Sa	Isa. 6. 1–9	Rev. 19. 9–end
16	S	THE THIRD SUNDAY AFTER TRINITY	
17	M	Exod. 13. 13b–end	Luke 15. 1–10
18	Tu	Prov. 1. 20–end	Jas. 5. 13–end
19	W	Gen. 5. 8–24	Jas. 1. 17–25
20	Th	Isa. 57. 14–end	John 13. 1–17
21	F	Jer. 15. 15–end	Luke 16. 19–31
22	Sa	Isa. 25. 1–9	Acts 2. 22–33
23	S	THE FOURTH SUNDAY AFTER TRINITY	
24	M	THE BIRTH OF JOHN THE BAPTIST	
25	Tu	Prov. 6. 6–19	Luke 4. 1–14
26	W	Isa. 24. 1–15	1 Cor. 6. 1–11
27	Th	Job ch. 7	Matt. 7. 21–29
28	F	Jer. 20. 7–end	Matt. 27. 27–44
29	Sa	PETER AND PAUL	
30	S	THE FIFTH SUNDAY AFTER TRINITY	

July 2024

		First Reading	Second Reading
1	M	Exod. 32. 1–14	Col. 3. 1–11
2	Tu	Prov. 9. 1–12	2 Thess. 2.13 – 3.5
3	W	THOMAS	
		Where Thomas is celebrated on 21 December:	
		Isa. 26. 1–9	Rom. 8. 12–27
4	Th	Jer. 8.18 – 9.6	John 13. 21–35
5	F	2 Sam. 5. 1–12	Matt. 27. 45–56
6	Sa	Hos. 11. 1–11	Matt. 28. 1–7
7	S	THE SIXTH SUNDAY AFTER TRINITY	
8	M	Exod. 40. 1–16	Luke 14. 15–24
9	Tu	Prov. 11. 1–12	Mark 12. 38–44
10	W	Isa. 33. 2–10	Phil. 1. 1–11
11	Th	Job ch. 38	Luke 18. 1–14
12	F	Job 42. 1–6	John 3. 1–15
13	Sa	Eccles. 9. 1–11	Heb. 1. 1–9
14	S	THE SEVENTH SUNDAY AFTER TRINITY	
15	M	Num. 23. 1–12	1 Cor. 1. 10–17
16	Tu	Prov. 12. 1–12	Gal. 3. 1–14
17	W	Isa. 49. 8–13	2 Cor. 8. 1–11
18	Th	Hos. ch. 14	John 15. 1–17
19	F	2 Sam. 18. 18–end	Matt. 27. 57–66
20	Sa	Isa. 55. 1–7	Mark 6. 1–8
21	S	THE EIGHTH SUNDAY AFTER TRINITY	
22	M	MARY MAGDALENE	
23	Tu	Prov. 12. 13–end	John 1. 43–51
24	W	Isa. 55. 8–end	2 Tim. 2. 8–19
25	Th	JAMES	
26	F	Jer. 14. 1–9	Luke 8. 4–15
27	Sa	Eccles. 5. 10–19	1 Tim. 6. 6–16
28	S	THE NINTH SUNDAY AFTER TRINITY	
29	M	Josh. 1. 1–9	1 Cor. 9. 19–end
30	Tu	Prov. 15. 1–11	Gal. 2. 15–end
31	W	Isa. 49. 1–7	1 John 1

August 2024

		First Reading	Second Reading
1	Th	Prov. 27. 1–12	John 15. 12–27
2	F	Isa. 59. 8–end	Mark 15. 6–20
3	Sa	Zech. 7.8 – 8.8	Luke 20. 27–40
4	S	THE TENTH SUNDAY AFTER TRINITY	
5	M	Judg. 13. 1–23	Luke 10. 38–42
6	Tu	THE TRANSFIGURATION	
7	W	Isa. 49. 1–7	Eph. 4. 1–16
8	Th	Jer. 16. 1–5	Luke 12. 35–48
9	F	Jer. 18. 1–11	Heb. 1. 1–9
10	Sa	Jer. 26. 1–19	Eph. 3. 1–13
11	S	THE ELEVENTH SUNDAY AFTER TRINITY	
12	M	Ruth 2. 1–13	Luke 10. 25–37
13	Tu	Prov. 16. 1–11	Phil. 3. 4b–end
14	W	Deut. 11. 1–21	2 Cor. 9. 6–end
15	Th	THE BLESSED VIRGIN MARY	
16	F	Obad. 1–16	John 19. 1–16
17	Sa	2 Kings 2. 11–14	Luke 24. 36–end
18	S	THE TWELFTH SUNDAY AFTER TRINITY	
19	M	1 Sam. 17. 32–50	Matt. 8. 14–22
20	Tu	Prov. 17. 1–15	Luke 7. 1–17
21	W	Jer. 5. 20–end	2 Pet. 3. 8–end
22	Th	Dan. 2. 1–23	Luke 10. 1–20
23	F	Dan. 3. 1–28	Rev. ch. 15
24	Sa	BARTHOLOMEW	
25	S	THE THIRTEENTH SUNDAY AFTER TRINITY	
26	M	2 Sam. 7. 4–17	2 Cor. 5. 1–10
27	Tu	Prov. 18. 10–21	Rom. 14. 10–end
28	W	Judg. 4. 1–10	Rom. 1. 8–17
29	Th	Isa. 49. 14–end	John 16. 16–24
30	F	Job 1. 1–24	Mark 15. 21–32
31	Sa	Exod. 19. 1–9	John 20. 11–18

September 2024

		First Reading	Second Reading
1	S	THE FOURTEENTH SUNDAY AFTER TRINITY	
2	M	Hagg. ch. 1	Mark 7. 9–23
3	Tu	Prov. 21. 1–18	Mark 6. 30–44
4	W	Hos. 11. 1–11	1 John 4. 9–end
5	Th	Lam. 3. 34–48	Rom. 7. 14–end
6	F	2 Kings 19. 4–18	1 Thess. ch. 3
7	Sa	Ecclus. 4. 1–28	2 Tim. 3. 10–end
		or Deut. 29. 2–15	
8	S	THE FIFTEENTH SUNDAY AFTER TRINITY	
9	M	Wisd. 6. 12–21	Matt. 15. 1–9
		or Job 12. 1–16	
10	Tu	Prov. 8. 1–11	Luke 6. 39–end
11	W	Prov. 2. 1–15	Col. 1. 9–20
12	Th	Baruch 3. 14–end	John 1. 1–18
		or Gen. 1. 1–13	
13	F	Ecclus. 1. 1–20	1 Cor. 1. 18–end
		or Deut. 7. 7–16	
14	Sa	HOLY CROSS DAY	
15	S	THE SIXTEENTH SUNDAY AFTER TRINITY	
16	M	Gen. 21. 1–13	Luke 1. 26–38
17	Tu	Ruth 4. 7–17	Luke 2. 25–38
18	W	2 Kings 4. 1–7	John 2. 1–11
19	Th	2 Kings 4. 25b–37	Mark 3. 19b–35
20	F	Judith 8. 9–17, 28–36	John 19. 25b–30
		or Ruth 1. 1–18	
21	Sa	MATTHEW	
22	S	THE SEVENTEENTH SUNDAY AFTER TRINITY	
23	M	Exod. 19. 16–end	Heb. 12. 18–end
24	Tu	1 Chron. 16. 1–13	Rev. 11. 15–end
25	W	1 Chron. 29. 10–19	Col. 3. 12–17
26	Th	Neh. 8. 1–12	1 Cor. 14. 1–12
27	F	Isa. 1. 10–17	Mark 12. 28–34
28	Sa	Dan. 6. 6–23	Rev. 12. 7–12
29	S	MICHAEL AND ALL ANGELS *or* THE EIGHTEENTH SUNDAY AFTER TRINITY	
30	M	*Where Michael and All Angels is celebrated on Sunday 29 September:*	
		2 Sam. 22. 4–7, 17–20	Heb. 7.26 – 8.6
		or Michael and All Angels	

October 2024

		First Reading	Second Reading
1	Tu	Prov. 22. 17–end	2 Cor. 12. 1–10
2	W	Hos. ch. 14	Jas. 2. 14–26
3	Th	Isa. 24. 1–15	John 16. 25–33
4	F	Jer. 14. 1–9	Luke 23. 44–56
5	Sa	Zech. 8. 14–end	John 20. 19–end
6	S	THE NINETEENTH SUNDAY AFTER TRINITY	
7	M	1 Kings 3. 3–14	1 Tim. 3.14 – 4.8
8	Tu	Prov. 27. 11–end	Gal. 6. 1–10
9	W	Isa. 51. 1–6	2 Cor. 1. 1–11
10	Th	Ecclus. 18. 1–14	1 Cor. 11. 17–end
		or Job ch. 26	
11	F	Ecclus. 28. 2–12	Mark 15. 33–47
		or Job 19. 21–end	
12	Sa	Isa. 44. 21–end	John 21. 15–end
13	S	THE TWENTIETH SUNDAY AFTER TRINITY	
14	M	1 Kings 6. 2–10	John 12. 1–11
15	Tu	Prov. 31. 10–end	Luke 10. 38–42
16	W	Jonah ch. 1	Luke 5. 1–11
17	Th	Exod. 12. 1–20	1 Thess. 4. 1–12
18	F	LUKE	
19	Sa	2 Sam. 7. 18–end	Acts 2. 22–33
20	S	THE TWENTY-FIRST SUNDAY AFTER TRINITY	
21	M	1 Kings 8. 22–30	John 12. 12–19
22	Tu	Eccles. ch. 11	Luke 13. 10–17
23	W	Hos. 14. 1–7	2 Tim. 4. 1–8
24	Th	Isa. 49. 1–7	John 19. 16–25a
25	F	Prov. 24. 3–22	John 8. 1–11
26	Sa	Ecclus. 7. 8–17, 32–end	2 Tim. 1. 1–14
		or Deut. 6. 16–25	
27	S	THE LAST SUNDAY AFTER TRINITY	
28	M	SIMON AND JUDE	
29	Tu	1 Sam. 4. 12–end	Luke 1. 57–80
30	W	Baruch ch. 5	Mark 1. 1–11
		or Hagg. 1. 1–11	

31	Th	At Evening Prayer, the readings for the Eve of All Saints are used. At other services, the following readings are used:	
		Isa. ch. 35	Matt. 11. 2–19

November 2024

1	F	**ALL SAINTS' DAY**	
		or, where All Saints' Day is celebrated on Sunday 3 November only:	
		2 Sam. 11. 1–17	Matt. 14. 1–12
2	Sa	Isa. 43. 15–21	Acts 19. 1–10
3	S	THE FOURTH SUNDAY BEFORE ADVENT	
4	M	Esth. 3. 1–11; 4. 7–17	Matt. 18. 1–10
5	Tu	Ezek. 18. 21–end	Matt. 18. 12–20
6	W	Prov. 3. 27–end	Matt. 18. 21–end
7	Th	Exod. 23. 1–9	Matt. 19. 1–15
8	F	Prov. 3. 13–18	Matt. 19. 16–end
9	Sa	Deut. 28. 1–6	Matt. 20. 1–16
10	S	THE THIRD SUNDAY BEFORE ADVENT	
11	M	Isa. 40. 21–end	Rom. 11. 25–end
12	Tu	Ezek. 34. 20–end	John 10. 1–18
13	W	Lev. 26. 3–13	Titus 2. 1–10
14	Th	Hos. 6. 1–6	Matt. 9. 9–13
15	F	Mal. ch. 4	John 4. 5–26
16	Sa	Mic. 6. 6–8	Col. 3. 12–17
17	S	THE SECOND SUNDAY BEFORE ADVENT	
18	M	Mic. 7. 1–7	Matt. 10. 24–39
19	Tu	Hab. 3. 1–19a	1 Cor. 4. 9–16
20	W	Zech. 8. 1–13	Mark 13. 3–8
21	Th	Zech. 10. 6–end	1 Pet. 5. 1–11
22	F	Mic. 4. 1–5	Luke 9. 28–36
23	Sa	At Evening Prayer, the readings for the Eve of Christ the King are used. At other services, the following readings are used:	
		Exod. 16. 1–21	John 6. 3–15
24	S	CHRIST THE KING (The Sunday next before Advent)	
25	M	Jer. 30. 1–3, 10–17	Rom. 12. 9–21
26	Tu	Jer. 30. 18–24	John 10. 22–30
27	W	Jer. 31. 1–9	Matt. 15. 21–31
28	Th	Jer. 31. 10–17	Matt. 16. 13–end

29	F	Jer. 31. 31–37	Heb. 10. 11–18
30	Sa	ANDREW	

December 2024

1	S	THE FIRST SUNDAY OF ADVENT	
2	M	Mal. 3. 1–6	Matt. 3. 1–6
3	Tu	Zeph. 3. 14–end	1 Thess. 4. 13–end
4	W	Isa. 65.17 – 66.2	Matt. 24. 1–14
5	Th	Mic. 5. 2–5a	John 3. 16–21
6	F	Isa. 66. 18–end	Luke 13. 22–30
7	Sa	Mic. 7. 8–15	Rom. 15.30 – 16.7, 25–end
8	S	THE SECOND SUNDAY OF ADVENT	
9	M	Jer. 7. 1–11	Phil. 4. 4–9
10	Tu	Dan. 7. 9–14	Matt. 24. 15–28
11	W	Amos 9. 11–end	Rom. 13. 8–14
12	Th	Jer. 23. 5–8	Mark 11. 1–11
13	F	Jer. 33. 14–22	Luke 21. 25–36
14	Sa	Zech. 14. 4–11	Rev. 22. 1–7
15	S	THE THIRD SUNDAY OF ADVENT	
16	M	Isa. 40. 1–11	Matt. 3. 1–12
17	Tu	Ecclus. 24. 1–9 or Prov. 6. 22–31	1 Cor. 2. 1–13
18	W	Exod. 3. 1–6	Acts 7. 20–36
19	Th	Isa. 11. 1–9	Rom. 15. 7–13
20	F	Isa. 22. 21–23	Rev. 3. 7–13
21	Sa	Num. 24. 15b–19	Rev. 22. 10–21
22	S	THE FOURTH SUNDAY OF ADVENT	
23	M	Isa. 7. 10–15	Matt. 1. 18–23
24	Tu	At Evening Prayer, the readings for Christmas Eve are used. At other services, the following readings are used:	
		Isa. 29. 13–18	1 John 4. 7–16
25	W	**CHRISTMAS DAY**	
26	Th	STEPHEN	
27	F	JOHN THE EVANGELIST	
28	Sa	THE HOLY INNOCENTS	
29	S	THE FIRST SUNDAY AFTER CHRISTMAS	
30	M	Isa. 9. 2–7	John 8. 12–20
31	Tu	Eccles. 3. 1–13	Rev. 21. 1–8

CALENDAR 2024

JANUARY · · B E³ E² E¹ / Su · 1 8 15 22 29 / M · 2 9 16 23 30 / Tu · 3 10 17 24 31 / W · 4 11 18 25 · / Th · 5 12 19 26 · / F · 6 13 20 27 · / Sa E 7 14 21 28 ·

FEBRUARY · · L⁻² L⁻¹ L¹ L² / Su · 4 11 18 25 · / M · 5 12 19 26 · / Tu · 6 13 20 27 · / W · 7 14 21 28 · / Th I 8 15 22 29 · / F Pr 9 16 23 · · / Sa 3 10 17 24 · ·

MARCH L³ L⁴ L⁵ P E / Su 3 10 17 24 31 / M 4 11 18 25 · / Tu 5 12 19 26 · / W 6 13 20 27 · / Th 7 14 21 28 M / F 1 8 15 22 29 G / Sa 2 9 16 23 30 ·

APRIL E⁵ T⁹ / Su · 7 14 21 28 / M · 8 15 22 29 / Tu · 9 16 23 30 / W · 10 17 24 · / Th An 11 18 25 · / F 4 12 19 26 · / Sa E 5 13 20 27 ·

MAY T W / Su · 5 12 19 26 · / M · 6 13 20 27 · / Tu · 7 14 21 28 · / W 1 8 15 22 29 · / Th A 9 16 23 30 · / F 3 10 17 24 31 · / Sa 4 11 18 25 · ·

JUNE T¹ T² T³ T⁴ T⁵ / Su · 2 9 16 23 30 / M · 3 10 17 24 · / Tu · 4 11 18 25 · / W · 5 12 19 26 · / Th · 6 13 20 27 · / F · 7 14 21 28 · / Sa 1 8 15 22 29 ·

JULY T⁶ T⁷ T⁸ T⁹ / Su · 7 14 21 28 / M 1 8 15 22 29 / Tu 2 9 16 23 30 / W 3 10 17 24 31 / Th 4 11 18 25 · / F 5 12 19 26 · / Sa 6 13 20 27 ·

AUGUST T¹⁰ T¹¹ T¹² T¹³ / Su · 4 11 18 25 / M · 5 12 19 26 / Tu · 6 13 20 27 / W · 7 14 21 28 / Th 1 8 15 22 29 / F 2 9 16 23 30 / Sa 3 10 17 24 31

SEPTEMBER T¹⁴ T¹⁵ T¹⁶ T¹⁷ T¹⁸ / Su 1 8 15 22 29 / M 2 9 16 23 30 / Tu 3 10 17 24 · / W 4 11 18 25 · / Th 5 12 19 26 · / F 6 13 20 27 · / Sa 7 14 21 28 ·

OCTOBER T¹⁹ T²⁰ T²¹ T⁻ / Su · 6 13 20 27 / M · 7 14 21 28 / Tu 1 8 15 22 29 / W 2 9 16 23 30 / Th 3 10 17 24 31 / F 4 11 18 25 · / Sa 5 12 19 26 ·

NOVEMBER A⁻³ A⁻² A⁻¹ / Su · 3 10 17 24 / M · 4 11 18 25 / Tu · 5 12 19 26 / W · 6 13 20 27 / Th · 7 14 21 28 / F AS 8 15 22 29 / Sa 2 9 16 23 30

DECEMBER A¹ A² A³ A⁴ X¹ / Su 1 8 15 22 29 / M 2 9 16 23 30 / Tu 3 10 17 24 31 / W 4 11 18 25 · / Th 5 12 19 26 · / F 6 13 20 27 · / Sa 7 14 21 28 ·

Legend (2024):

A = Ash Wednesday, Ascension, Advent
A⁻ = Before Advent
A⁻¹ = also All Saints, 2024 and 2025 (if transferred)
A¹ = Christ the King
An = Annunciation
AS = All Saints
B = Baptism
E = Epiphany, Easter
E⁴ = also Presentation, 2024 (if transferred)
G = Good Friday
L = Lent
L⁻ = Before Lent

M = Maundy Thursday
P = Palm Sunday
Pr = Presentation
T = Trinity

CALENDAR 2025

JANUARY X² B E¹ E² E³ / Su · · 5 12 19 26 / M · · 6 13 20 27 / Tu · · 7 14 21 28 / W 1 · 8 15 22 29 / Th 2 E 9 16 23 30 / F 3 · 10 17 24 31 / Sa 4 · 11 18 25 ·

FEBRUARY Pr L⁻³ L⁻² L⁻¹ L⁻ / Su · 2 9 16 23 · / M · 3 10 17 24 · / Tu · 4 11 18 25 · / W · 5 12 19 26 · / Th · 6 13 20 27 · / F · 7 14 21 28 · / Sa 1 8 15 22 · ·

MARCH L¹ L² L³ L⁴ L⁵ / Su · 2 9 16 23 30 / M · 3 10 17 24 31 / Tu · 4 11 18 25 An / W · 5 12 19 26 · / Th · 6 13 20 27 · / F · 7 14 21 28 · / Sa 1 8 15 22 29 ·

APRIL L⁵ P T² / Su · 6 13 20 27 · / M · 7 14 21 28 · / Tu 1 8 15 22 29 · / W 2 9 16 23 30 · / Th 3 10 17 24 M · / F 4 11 18 25 G · / Sa 5 12 19 26 · ·

MAY E⁴ E⁵ E⁶ / Su · 4 11 18 25 · / M · 5 12 19 26 · / Tu · 6 13 20 27 · / W · 7 14 21 28 · / Th 1 8 15 22 A · / F 2 9 16 23 30 · / Sa 3 10 17 24 31 ·

JUNE W T¹ T² / Su · 8 15 22 29 · / M · 9 16 23 30 · / Tu 3 10 17 24 · · / W 4 11 18 25 · · / Th 5 12 19 26 · · / F 6 13 20 27 · · / Sa 7 14 21 28 · ·

JULY T³ T⁴ T⁵ T⁶ / Su · 6 13 20 27 / M · 7 14 21 28 / Tu 1 8 15 22 29 / W 2 9 16 23 30 / Th 3 10 17 24 31 / F 4 11 18 25 · / Sa 5 12 19 26 ·

AUGUST T⁷ T⁸ T⁹ T¹⁰ / Su · 3 10 17 24 31 / M · 4 11 18 25 · / Tu · 5 12 19 26 · / W · 6 13 20 27 · / Th · 7 14 21 28 · / F 1 8 15 22 29 · / Sa 2 9 16 23 30 ·

SEPTEMBER T¹² T¹³ T¹⁴ T¹⁵ / Su · 7 14 21 28 · / M 1 8 15 22 29 · / Tu 2 9 16 23 30 · / W 3 10 17 24 · · / Th 4 11 18 25 · · / F 5 12 19 26 · · / Sa 6 13 20 27 · ·

OCTOBER T¹⁶ T¹⁷ T¹⁸ T⁻ / Su · 5 12 19 26 / M · 6 13 20 27 / Tu · 7 14 21 28 / W 1 8 15 22 29 / Th 2 9 16 23 30 / F 3 10 17 24 31 / Sa 4 11 18 25 ·

NOVEMBER A⁻³ A⁻² A⁻¹ A¹ / Su · 2 9 16 23 30 / M · 3 10 17 24 · / Tu · 4 11 18 25 · / W · 5 12 19 26 · / Th · 6 13 20 27 · / F · 7 14 21 28 · / Sa AS 8 15 22 29 ·

DECEMBER A² A³ A⁴ X¹ / Su · 7 14 21 28 / M 1 8 15 22 29 / Tu 2 9 16 23 30 / W 3 10 17 24 31 / Th 4 11 18 25 X / F 5 12 19 26 · / Sa 6 13 20 27 ·

Legend (2025):

(T² = also Peter and Paul, 2025)
(T¹³ = also Holy Cross Day, 2025)
(T¹⁴ = also Matthew, 2025)

(T¹⁸ = also Michael and All Angels, 2024)
T⁻ = Last Sunday after Trinity
W = Pentecost (Whit Sunday)
X = Christmas